ART DECO
TABLEWARE

ART DECO TABLEWARE

British Domestic Ceramics 1925 – 1939

JUDY SPOURS

STUDIO
VISTA

Facing title page *Cups, saucers and plates from three Doulton and Co. china tea services of c. 1932 in the* Fairy *shape: striking border and triangle pattern* (top); *the extremely stylized half sunburst of* Tango (centre); *and simple green and platinum effect of* De Luxe (bottom). (Page 128)

© Text and captions Judy Spours 1988
© Photographs pages 174–5, 195, 206, 207, 210–11 Wedgwood Museum Trust
© Photographs pages 6, 102, 110, 122, 126–7 Royal Doulton UK Ltd
© All other photographs Ward Lock Limited 1988

First published in Great Britain in 1988 by Ward Lock
First paperback edition 1991

Studio Vista
Villiers House
41–47 Strand
London WC2N 5JE

Designed by Anita Ruddell

Text set in Novarese ITC
by A.K.M. Associates

Printed and bound in Singapore by Toppan Printing Co.

British Cataloguing in Publication Data

Spours, Judy
    Art deco tableware : British domestic
    ceramics 1925–1939.
    1. Ceramic tableware —— Great Britain
    2. Art deco —— Great Britain
    I. Title
    738'.0941   NK4695.T33

    ISBN 0-289-80047-1

The author and publishers would like to express their thanks for permission to reproduce quotations from the following: *Art Deco of the '20s and '30s* by Bevis Hillier, The Herbert Press; *An Inquiry into Industrial Art in England* by Nikolaus Pevsner, Cambridge University Press; *Wedgwood Ceramics 1846-1959* by Maureen Batkin, Richard Dennis.

While every effort has been made to trace publishers of works quoted, we apologize for any omissions.

Contents

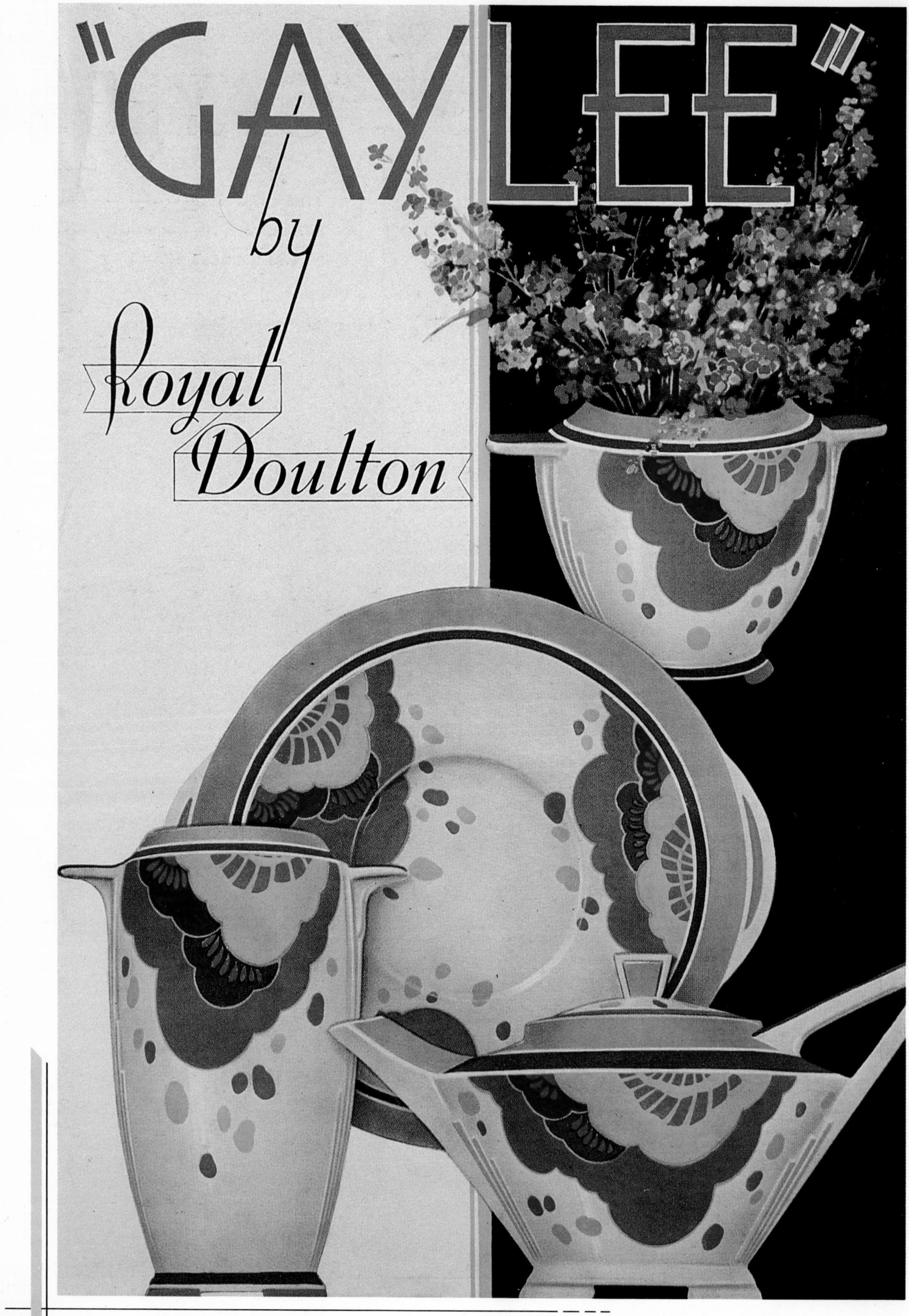
"GAYLEE"
by
Royal
Doulton

Introduction

Over the past few years, a handful of British industrial potteries and pottery designers operating between the two World Wars have become well known, and their work documented. Clarice Cliff, Susie Cooper, and Carter, Stabler and Adams at the Poole Pottery are, for example, familiar names to those interested in new ceramic designs of the period. They are amongst the most important and productive and are discussed here, but their designs represent only a tiny proportion of the great quantity of interesting new ceramics made in Britain at the time. The first intention of this book is to document and describe a wide range of the rest. The tableware designs of over a hundred potteries are discussed, from those of great manufacturers of the stature of Worcester and Wedgwood to small companies who are almost unknown today except as the name printed on the back of an old plate found in a cupboard or on an antique market stall.

The book is concerned with industrially-produced pottery, not with the hand-thrown examples produced in small numbers by individual artists and known as 'art' or 'studio' pottery. Further, it concentrates on tablewares – the ordinary cups and saucers and plates in everyday use – rather than on decorative items, although these are mentioned where they are of particular interest. Tablewares were themselves often highly decorative during this Art Deco period, and they in any case represent the largest and most important output of the pottery industry.

The inter-war years were a period of important social and artistic change, and this is reflected in the tableware produced, with those manufactured between 1925 and 1939 being the most exciting. The term Art Deco is commonly used to describe new designs of this period, referring to a style which had its origins in the 1920s but reached its zenith in the 1930s. It derives from the title of the 1925 Paris *Exposition Internationale des Arts Décoratifs et Industriels Modernes*, although it only became an accepted and well-used term in the 1960s. The definition of Art Deco is notoriously vague, and is best quoted from Bevis Hillier, whose 1968 book on the subject is a key text:

An advertisement for tablewares and ornamental pieces in Royal Doulton's Gaylee pattern of c. 1933, hand-painted on the Dandy earthenware shape. (Page 129)

. . . an assertively modern style, developing in the 1920s and reaching its high point in the thirties; it drew inspiration from various sources, including the more austere side of Art Nouveau, cubism, the Russian Ballet, American Indian Art and the Bauhaus; it was a classical style in that, like neo-classicism but unlike Rococo or Art Nouveau, it ran to symmetry rather than asymmetry, and to the rectilinear rather than the curvilinear; it responded to the demands of the machine and of new materials such as plastics, ferro-concrete and vita-glass; and its ultimate aim was to end the old conflict between art and industry, the old snobbish distinction between artist and artisan, partly by making artists adept at crafts, but still more by adapting design to the requirements of mass-production.

'Art Deco' has become even more imprecise in recent years: a reviewer of a book about American Art Deco in the *Tatler* of November 1986 described it as 'the lazy catch-all for a multiplicity of styles which have nothing in common save their contemporaneity'. This problem has arisen partly because of the nature of Art Deco designs, which take inspiration from as many or as few of the decorative sources pinpointed by Hillier as they see fit. This produced varied results, as is certainly the case with British pottery of the period. Art Deco is a fundamentally nostalgic style – a 'stylization' of motifs taken from elsewhere – and the British pottery manufacturers produced and marketed their own idiosyncratic inter-pretations of this principle.

As the 1930s progressed, more serious and restrained designs were produced than those of a purely Art Deco character, and something of an English 'Modernist' style began to emerge. In his book *The Spirit and Splendour of Art Deco*, Alain Lesieutre distinguishes Art Deco from the intentions of the avant-garde International Modern Style (also known as Modernism) which was developing in the early decades of the twentieth century. He states that 'Deco sustained the values of the past, while Modernism was committed to the future.' The tension between designs inspired by the past and less derivative ones made for the future existed strongly in the minds of British pottery manufacturers and their critics. And it appeared that before the potters could seriously consider the stringent Modernist and forward-looking ideas that were gaining ground artistically and commercially, they needed to indulge in the less demanding Art Deco style.

As a result, the modern tablewares produced between 1925 and 1939 are of an enormous and fascinating variety – some are beautiful and tasteful, others colourful and amusing, and yet others are extreme and *kitsch*. The 'Art Deco' of the book's title is thus employed as the most familiar and evocative description of designs of the period, but in fact the book covers a wide range of modern tablewares, many of which do not fit easily under this term.

The tablewares were produced against a background of intense debate about these developments in modern design in Britain, and in particular about design for machine-produced goods. It is impossible to understand or appreciate what the pottery industry was making at the time without some awareness of this debate, and the book therefore attempts to provide a direct context in which to place the tablewares. The descriptions of individual potteries themselves tell something of the story, but are interspersed with information about the wider social and design scene. Together they aim to present a chronology, a continuing story of the development of design in the pottery industry. This approach differs, I believe, from that of many other histories, which choose rather to document the formal history of design as distinct from the actual products of a period. By combining the two, I hope that the reader will be able to place a single and particular piece of pottery in an accurate twentieth-century context. The background can nevertheless only be outlined here, but the Bibliography refers the reader to a number of excellent and comprehensive histories of twentieth-century design.

In presenting this background, and in describing the tablewares, I have where possible and appropriate used contemporaneous quotations from reports of meetings in the Potteries or from trade journals, particularly the *Pottery Gazette*. The intention here is two-fold: to provide the atmosphere of the 1920s and 1930s, and to gain the perspective of how design matters were viewed from a manufacturing standpoint. Design in industry is inextricably linked with market forces – sales and profits – and nowhere is this more evident than in the pottery industry, which boasts hundreds of years of traditional manufacture. Thus the opinions of the *Pottery Gazette* must be read as those of a publication which served the often biased interests of this industry.

The industry itself was, and still is, concentrated in the geographical area known as the Potteries, in and around Stoke-on-Trent, although there were important outposts, such as Worcester. Stoke-on-Trent is a city federated in 1910 out of six neighbouring towns – Burslem, Hanley, Tunstall, Longton, Stoke and Fenton. It became a city in name only: each town retains its individual identity and its parochial interests and atmosphere. In the 1920s, as many as four hundred pottery firms were blasting out smoke across Stoke-on-Trent from over a thousand chimneys. It was not a picturesque sight, as Maurice Rena described in an article in *The Studio* of 1936:

> Within the towns themselves there is no relief from ugliness. Narrow streets of small, uniform houses, strongly and roughly built in the true artisan tradition of the last century, succeed each other, to give place to factories all similar in appearance as regards dirt and antiquity, yet of every shape and size thrown together in haphazard fashion, cheek by jowl. The characteristic monuments of the place, by which it differs radically from only too many similar industrial centres, are the innumerable tall, conical-shape kilns, focus-points of grime, which rise up on all sides.

It was against this backdrop that the potters were to create their colourful new designs, despite having been told by William Morris back in 1881 (and repeatedly by others since), at an address he gave at Burslem Town Hall, that 'Those who are to make beautiful things must live in a beautiful place.'

The pottery companies are presented in varying amounts of detail. Those I consider to be of particular interest, but which have been little published elsewhere, are afforded as much space as possible; those that are important or popular enough to have been published comprehensively elsewhere are discussed comparatively briefly, although I hope with a new and constructive

Items of Mintons dinner-, tea-, coffee- and breakfast-wares decorated with pink or green opaque Solano glazes, designed from 1937 by John Wadsworth, centred by an advertising sign for Solano Ware. (Page 136)

point of view. Only limited information is provided about companies that produced new designs of no particular distinction, and there are also a few firms that warrant more detail but for which I was able to find sparse material, often because company records and pattern books have been destroyed, and interest in the firms from the contemporary trade press was scant. I have given very brief historical notes for the most important firms, but the name and location of each pottery, plus the trade name used as part of the backstamp on the wares of the period where appropriate, are given throughout.

Individual pattern and shape names are given, with a description of their appearance, wherever possible, in order to help collectors. Using this information, it should be possible to match up a pattern or shape name to an actual piece of pottery. In a few instances, a pattern name will be found on the bottom of a piece of pottery, recorded as part of the backstamp. However, accurate identification can be a difficult and imprecise art, and I have been able to name and describe but a few of the thousands upon thousands of designs produced.

My main intention has been to detail for each company a number of designs which represent their best and most exciting tablewares or which are characteristic of their production at the time. This principle has been extended to the photographs, which illustrate a few of the tablewares of many of the companies discussed in the text, so that the particular style of a manufacturer can be appreciated and recognized.

Although the book discusses a large number of potteries, about one hundred, they still represent only about a quarter of the entire Stoke-on-Trent industry. Many of these others were manufacturing tiles, sanitary wares, laboratory wares, and so on, although some omitted here did produce new tablewares. I hope that future publications will both extend my discussions and choose to concentrate on some of the additional potteries which may also be of interest to the historian or the collector.

Acknowledgements

I am indebted to the people of the Potteries, who helped and encouraged me during my research visits to Staffordshire.

I would like to thank Kathy Niblett, Assistant Keeper of Ceramics, and Pat Halfpenny, Keeper of Ceramics, of the City Museum and Art Gallery, Stoke-on-Trent, for generously sharing their scholarship and allowing me access to the Museum's reserve collections and study material. I am also grateful to the staff of the Stoke-on-Trent City Central Library for their guidance through material in the Horace Barks Reference Library.

At the Potteries themselves I was given expert help when looking at extant tablewares and factory pattern books and records, and many stimulating and informed ideas about the pottery of the period. I am very grateful to everybody who advised me, and who gave permission for pieces in their collections to be photographed. In particular, I would like to thank Valerie Baynton, Curator of the Sir Henry Doulton Gallery, Joan Jones, Curator of the Minton Museum, and John Morton, Royal Doulton's Museums Officer; Gaye Blake Roberts (Curator), Lynn Miller (Information Officer) and Sharon Gater (Research Assistant) of the Wedgwood Museum; Anne George of Coalport; Robert Copeland, Historical Consultant of Royal Worcester Spode; Wendy Cook (Assistant Curator) and Harry Frost (Curator) of the Dyson Perrins Museum Trust, Worcester. I am very grateful to Harold Holdway for sharing his invaluable knowledge of W. T. Copeland and the pottery industry as a whole; Vega Wilkinson for her warm advice and hospitality; and Paul Niblett, for advising me about the pottery of A. E. Gray.

Numerous antique dealers told me about pieces of tableware in their shops and on their stalls, and I am most grateful. Particular thanks to John Miles of Bizzare, Birmingham, Howard and Pat Watson of Castle Antiques, Warwick, and Alastair Hendy of Alfie's Antique Market, London, for permission to photograph tablewares from their collections, and to the other dealers who helped in this way. Piers Bizony and Richard Van Spall of the Long Room Studio took the book's excellent photographs – many thanks to them and to Ward Lock's Design Manager, Anne Sharples, for their work on the illustrations.

I would like to thank the staff of the British Library and its Newspaper Library in Colindale; Paul Atterbury for commenting on my text; and Hazel Harrison for her copyediting. I am indebted to my publishers, Ward Lock, for asking me to write the book and for their continued support, especially that of my editor, Helen Douglas-Cooper. Thanks to my friend Sarah Nichols of Leeds City Art Galleries for her interest in and enthusiasm for the book. The encouragement, patience and good opinions of my husband, John Kassman, were indispensable.

London, January 1988

CHAPTER ONE

Tableware Design
After World War I

In the opinion of pottery manufacturer and designer John Adams, writing in 1926, late nineteenth-century transfer-printed decoration produced 'some of the most atrocious ceramic design the world has ever seen'. There was a tendency in the late nineteenth and early twentieth centuries to reproduce predominantly eighteenth-century styles or the ceramic masterpieces of other countries, particularly China and Japan, rather than to concentrate on the creation of new forms. Such imaginative schemes as did exist, often still demonstrating the influence of Art Nouveau and the Aesthetic Movement, were mainly reserved for ornamental pieces, and were rarely used for mass-produced, cheap tablewares.

By the end of World War I, an extensive debate about the design of everyday ceramics was well underway, and was to echo through the industry until World War II, to be revived again in the late 1940s. During World War I, export markets had largely been cut off, and production for the home market, particularly of decorated wares, much reduced. The market did not pick up as well as expected in the years immediately following the war, and there was also growing concern that the paucity of British tableware designs would result in foreign competition – and to make matters worse, that this would come mainly from Germany.

No one could deny, however, that Germany offered lessons in design that the British would be well advised to learn. In 1907 the Deutsche Werkbund had been founded in Munich to promote a productive liaison between art and industry. The organization, which brought together experts from varied disciplines – architecture, industry, economics, teaching and design – was committed to solving the problems associated with a newly emerging figure – the industrial designer. The Werkbund had itself been influenced by the British Arts and Crafts Movement, now in decline, but although the latter's goal of reconciling art and technique had been productive with regard to the individual craftsman, its rather vague premise that the craftsman should inspire machine production was not adequate to effect real change in industrial design.

A selection of hand-painted coffee cups and saucers by A. E. Gray. Floral patterns were produced from the mid-1920s (bright colours), through to the 1940s (more muted shades). Two here are backstamped as designed by Susie Cooper (top right and centre left). The banded patterns were produced from the late 1920s; and the two with raised enamelled polka dots on coloured groundlay (centre right and left) are the Stella *pattern of 1937. (Pages 32–6)*

In 1915 the Design and Industries Association (DIA) was founded in Britain with the expressed intention of influencing and improving design for mass-production, 'accepting the machine in its proper place, as a device to be guided and controlled'. Its founder-members were anxious to extend and tailor design principles for industrial manufacture, in reaction against the anti-mechanistic teachings of the Arts and Crafts Movement. Indeed, one of the powers behind the DIA was W. R. Lethaby, architect, designer and ex-Professor of Design at the Royal College of Art, who had been an important proponent of Arts and Crafts thinking, but who now saw that the time was ripe for a move forward. Among the 199 founder-members were the silversmith Harold Stabler, and John Adams (both later of the Carter, Stabler, Adams pottery at Poole, Dorset), Ambrose Heal of London's Tottenham Court Road shop, Noel Carrington, Harry Peach, the retailer and designer, John Gloag, and Harry Trethowan, buyer for Heal's china and glass department and later to become the DIA's spokesman on ceramics.

The DIA's first publication in 1915 contained the statement: 'The first necessity of sound design is fitness for use', and the rather puritanical phrase 'fitness for purpose' subsequently became the Association's touchstone of good design. The underlying idea that functionalism derives from a living, rather than an academic, tradition of design was an extension of Arts and Craft's thinking. With regard to ceramics, the phrase was expressly used to encourage manufacturers to think in terms of simple, modern and utilitarian shapes rather than decoration, but the DIA was so serious in its pursuit of functional modern style that it left itself little room to accommodate individuality and frivolity. In consequence, its members and sympathizers were to be horrified by some of the 'barbarous patterns' produced by the pottery manufacturers in the 'thirties, which showed little or no regard for simplicity and shape.

The DIA was a direct response to the Deutsche Werkbund, which had impressed a number of the founder-members through its publications and its exhibition in Cologne in 1914. In March 1915, the British government, through the Board of Trade, took the remarkable step of sponsoring a wartime exhibition of German industrial design, held at Goldsmiths' Hall in London, and in spite of the fact that these were 'alien enemy products', a speaker to the English Ceramic Society in 1916 had to admit:

> Generally speaking, the pottery exhibited appeared to me to be considerably superior to anything produced of a similar character in the Potteries at the present time . . . our rivals have discovered that a cheap thing need not of necessity be nasty: it can be well and fitly designed.

The recognition of 'fitness' in design was used to good advantage by the DIA to further its British ideals. In an address given at Stoke-on-Trent in January 1918 to the Potteries Group of the DIA, Honorary Secretary Mr Hamilton T. Smith spoke to his audience in the following World War I metaphor:

> British Commerce has been entrenched for a century, but your competitors are everywhere preparing to storm your entrenchments. Perhaps you think

> you are safe – we always do until the catastrophe, but, believe me, the years that are coming will be critical times. Technically, British goods are better than the foreigner's, but his chemists are experimenting day and night to catch up, and the British manufacturers' last line of defence will have to be design – living, progressing and constantly developing. This may prove to be the only way of keeping your lead.

Such language was apposite in 1918, the battles of World War I having proved decisively that entrenchment was *not* a secure option. Smith criticized the potters for being over-involved with the science of manufacture, and unadventurous in design. Moreover, they did not take their art directors seriously enough, and they were not following their own shining example – Josiah Wedgwood, who had employed the great artists of his own day to design pots. What was emerging here and in later discussions in the Potteries was the search for a style which was modern and satisfying as well as meeting the post-war demand of being quintessentially English.

Smith's most telling attack was on the manufacturers' last complacency in producing only in direct response to what the public wanted to buy.

> Manufacturers say they provide what the public demand; but are they sure of that, and more important, are they sure that even if it were so it is the right position for them to take up? . . . If the maker fails to sell things such as we are advocating, it is not the fault of the public, it is want of co-operation between the maker and the distributor. The public can only choose from amongst what is offered by the distributor; they are seething with discontent at the offer but are inarticulate.

This public wrath was, of course, imagined well before the days of consumer research in Britain, and history has proved that Smith was somewhat overstating his case. Many other such criticisms of the industry were made, notably by DIA members, and caused uproar and resentment in Stoke-on-Trent, where many potters saw the DIA as an out-of-town bunch of 'interfering busy-bodies' who were trying to impose on them the atrocious and unnatural new-fangled art of the 'most extraordinary paintings' they saw in contemporary exhibitions. In a paper given in 1921 to the Ceramic Society, entitled 'Pottery Design from the Manufacturer's Point of View', H. J. Plant declared that the types of tableware decoration much appreciated by the public were:

> . . . borders with naturalistic rose sprays tastily displayed underneath, also roses with narrow brown borders underneath, festoons, scattered flowers connected by choice bits of ornament . . .

And so on. His paper ends with some no-nonsense advice to the artist, who '. . . must mix a large proportion of common sense with his colours.' Mr Plant's views may well appear philistine in retrospect, but he represented the innate conservatism of the pottery manufacturers, who had yet to be convinced of the *commercial* expediency of changing their ideas.

If a businessman is to experiment he must be persuaded that he will see a return on his investment. As it was, the DIA, for all its proselytizing about good, simple shapes and decoration, had not yet reconciled the artist to industry or

Hand-thrown stoneware vases by Carter, Stabler and Adams at the Poole Pottery, dating from the 1920s. The shapes were probably designed by John Adams and the geometric patterns, under a matt glaze, by Truda Adams (later Carter). (Page 24)

vice versa; nor had it been able to set up sufficient educational means to that end. The manufacturers felt, with some justification, that the artists who were to inspire their industry had no knowledge of or interest in it. They were cushioned in the art colleges, mainly in London, and imbued with Arts and Crafts ideology, or were somewhere deep in the British countryside making hand-thrown pots. The great studio potter Bernard Leach was a case in point. When he returned to England in 1920 after his study of pottery in Japan, he settled in St Ives, Cornwall, not in Stoke-on-Trent. Even as late as July 1933, John Betjeman was writing in the *Architectural Review* about:

> . . . the sharp division between gentlefolk craftsmen who prefer to hide from commerce in the Cotswolds and pioneer in design alone, and those artists who wish to co-operate with the manufacturers . . . let us see those escapists who remain, out in the open, lending their expertise and sense of design to manufacturers.

Moreover, the potters felt that these criticisms were being levelled at them after a war during which development of design had hardly been possible, since their concern had been to produce utilitarian wares – the firm Grimwades, for example, had produced items of tableware bearing a message from the Prime Minister asking for economy of food consumption.

Other more malleable people could see the opportunities presented by the DIA's pioneering. In an earlier paper to the Ceramic Society, in 1918, the potter A. E. Gray admitted:

> Of the artistic merit of modern pottery one can say with confidence that there is room for much improvement, particularly in the cheaper goods, and that is the class of goods I think we ought to direct our particular attention to. We seem to have moved in a vicious circle in that grade of pottery, copying one another, undercutting prices and cutting down wages, with most serious results so far as design is concerned.

Gray was intelligent enough to realize, as a small earthenware decorator without the clout of a Spode or a Wedgwood in the expensive china markets, that if times got hard (and they were to do so some ten years later), future competition would hinge on design. He had taken the DIA's point, although as a decorator rather than manufacturer he was not in a position to develop new shapes. It is interesting to note that he was also conscious of the fact that satisfying decorations were more important than the quality of the wares themselves.

> I am inclined to think that good decoration on more or less indifferent ware is more acceptable to the buying public than technically perfect ware of less attractive design.

But this still did not solve the problem of simplicity of shape which the DIA was anxious to advance. Experimentation with new shapes, which involved investing in new moulds, was a costly business, and was naturally resisted by the manufacturer, who was not convinced that such experiments would prove worthwhile financially.

In the first two decades of the twentieth century, few significant changes in modern pottery design were to be seen in the work produced in Britain, although developments on the Continent during this period were at times startling. In Vienna, the most radical design ideas prompted artists of the Wiener Werkstätte (founded in 1903) to produce minimal pottery designs before 1910; the influence spread to the German Deutsche Werkbund, and artists in Prague made revolutionary Cubist pottery designs from 1908. By the early 1920s, very stark geometric decorations, and some uncompromisingly angular shapes, were frequently seen in examples of tableware produced by designers such as Wilhelm Kåge at the Royal Copenhagen Porcelain Factory; Jean Luce and Georges Rouard in France; the architect Gio Ponti in Italy; artists of the German Bauhaus (founded in 1919 by architect Walter Gropius, and extending the work of the Deutsche Werkbund); and by Constructivist abstract designers working in Russia. England, however, remained virtually immune to the influence of these progressively modern foreign examples.

□ W. Moorcroft (*Washington Works, Burslem*)

One English company had, however, taken a useful lead in the production of simple tableware shapes 'fit for their purpose' as early as 1913. Moorcroft Pottery is best known for its spectacular ornamental pieces: stunning Art Nouveau vases decorated with landscapes and mushrooms, and the rich flambé wares introduced by William Moorcroft in 1919. However, 1913 saw the launch of Moorcroft's *Powder Blue* domestic tableware. The extremely simple, rounded shapes, reminiscent of some eighteenth-century wares, were decorated simply in an all-over speckled blue (rather like a brightly coloured bird's egg), the insides of the hollow-wares remaining white. Moorcroft was an 'art' rather than 'industrial' pottery, and the pieces of *Powder Blue* were hand thrown to produce the simple earthenware shapes.

The design was so successful that it remained in production for fifty years (vindicating the view that very simple wares do sell), and even received that highest of accolades, the admiration of Sir Nikolaus Pevsner. Moorcroft's advertisements of the latter 'thirties quote his opinion of *Powder Blue*, expressed in his *An Inquiry into Industrial Art in England*, published in 1937:

> W. Moorcroft's famous Blue, one of the best contemporary sets, was designed in 1913, and is, in spite of that, as 'modern' as anything created now, and as 'modern' as Jos. Wedgwood's sets, i.e., undatedly perfect.

Moorcroft's methods of largely hand-thrown production had in fact little to do with the machine age, although he regarded himself as an industrial potter, but he is one of the designers and manufacturers whose productions were sufficiently numerous and commercial to provide a link between 'art' pottery and genuine industrial manufacture. In the light of the problems inherent in producing good designs for industrial manufacture that were faced by the British pottery industry, the achievements of William Moorcroft's enterprise are well worth examining.

A wide selection of tablewares, including candlesticks, in William Adams and Sons' hand-painted earthen Titian Ware, launched by 1920. This pattern of fruit and lining proved popular and successful, and remained in production through to the 1940s. (Page 28)

□ Carter, Stabler and Adams   (*Poole Pottery, Dorset*)

Another company in a similar position, and one that was consistently lauded for its good innovative designs from an early date, was Carter, Stabler and Adams, situated well away from the smoke of Stoke-on-Trent down in Poole, Dorset. The pottery was established in 1873 as Carter and Co. to produce tiles, mosaics and architectural ware. Production of domestic pottery developed, and from 1913 Poole produced pottery designed by the Bloomsbury artists of the Omega Workshops. In 1921 the company was established as an exciting commercial venture. Charles Carter had brought in Harold Stabler, the leading gold- and silversmith and founder-member of the DIA, and his wife Phoebe, a successful designer and modeller who had worked with Doulton. Both had a keen interest in ceramics, and had designed and made ceramic figures and groups in their London studio. The Stablers introduced the third partner of the firm, John Adams, a talented and experienced potter from Stoke-on-Trent. He had studied at Hanley School of Art, worked in Bernard Moore's decorating studio, won a scholarship to the Royal College of Art (RCA) and stayed on to teach there for a couple of years. At the RCA he met his wife Truda (who remarried to become Truda Carter in 1931), who was to become the firm's influential and highly original designer.

Throughout the 1920s the notable pottery produced by the company was hand-thrown ornamental stonewares, typically decorated with floral and geometric patterns under a matt glaze. Shapes were designed largely by John Adams, with the more angular ones by Harold Stabler, and the stunning decorations were by Truda Adams. Her designs were sophisticated in comparison with many of those produced in the Potteries at the time, demonstrating both her fine understanding of the Art Deco style and an individualistic interpretation of it. Her palette of colours was subdued, avoiding the garish, bright effects often seen in English pottery of the period, and having more in common with pieces produced on the Continent. The company won some of the highest awards at the 1925 Paris *Exposition* for these hand-decorated wares.

However, Carter, Stabler and Adams does present a problem of definition, namely can they be considered an industrial pottery or were they essentially an art pottery? This was a problem which concerned the partners themselves, since their very real interest in the development of industrial design could be seen as conflicting with the style of their own manufacturing business. They were loath to be dubbed 'art' potters, and pointed out with some justification that their products were of smooth finish and uniform in shape and did not have the rough and irregular outlines and finish of true art pottery. The *Pottery Gazette*, writing about the firm in 1926, was prepared to accept that they were somewhere in between:

> . . . the productions of Carter, Stabler and Adams, Ltd. are, in a very real sense, a sort of compromise between studio pottery, on the one hand, and pottery produced under factory conditions on the other.

In many ways, though, the firm's productions of the 1920s and early 1930s can be seen as the very obverse of industrial manufacture, and the following passage from a *Pottery Gazette* article of 1929 expresses the opinion that the quality of the designs derived from the very fact that they were produced *away from* large-scale industrial production:

> The domestic pottery that is produced here bears evidence of an atmosphere that is in every way responsive to artistic sensibilities, and detached, as the pottery workers are, from anything savouring of the more industrial phases of clay manipulation, and operating, as they do, under the necessity of evolving ideas from within, one finds in their finished productions much more that is suggestive of creative talent than of a desire to produce something that falls into line with a vogue the origin of which is to be found elsewhere.

Certainly, in terms of the tablewares with which we are largely concerned, they produced nothing on anything like a commercial scale at this time: their productions were decorative rather than utilitarian. Some small morning tea- and coffee-sets were produced in the 1920s, but predominantly for presentation purposes. In 1933 Harold Stabler produced a tableware shape called *Studland*, a plain body with quite elaborate and angular handles. It was either spray glazed in dark green, Sapphire blue or powder blue, producing a mottled effect reminiscent of Moorcroft's established *Powder Blue* wares, or painted up with modern leaf and floral patterns. These hand-made pieces were not produced in any quantity and remained exclusive. Other restricted-production tableware shapes introduced at about the same time included the rounded *Picotee* and the ribbed-bodied *Everest* ware with solid diamond-shaped handles, decorated in plain glaze colours.

It was not until 1936 that John Adams designed a shape, *Streamline*, intended to be used for competitive, standard tablewares. In her history of the company, Jennifer Hawkins describes a large private commission which Carter, Stabler and Adams received from South Africa in 1936. The undecorated white wares had to be bought in from Poultney and Co of Bristol, and John Adams thus realized the necessity of producing his own competitive and industrially produced tablewares. *Streamline*'s design was based on the wares used for the South African commission.

The name aptly describes the intention of the shape, which was simplified, rounded and traditional, modern but not so fashionable that it would quickly become outmoded. The first few examples were hand-thrown, although it was subsequently standardized and machine-made, providing the firm's first real commercial success in tableware. It was decorated with combinations of two-coloured glazes, the first a sombre sepia brown partnered with mushroom, followed by various combinations of a mottled grey, peach, pale green and lime. (After World War II these combinations were known as *Twintone*, and the tableware continued in production for many years.) Most were decorated in these plain colours, although some were augmented with small floral motifs devised by Truda Carter (as she had now become).

Other supplementary tablewares were also produced – for example, a fish and hors d'oeuvres set decorated with hand-painted fish, preserve jars, cream

Part of a pink/purple lustre earthenware tea service by A. E. Gray, probably designed by Gordon M. Forsyth and produced in the late 1920s. (Page 33)

and sugar sets – many to designs by art-school friends of the firm's partners. Decorative wares of the second half of the 1930s included bookends in stylized forms of animals such as elephants and monkeys; cuboid vases; snail-shell candlesticks; wall-mounted flying seagulls, and a Modernist sculpture of a yacht. Again, these were designed by John Adams, Truda Carter and a variety of outside artists.

By 1936 the *Pottery Gazette* was able to say of the more commercial *Streamline* tableware and decorative items that '. . . the movement which is now manifesting itself in this direction may ultimately go far . . . only the fringe of the field has yet been explored'. Indeed, after World War II, tableware designs were further standardized, and Carter, Stabler and Adams's commercial productions increased until their identity became firmly that of an industrial, rather than an art, pottery.

□ William Adams and Sons (*Titian Ware—Tunstall and Stoke*)

An interesting example of a more typically gradual advance in ideas about tableware design and its marketing during this period is *Titian Ware*, made by William Adams and Sons, who were originally established at Burslem in 1657. The company had obviously accepted some ideas about simplicity of design, and were aware of a growing vogue for rustic pottery designs with simple floral motifs. However, as an old-established firm they were reluctant to break fully from tradition by any dramatic changes in design.

Adams decided to relaunch their successful eighteenth-century designs of fruit and floral decorations on simple period shapes with the addition of a new glaze, rich ivory in colour, which gave the ware its name. The resulting earthen tableware was launched by 1920, and is interesting not least because it was successful enough to be developed over the following years, with production continuing until the early 1950s. The original eighteenth-century designs were adapted and enhanced, particularly by brightening up the colours used for the patterns. This formula of slightly modernizing traditional wares was adopted by many other potteries, as we shall see – most importantly those operating at the top of the fine china market, such as W.T. Copeland and Worcester.

Most important of all, *Titian Ware* was hand-painted. The revival of handcraft techniques was influenced by the Arts and Crafts Movement, and although it did not satisfy all the DIA's design wishes, they favoured the trend because it lessened the existing dependence on badly designed lithographic prints. The potters themselves were convinced of its virtues once they realized that they could employ paintresses at wages low enough for the enterprise to succeed in business terms. For all these reasons *Titian Ware* provides an interesting link between the pottery designs of the ten years after World War I and those of the ten years which followed. It was advertised and presented in catalogues with the following script:

This style of Free-hand Painted Ware was made by the Adams firm about 1760; first in different shades of Blue, and later in colours. The addition of Titian Glaze blended with the colours gives a very beautiful effect.

The tableware was relatively cheap, and in the somewhat awkward words of its advertisements, 'Atones in Beauty for what it lacks in Expensiveness'.

William Adams produced few tablewares that can really be called Art Deco, but the *Titian Ware* designs, although conceived before 1920, came to have an unmistakable 1930s feel. Pattern books from the early 1920s already show experiments in brightening the colours used for the existing designs. Perhaps the most successful design of all relied on simple, widely spaced motifs of fruit lined off into a wide border at the edge of the wares, with an additional fruit used at the centre of the flatwares. Tea-, coffee-, dinner-wares and decorative items such as candlesticks were all produced to this pattern.

In May 1920 *Titian Ware* was illustrated and featured in an article in *Our Homes and Gardens* magazine entitled 'What the Potters are Making: Some Modern Examples that reach Excellence in Form and Decoration'. None of the examples showed any radical advancement in design, but Adams's 'Hand painted patterns on ivory coloured ware, Fruit in yellow, blue and dull mauvey red. Black line above and red line below' (which were later to be shown by Adams at the 1925 Paris *Exposition*), found favour. The writer of the accompanying text had digested fully the edicts of the DIA, and of the newly formed Art Section of the Ceramic Society, and evidently found *Titian Ware* to be a cut above the average eighteenth-century reproduction ware. In his report on British ceramics at the Paris *Exposition* (see p. 42), Gordon Forsyth described *Titian Ware* favourably as 'modest' (a very positive word in his vocabulary) and the decorative designs as 'excellent in scale to the pieces', though he also added that they represent 'restrained country cottage designs' (a negative description!).

By 1930 *Titian Ware* was subject to some of the kitsch type of presentation favoured by Clarice Cliff and others at the same date. Advertisements showed it in front of a backdrop of Titian's *Portrait of a Man* in the National Gallery, London, with the caption 'A Modern Old Master'.

In May 1930 the Stoke-on-Trent Historical Pageant, organized as part of Wedgwood's bi-centenary celebrations, witnessed an extraordinary 'Allegorical portrayal of the Modern Potteries' Industries' in which HRH the Ceramic Queen (actually Lady Joseph, wife of the chairman of the organizing committee) and her royal bearers of Pottery products lead a stately procession. Photographs in the *Daily Dispatch* show 'living examples' of *Titian Ware* – namely a bob-haired girl dressed in an appalling pseudo–Victorian Bo-Peep dress decorated with *Titian Ware* fruit patterns. In another section, some fifty young women were dressed – extremely unflatteringly – as Portland Vases, appearing in photographs with arms neatly curved to form the vase handles. The procession included such representatives of the industry as 'Ole King Coal' and a dance of the living tableware ended appropriately with a rousing chorus of 'O God, our help in ages past'. Princess Mary, who attended the ceremony, is recorded as remarking (with admirable tact): 'Everything is very beautiful'.

The *Titian Ware* pattern books of the 1930s show that old shapes were resolutely adhered to but that colours brightened considerably, sometimes into such all-over patterns as brilliant blue, pink and yellow daisies and strong wash-banded designs. The flowers and fruit became more elaborate in such

A superb earthenware tea set designed by Susie Cooper for A. E. Gray c. 1928–29, with vivid hand-painted Art Deco pattern. (Page 34)

designs as *Maytime* – a vivid and somewhat haphazard collection of predominently orange, yellow and green motifs. Other designs which incorporated Art Deco sunburst motifs and the popular 'stepped' forms of Aztec architecture appeared in the books, although there is no evidence that they were actually produced in any quantity. Reproductions of 'Della Robbia' borders with embossed and painted fruit and flowers – the most widely produced bearing acorns – were exhibited at the time, together with a design of dancing cupids in relief, painted with festoons in greys, pale pink, green, yellow and a touch of magenta. In 1930, sales were healthy enough to warrant the employment of over a hundred young women executing freehand designs on *Titian Ware*. Other reproduction lines in tableware were added, such as *Calyx Ware* (the word calyx implies a covering, again emphasizing the glaze, which here was a faint greenish-blue), an adapted copy of an oriental style of decoration of the period 1760–90. Shapes used were also traditional, and the hand-painted decoration was applied both on the glaze and under it in various productions.

By the early 1940s a more extensive change had been forced upon Adams, and the firm's new designs were entirely different, absorbing elements of Modernism in pottery decoration. For example, *Newport Titian* consisted of tableware with a central curved, stylized leaf clump in brown and pale blue, surrounded with a wide wash border on the rim in apple green, overpainted with dark blue dashes. But even at this point, the old Titian Ware patterns were still in production, and Adams had achieved something of a coup in surviving the period as an earthenware manufacturer without stretching to the extremes of design and novelty production that were to prove essential to the survival of smaller factories.

□ A. E. Gray (*Glebe Works, Hanley; Wheildon Road, Stoke from 1934*)

Although reproduction styles for interior decoration remained popular with some throughout the 1920s and 1930s (we still have not escaped them), people were at least now encouraged to thin them down to bare essentials. In May 1922, for example, *Our Homes and Gardens* discussed the problem in an article entitled 'Superfluity in the Drawing-Room: A Rigorous Clearance the only Solution'. The problem then arose that the absence of clutter and consequent lack of colour in rooms was unacceptable to average British taste. In an article dated April 1925, the same magazine declared:

> . . . there remains the necessity of a certain relief, a note of colour, the mitigation of too great austerity in outlines of table and cabinet. The decorative qualities of china which is a household necessity for meals or toilet may be made to give that note of gaiety and brilliance which the many superfluous trifles were intended to do.

The discussion goes on to look at the virtues of imported French and Italian 'peasant' pottery, and the appeal of colourful red and yellow tea-sets against 'the whitewashed walls of a simple cottage'. Czechoslovakian potteries also excelled in rustic pottery designs, simple, floral, brightly coloured and hand-painted, and these were imported into Britain in quantity after World War I, and became very popular. The dual problems of drab interiors and the import of foreign wares (as many had predicted) can be seen as the catalysts in a demand for brightly coloured wares of homespun style that, as we shall see, were to become more fashionable still in a few years time.

One of the first to respond to calls for new design and colour was the energetic A. E. Gray, whose well-balanced reactions to the contemporary design debate and quickness to recognize market trends made him something of a pioneer of hand-painted wares in the early 1920s.

Gray began his career as a salesman in a glass and china shop in Manchester. The poor design of the wares he was obliged to sell prompted him to turn to manufacture in an attempt to raise standards, and he established a wholesale ceramic decorating business in 1907. By 1920 lithographic transfers formerly used to decorate his wares had been virtually abandoned in favour of bright, hand-painted patterns. Gray was a leading light in the growing handcraft movement which was to take the earthenware industry by storm in the late 1920s and early 1930s.

But although his firm was producing original earthenware designs and he himself, as a former salesman now on the advisory committee of the British Industries Fairs, was vociferous about design, the wares were comparatively rarely discussed in trade journals. To make matters worse, all the company's pattern books were destroyed, so that records and information about the firm are very sparse. However, the history and productions of A. E. Gray have been pieced together by Paul Niblett, resulting in a unique documentation of a small Stoke-on-Trent firm. I am indebted to his scholarship, and to his chapter in *Hand-Painted Gray's Pottery* which forms the basis of this discussion.

Most of Gray's paintresses were engaged from the local art schools (see Chapter 2), and he was also wise enough to employ talented designers to provide patterns for the hand-painted wares. One such was John Guildford, who was working for the company as decorating manager by 1920, and designed many of the early wares. (He subsequently designed and signed pieces for Barker Bros – see p. 97.)

In 1922 Susie Cooper, whose own pottery company was later to become famous (see Chapter 7), joined the company after attending evening classes at Burslem School of Art. As an assistant designer, some of her first work for the company was executing patterns for *Gloria Lustre* ware, which was designed for Gray by Gordon Forsyth in 1923. Lustre wares have a shiny appearance derived from a thin coating of metal, which results from the application of liquid lustre, a mixture containing metallic compounds, after firing. The metals used, producing different colours, include gold, silver, platinum, copper and titanium (from which a transparent mother-of-pearl effect is achieved). Gray's produced an enormous number of lustre wares, predominantly in purple, pink, copper and silver colours, the *Gloria Lustre* range being in a mixture of colours. Lustre was applied to both earthenware and bone china, and although Gray's produced some coffee and fruit sets, the medium was reserved mostly for ornamental wares as the lustre surface could not stand up to constant washing.

Printed and enamelled china tea-
and coffee-ware by Shelley
Potteries: Eve *shape of 1932*
decorated with geometric pattern
(top); Eve *shape with delicate*
landscape and fruit tree pattern
(left) (page 58); *and* Vogue
shape of 1930 with elaborate
stylized floral pattern (right).
(*pages 56–8*)

By 1924 Susie Cooper's own talent as a designer had begun to emerge, and her early colourful floral, abstract and banded patterns appeared on Gray's wares until 1929, often with her name as designer incorporated in the back stamp. Her floral handcraft designs for Gray's were bold, bright and rustic, but left plain ground on the wares, unlike those by later designers for the company, which were often painted overall, leaving no background. She introduced abstract, Cubist decorations in about 1928, although they were comparatively shortlived, but her vivid banded wares conceived at about the same time set a design precedent. Different coloured bands of enamel paint were applied in horizontal circles around the wares: favourite colour combinations at the time were, for example, green, red, yellow and black.

A hand-painted ginger jar of 1926 designed by Susie Cooper has come to represent her work of this period. The colours are already quite subtle although still bright (rust, turquoise, ochre); the background is abstract with zigzagged areas in Art Deco style; three panels are painted with stylized animals – an ibex, a ram and the leaping deer which was later to decorate so many of her wares and to illustrate her own company's backstamp. By the time she left Gray's in 1929 to form her own decorating business, Susie Cooper was well-versed in the advantages of hand decoration (although even at Gray's a few of her designs were converted into striking new lithographs).

Gray's undecorated white ware came from a variety of manufacturing sources, including T. G. Green, Alfred Meakin and Wood and Sons, but the company who seemed best to supply his needs was Johnson Bros, whose simple, elegant shapes were much admired by design commentators of the period (see p. 105). Gray's combination of good simple shapes and bright floral and banded hand-painting was consistently praised, as were his efforts in 'working in the cause of good design'. By the mid-1930s, with some splendid manufacture behind him, he was still working to this end, speaking on the subject of design whenever possible. The following, for example, is taken from a transcription of a meeting of the Royal Society of Arts in 1934:

> A great deal had been said about art in industry. He |A. E. Gray| had had a little experience. He had served 20 years in the retail trade, and then the urge came to get into the potteries and do something himself . . . The artist had got to approach the thing in the same way and go into industry. It was no use talking from outside because he must know not only the material and its possibilities, but also its limitations and the craftsmen within the industry. He must design something which it was possible for the craftsman to produce, and not to degrade him by asking him to do something below his possibilities. One must think of design in pottery, not as a whole, but in connection with the home generally, and must fit it in with the background of furnishings, textiles, etc.

Gray's opinions highlighted the problems which were central to the continuing debates about design for industry in the 1930s (see Chapter 7). By this time, he had proved his point by employing artists of the calibre of Susie Cooper, and later such talents as Sam C. Talbot, designer from about 1931.

As tastes changed in the 1930s, Gray's production of bright floral wares

decreased, to be replaced by simpler patterns. A number of the most beautiful used groundlay coloured backgrounds, painted in one shade onto the wares and decorated with tiny raised enamelled polka dots, as in *Stella*, used for coffee services from about 1937. By the end of the 1930s, along with other progressive decorators, Gray was turning his attention back to lithography. His design success was no doubt partly a result of his coming to pottery from another trade and starting afresh; unhampered by the traditions and company image which affected the productions of companies such as William Adams, he was free to put his modern ideas into action.

□ Ashtead Potters   (*Victoria Works, Ashtead, Surrey*)

The Ashtead Potters had no tradition at all from which to escape – their pottery was established in conjunction with the Rural Industries Board after World War I, specifically to employ disabled ex-Service men. It was felt that the nerves of the men would not tolerate the intensive industrial conditions of Stoke-on-Trent, so the pottery was built in the Surrey village of Ashtead. It was, however, equipped with the latest technology: this was not planned to be merely a cottage industry. Not a single man had been trained as a potter before the War, and their lack of experience was complicated by their physical and nervous conditions. In an article of May 1925 in *Our Homes and Gardens*, Sir Lawrence Weaver described their circumstances:

> . . . thirty-four men, ranging in disability from 20 per cent to 100 per cent., suffering from old gunshot wounds, neurasthenia, valvular disease of the heart and what not – with pre-war occupations of fantastic variety, such as groom, analyst's assistant, valet, steelworker, fishmonger and gardener – not one of them versed in any artistic craft – had to be trained in the art of the potter after years of misery in hospital.

The approach of the potters was systematic and educational, not only in the technical skills they needed to develop, but also in the artistic judgement they would need to acquire to produce saleable decorative wares. They studied the pottery of Bavaria, Italy and Spain; they studied the traditions of the Staffordshire potters; and the decorators in particular spent time looking at the ceramic displays in the Victoria and Albert Museum, London.

Because the Ashtead potters were creating all their forms from scratch (either moulded or on the wheel), they did not have to concern themselves with finding new decoration for old shapes, and were able to bear in mind the current enthusiasm for simple, clean lines for useful earthenware household objects. The results were quite remarkable – pleasing and straightforward designs, decorated in bright colours, predominantly in striking geometric and banded patterns. By 1920 they had produced designs as advanced as other companies were creating in the mid-1930s. Their adherence to ideals of simplicity in ceramic design resulted in tableware with one-colour glazes, otherwise undecorated, in such colours as oatmeal, grey, jade green or yellow, probably influenced by the understated success of Moorcroft's *Powder Blue*.

Their pottery decoration was clearly more influenced by foreign designs than by British products, which accounts for its relative modernity – design was considerably more 'advanced' and imaginative in other parts of Europe. However, their products are recognizably English, demonstrating a modesty and lack of extremes which distinguished them from comparable European examples.

Ashtead demonstrated the marked success possible without the benefits (or drawbacks) of traditional manufacture: they produced distinctive and uncompromising pots. Their wares were stocked by Heal's, Waring and Gillow, Harrods and the Army and Navy stores, and the buyers of these firms were not acting charitably. Most interestingly, other simple, fine designs were also sold by Woolworths, inspiring Harry Trethowan, in his capacity as President of the China and Glass Retailers' Association, to comment in 1929: 'and so at Woolworth's, we may indulge our good taste, and make our selection to our entire satisfaction for a nimble sixpence.'

Ashtead employed talented outside designers, for example, Phoebe Stabler (wife of Harold), who designed ceramic figures for the company in the 1930s. In common with Gray's, Ashtead also early on used the device of designers signing their own work, a marketing idea which was to be exploited to the full by Clarice Cliff and others in the early 1930s. Their own brand of Modernist ware is typified by their edition of the 'Lion of Industry', modelled by Percy Metcalfe in the early 1920s, one of which was 'put in his own room' by the Prince of Wales. The lion is distinctively English, but sculpted in stylized 'Cubist' form, with its mane squared off like a helmet, reminiscent of battledress. It represents both the spirit of the age and the spirit of the potters, who were no doubt motivated more strongly than most to put the past behind them.

□ The exhibitions of the early 1920s

In 1920 the DIA mounted an 'Exhibition of Household Things' at the Whitechapel Gallery, London. It was the first time they had exhibited articles of daily use, and 'fitness for purpose' was of paramount importance in their selection. There were no trade stands and, in the words of the exhibition catalogue: 'The selections have been made by artists and expert members and by those who have made a sincere study of domestic problems.' Tableware was listed as 'Crockery', a somewhat disparaging term emphasizing its utilitarian nature. The selectors' opinions about what constituted a successful item of tableware are sensible in the extreme, and no doubt many observers from the Potteries found them pompous, puritanical and damning – the antithesis of their back-to-back rose decorations on pretty and elaborate tea-services. The selectors' strict approach is worth quoting in full:

1. Simple shapes are the best; they are stronger and more easily cleaned.
2. Flutings and raised ornament and unnecessary twists and curls have been avoided; these things often disguise bad shapes and are always tiresome to clean.

China tea-ware by Shelley Potteries in the Queen Anne *shape of 1926, decorated with four print and enamel floral and 'cottage garden' patterns, c. 1927–30. Those bottom right and left* show the characteristic use of tall English garden flowers to add height to the patterns. *(Page 53)*

3. Bottle-shaped, narrow-necked utensils should be shunned both in crockery and glass.

4. Teapots and jugs are well-balanced; teapot lids have in many cases deep flanges that prevent them easily falling off, and the spouts are made to pour out of.

5. Inside surfaces of vessels which hold food are smooth and free of corners and crevices; thus a vegetable dish is so shaped that it is easy to serve the last potato.

6. Handles are unobtrusive and not easily broken.

7. In a word, we are trying to prove that domestic pots of all grades may be beautiful in the truest sense, and it is for the public to see that a demand is created for articles of everyday use that are simple, fitted for use, and delightful in their conception . . . In this way there will be some addition made to the joy of living.

Many of these points are obviously very important, but the implied judgements of 'good' and 'bad' and 'right' and 'wrong' are irritating and, more important, restricting. To the average small pottery manufacturer it must have seemed an impossible task to produce tableware which would soften the expression on the collective face of the DIA and provide 'joy of living', and many must have felt an irresistible temptation to go to the other extreme. The public at large might well have felt the same, as magazines of the period took up the theme with a vengeance, making endless similar judgements in articles about ceramics with such titles as 'Things Good and Bad', which they virtuously published alongside others condoning the collecting of old Staffordshire figures!

This is not to say that the DIA's design principles were wrong-headed: indeed, one might wish that they had been more widely accepted. One of the problems was that their campaigns were not backed by adequate example or education, either in the Potteries or of the public, and the puritanical message of 'fitness for purpose' was unlikely to be popular with a post-war population looking for a little frivolity. Many in the Potteries strongly believed that visual fun was more important than the easy availability of the last potato in the vegetable dish. As the *Pottery Gazette* was later to comment:

As regards pottery, people want colour. Contrast the feminine fashions of to-day with those of pre-war days; the soft shades of yesterday are cast aside; vivid, unadulterated colour is demanded. Probably we still react against the dullness of the War period; possibly we feel that colour in clothes and the things we use helps to counteract depressing industrial conditions. Whatever the reason, the demand is there, and the manufacturer must try to satisfy it.

Colour, which had made its mark with the rustic pottery fashion, was in the design ascendancy, often to the detriment of practical shape. As a result, the design pundits were in a state of near despair by the late 1930s, with their stern sensibilities assaulted by solid triangular cup handles, cuboid teapots, no end of deliberately 'unnatural' uses of the medium of clay, and colours that made their heads spin.

The British Institute of Industrial Art, formed in 1920, presented its

'Exhibition of Industrial Art To-Day' at the Victoria and Albert Museum in 1923. Despite the title of the exhibition, the greater proportion of the pottery displays was devoted to art, rather than industrial, pottery, with pieces by Bernard Moore, Katherine Pleydell Bouverie and others. Presumably it was hoped that some of this 'artistic' pottery would rub off on the industry, as the industrial pieces displayed, largely from such firms as Wedgwood, Crown Staffordshire, A. J. Wilkinson and S. Fielding (Crown Devon) were described in the catalogue as 'conventional'. They did also display a number of vividly hand-painted wares, mostly floral or banded, dominant amongst them works by Susie Cooper for A. E. Gray, and one or two examples of students' hand-painted work from Stoke-on-Trent School of Art.

This exhibition was hardly inspiring, particularly when it is realized that the British Institute of Industrial Art had been founded largely to undertake exhibitions that would raise the standards of industrial art and link industry with the activities of museums and art galleries. It opened with a permanent gallery in Knightsbridge and three temporary displays of modern products at the Victoria and Albert Museum.

The real showcases of industrial production, where the manufacturers themselves had confidence in the displays, were the annual British Industries Fairs (BIFs). These were organized by the Board of Trade solely for British manufacturing firms, with the specific intention of attracting export trade. The Fairs were designed for the placing of firm orders to buy, rather than exhibitions merely for the sake of art, and were thus treated with due seriousness by the manufacturers. The trade press reported extensively on each BIF, and the orders placed year by year gave a good indication of fluctuations in overall trade in the industry. The pottery displays were extensive – divided into sections dealing with china, earthenware, art pottery, cooking, hotel and restaurant wares, teapots and jugs – and all important retailers from home and abroad attended the Fairs. When the huge and much publicized British Empire Exhibition was staged in 1924, its display of pottery were in consequence less representative of the products of the whole industry than those found at the BIF in the same year. The *Architectural Review* had to conclude of the British Empire Exhibition, in June 1924, that '. . . the design and colour of British industrial art is depressingly bad. It lacks ideas, spontaneity, and tone . . . .'

The overall impression given by these exhibitions was that the standard of British industrial pottery, particularly tableware, was in general neither high nor original, and the trade stands at the British Empire Exhibition did not bode well for Britain's showing at the Paris *Exposition Internationale des Arts Décoratifs et Industriels Modernes* in 1925. Although the *Exposition* was attended by nearly six million visitors, many of the important British pottery manufacturers did not bother with it at all; France was not an important export market for them so they perceived the show as commercially useless. And they certainly did not attend for the sake of art.

Those who did show made notably little impact. A somewhat embarrassed report in the *Pottery Gazette* of July 1925 tried to pass off the British showing on the rather absurd grounds that others might want to steal their (distinctly limited) new ideas, but in fact the adjudicators' committee of the *Exposition* probably turned down a proportion of British goods before they reached the display cases as they did not fulfil basic standards of originality.

The chapter on pottery in the official report on the *Exposition* (produced by HMSO) was written by Gordon Forsyth, who mildly commended William Adams for the scale of their patterns to the various sizes of tableware, Wedgwood for high-quality manufacture, Worcester for their simple china shapes, Mintons for their study of French Sèvres designs, Carter, Stabler and Adams for 'freely painted designs of modern character' and Ashtead for interesting and simple pottery. He was most enthusiastic about Doulton's flambé ware ('No firm deserves greater praise than Messrs. Doulton's for their constant endeavour to produce pottery of a high artistic order') and A. E. Gray's dinner-ware ('This ware is excellent in its simplicity, great use being made of small bright touches of on-glaze enamel colour, which gives a clean and wholesome effect – so necessary to utilitarian ware'). Although he was trying hard to give credit where credit was due, he had to conclude that while other countries, particularly Denmark, showed 'originality of design' and 'vigorous modern conceptions':

> The British Section as a whole was inclined to be rather staid and dull. There was in the Pottery Section a real lack of spirit of adventure on the artistic side ... A little virility in the treatment of clay by our distinguished potters would have created a sensation ...

The *Pottery Gazette* was of much the same opinion, but its summing up of the *Exposition* gives little indication that the British potters could be persuaded to move forward with Forsyth's spirit of adventure:

> ... if the exhibits were to be adjudged solely from the point of view of art, as divorced from the technique by which they are supported, other nations might support a claim for pre-eminence as regards newness of artistic ideas. After all, however, newness is not everything; and to be ever striving to create something new in art must necessarily lead, at times, to the creation of freaks and monstrosities. Someone has suggested that, for the purposes of the present Paris Exhibition, 'bad new' might have received more consideration than 'good old'. But, at any time, we ourselves would far prefer the latter, even at the risk of being regarded as unprogressive.

CHAPTER TWO

New Fashions in the Potteries

□ Gordon M. Forsyth and the Stoke-on-Trent School of Art

The potters of Staffordshire may have been reluctant to listen to the DIA, but the one man who did succeed in holding their attention on matters of design was Gordon M. Forsyth. He was born in Fraserburgh, Scotland, in 1879, studied at the Royal College of Art, London, under W. R. Lethaby, and in 1902 was appointed Art Director at Minton, Hollis and Co., where he designed tile faience and mosaic decoration. He moved to Pilkington's Tile and Pottery Company as chief artist in 1905, returning there after World War I, and in 1920 he was appointed Superintendent of Art Instruction for the Stoke-on-Trent School of Art – a post which he held until 1944/5 and which was to make him the greatest single influence on design in the Potteries throughout the 1920s and 1930s.

The first schools of design officially recorded in the Potteries were established in Hanley and Stoke in 1847. During the second half of the nineteenth century, individual schools were established in all six towns, Burslem, Stoke, Hanley, Fenton, Tunstall and Longton, as well as in neighbouring Newcastle-under-Lyme. (Arnold Bennett, the novelist and amateur painter, attended art classes at the Wedgwood Instititute in Burslem in 1885.) With the Federation of the towns in 1910, the schools came under one jurisdiction, with Burslem, the most progressive, as the principal school.

Forsyth's appointment was greeted with enthusiasm; he had a long training as a working potter and therefore had a sound knowledge of both practice and theory. He clearly recognized that he was in a strong position to affect design in the pottery industry from within, which was to achieve much more in this closed community than advice proffered from outside. By giving his students a firm art training and actively encouraging them to use their skills in industry, a raising of design standards was bound to occur, albeit gradually.

The art classes under Forsyth's direction were split between the various school locations. Stoke specialized in clay working – throwing, turning, experimental firing and glazing; Hanley was used for design evening classes only; at Burslem both day and evening classes were held; and Longton was a relatively small outpost. In 1925 a junior art department was established at Burslem to raise the standard of apprenticeship and to feed talented students back into the pottery industry. Harold Holdway, later to become an influential Chief Designer at W.T. Copeland, won a scholarship to the junior art department at the age of 13, soon after its inception. His education there consisted of half art training and half general subjects, and after two years he was also introduced to factory training, to enable him to tie his artistic skills to the techniques of the potteries. Holdway's sketchbooks from his schooldays show an astonishing range of drawing skills for such a young child – drawings from life, detailed human anatomy, landscapes, copies of flowers, animals both naturalistic and stylized, and of course steam trains and fast cars, the natural modern enthusiasms of a young man.

Forsyth made sure that his students' art training was sophisticated and academic, and he was careful to strike the most productive balance between tradition and Modernism in pottery design. He never detracted from the past design achievements of the potteries, suggesting that they were a firm basis from which to draw inspiration for the new, and he used the schools rather as a research department, encouraging the students to experiment with new decorations. He was keenly aware, both from the opinions expressed at local Ceramic Society meetings and from his own experience as a working potter, that these were the ways to the Stoke-on-Trent heart, and by December 1925, at a meeting of the Art Section of the Ceramic Society, he was using the idea of reliance on tradition to good advantage:

> The war seems to have marked the end of a definite period in art, and we now appear to be at the beginning of the development of a new style. The universality of this striving for new artistic expression leads one to believe that it has the quality of permanency; it is something very much bigger than a mere change of fashion; it was heralded by a complete revolution against our usually accepted ideas of art, and it has settled down to the more solid basis of sound and rational craftsmanship. To get this quality, artists have turned back to the primitive for inspiration – a very natural procedure, for which there are several historic precedents in the greatest art movements of the world.

The passage illustrates Forsyth's delicate approach to the problems of design in the Potteries, and in the same lecture he went on to make it perfectly clear that he understood the industrial and business demands of manufacturers and the difficulties they faced in adapting to change. Above all, he was able to talk in terms of 'we' rather than 'you'.

At this time Forsyth believed 'primitive' models, often in the form of the 'peasant' floral hand-painted designs already discussed, to be a good advancement in design. They certainly provided a welcome escape from the lithographic transfer designs that had plagued the industry during the preceding years, even if they did not take care of all the problems of simplicity of shape. Forsyth's wide experience of the industry meant that he was able to be content with a relatively slow advancement of ideas, and was not tempted into the DIA pitfall of demanding a virtual overnight revolution in design thought. By the late 1930s, his voiced opinions were to become more stringent, but only in good time, when the industry had made the new design discoveries for itself.

The simple floral designs were produced in abundance by the young paintresses who attended evening classes at the schools. Descriptions of evenings in the art schools show the atmosphere as easy going, lively, colourful and – for working-class young women in Stoke-on-Trent – Bohemian. Young women would flood in sporting bobbed hair and cloche hats to sit in the conservatory copying flowers, or exercise their brushwork skills with the fashionable and vivid motifs of the jazz age.

Forsyth's emphasis on hand-painting capitalized on the lead given by some manufacturers, notably Josiah Wedgwood (and Sons), and largely helped to establish a working practice which was to become widespread in the potteries throughout the late 1920s and 1930s. Its drawback was that it to some extent delayed any concerted effort to come to terms with total machine-production. Looking back from the vantage point of 1937, Sir Nikolaus Pevsner, in his *Inquiry into Industrial Art in England*, was able to conclude:

> Mr Forsyth's own sympathies in pottery decoration seem to be rather with the development of modern hand-painting than with mass-production methods. It is noteworthy that hand-paintresses trained by him have been able to hold their own against the progress of un-skilled labour in pottery making . . . the excellence of the Burslem School and its influence on industry appears to be to a large extent the work of one personality rather than of any special system of organization.

Pevsner also emphasized, however, the strong relationship which Forsyth had with the industrialists and the fact that his training methods had secured the interests of some of the best manufacturers. Forsyth not only had good personal links with the industry, but went to some lengths to involve his students in the community (decorating hospitals and churches), and to maintain his useful friendship with the editor of the local evening paper, who printed copious news stories about the art schools. As a result, he was able to make art education an accepted practice in the community as well as to advise his students on the best potteries to approach, and the manufacturers on the best students to employ. For example, he asked A. E. Gray to employ the young Susie Cooper, and among his other notable pupils were Harold Holdway of Copeland, and Victor Skellern and Millicent Taplin of Wedgwood. In 1930, the *Pottery Gazette* commented:

> There is now a sympathetic bond between the manufacturers and the art schools, which was entirely absent in years gone by. We understand that hardly a day passes without some inquiry, some request for help being made by the manufacturers to the art schools. Sometimes there may be a call for an apprentice; sometimes for a fully fledged designer. The antagonistic criticism which was formerly levelled against the art schools has almost entirely disappeared.

,th did not exactly hurry the course of Modernism (and as Pevsner
,ests, he may have been slow to take up the cause of good new lithographic
ζn), but he successfully advanced new ideas within the traditions of an
стry suspicious of change, and equipped his students to be able to take
their own educated decisions about new design.

□ Cube Teapots (*Campbell Yard, Leicester*)

Concurrent with this emphasis on education and handcraft in 1925 was a
growing awareness in the minds of the businessmen of the novelty value of new
shapes and of the importance of advertising techniques to promote them. The
curious Cube Teapot Company was perhaps the first to capitalize on this
combined potential.

One of the ceramic items closest to the British heart is undoubtedly the
teapot, indispensable to the tea-drinking life, and also a source of constant
irritation – lids are liable to fall off and spouts inclined to dribble. At the back of
every British industrial potter's mind must be the thought that if only he could
produce the technically perfect or the irresistibly fashionable teapot his
fortune would be made.

When Cube Teapots established themselves on the scene in the early 1920s,
their product, although hailed as 'revolutionary' by the *Pottery Gazette* in October
1925, was not entirely new. Back in 1878, after the sensational 1862
International Exhibition, which included Japanese ceramics, Worcester had
made an 'oriental' cuboid teapot with extravagant and colourful decoration of
storks and bamboo with a handle moulded as a lizard. Other pottery
manufacturers made similar shapes, and the brilliant designer Christopher
Dresser (1834–1904) produced metal tea and coffee pots of stark geometric
shape in the 1870s and 1880s. Then an indented cube-shaped teapot in silver,
with wooden handle and finial, was designed and patented by Robert Johnson
in 1916, and marketed to the public as easy to pack and store. However, very
little commercial ceramic design had emerged in Britain by the mid-1920s
which could lay any claim to Art Deco or Cubist fashions, and the undecorated
Cube, as it came to be known, did appear revolutionary pictured alongside floral
and rounded 'eighteenth-century' style teapots. The *Cube*'s attributes are
succinctly described by the *Pottery Gazette*:

> This teapot, the inventors claim, eliminates all the faults of its predecessors,
> while it adds to itself new and necessary virtues. Although its shape follows
> that of a cube, it is not so geometrical in design that it loses all vestige of
> daintiness; in fact, to many, in view of the present desire for simplicity in
> decoration, its concealed spout, sunken lid, and built-in handle give an
> added charm.

From this it would seem that Cube Teapots had managed to pull off an early
modern design coup – to be praised for geometric yet simple design. The
company patented the shape for teapots, jugs, early morning sets and picnic
sets in 1925, and successfully leased it to a large number of manufacturers

*Cube Teapot sets designed for the
Cunard Steamphip Co. Ltd: in
banded and lined Foley China
(top) by E. Brain; and in matt-
glazed stoneware by George
Clewes and Son of Tunstall.
(Pages 47–9)*

throughout the period until World War II. Some, such as Wedgwood, Minton, and Copeland, were operating at the top end of the market and were therefore unlikely to adopt fly-by-night designs, and their choice of the shape endowed the *Cube* with respectability. However, these companies had a particular and lucrative market in mind, where the shape was practical not just for its design and pouring methods but also for its suitability for storage – hotels, and most importantly, the great passenger shipping lines.

The cube sets could be neatly, safely and economically stacked, with no spouts to break off with the rocking of the ship or in the chaos of mass washing-up. Minton produced hotel china from 1931, including a traditionally decorated *Cube* for the Cunard Line; Copeland produced examples around 1930 for Cunard and hotels around the globe, and Wedgwood were early leasers of the shape from 1925. In mid-1927, the Wedgwood pattern books for earthenware show designs for the Cube decorated with large 'peasant' florals – a slightly incongruous mix of styles.

Cube Teapots were also ahead of their time in advertising, adopting fierce campaigns which in 1925 were very unusual among pottery manufacturers (although Shelley was to develop advertising to a fine art only a year or so later). Sophisticated advertising techniques incorporating graphics and slogans were part of a new genre which had been developing in the US since World War I. The American post-war boom in the mass-production of consumer goods meant that the buyer was suddenly spoilt for choice and receptive to both information and persuasion about which model to opt for. American advertising was therefore very closely linked to the concept of 'industrial design', and its methods were beginning to filter through to Britain. The *Pottery Gazette* describes some of the advertising gimmicks employed for the *Cube*:

> They . . . have a moving demonstration display, showing the perfect pouring of the "cube" by tea perpetually pouring from the teapot into a cup. This they send out on loan. They have, also, a series of window displays in different sizes, depicting in a very realistic fashion the old era – a teapot with broken spout, and stained tablecloth, etc. – and the new era with the "cube" teapot, an immaculate table, a tidy maid, and a satisfied mistress.

An extensive press advertising campaign depicted, for example, happy shoppers emerging *en masse* with square packages above the caption: 'They're all pouring out with "Cube" Teapots!'; leaflets for the retailer, and energetic claims for the design's modernity contributed to a successful sales endeavour. Cube Teapots clearly felt that they could claim that they had hit upon the ultimate in teapot technology, describing their achievement as 'The Brilliant Climax in Teapot Construction', and were alert to possible criticism from the design purists. They soon modified their design to produce the 1926 *Cube*, which, according to the *Pottery Gazette*, 'is provided with a somewhat more roomy handle than its predecessor, an improved lock lid, an unrestricted opening and rounded interior, facilitating easy cleanout and, above all, a spout that is claimed to be absolutely non-drippable.' As a result, in 1926 they secured a gold medal for the teapot at the Nation's Health Exhibition.

Despite this success, the advertising campaign did not relax. An advertisement of 1928, for example, bears the caption: 'Why continue to advertise "Cube" perfect pouring teapots when they already enjoy the *largest sale of any* patent teapot in the world? It is to keep this *fact* before you . . .' By 1932, new and even absurd *Cube* designs were produced by the company, for example, a cuboid egg-stand which doubled up rather unsympathetically to 'rest cigars and cigarettes', the 'channel' surrounding the egg-cup used for ash.

Whether or not the extravagant claims made by Cube Teapots for their product's pouring abilities were justified is still a matter of debate: as for most teapots, its fans claim it pours perfectly, its opponents that it dribbles and, worse still, that its inset handle causes the user to burn his knuckles on the side of the pot. Nevertheless, cuboid teapots are still to be found in hotels, restaurants, trains, boats and planes, but perhaps found their final functional resting place as a component of the electric tea-maker. The streamlined design of today's models would have been impossible without a spoutless teapot into which boiling water could be automatically poured, as becomes obvious when one looks at the earliest automatic tea-making machine of 1902, an arrangement of springs and levers with a conventional teapot standing Heath-Robinson-like at its side.

□ Shelley Potteries (*The Foley, Longton*)

In the early 1920s the majority of pottery manufacturers who even bothered to advertise their products did so irregularly and in a restrained manner, often using no illustrations. Their advertisements, usually in the trade presses, were reminders of the general reputation of their companies rather than genuine efforts to persuade retailers to buy specific new goods. This modest approach was all that was needed by the large, well-known companies who had been producing traditional wares for a hundred years or more, but for the small or medium-sized manufacturer with a new idea up his sleeve more sophisticated techniques were needed to get the message across, as Cube Teapots realized, and Shelley Potteries were to develop still further.

The Shelley family entered into partnership with Wileman and Co. in 1872, and although the Shelley backstamp originated in 1910 and was used on wares, the pottery only changed its name to Shelley in 1925. The firm's managing director at this time, Percy Shelley, had had a business education, and one of his three sons, all of whom worked in the business, held a Bachelor of Commerce degree from Birmingham University. On the creative side of the enterprise, the talented art director Walter Slater was now assisted by his son Eric, who had studied at Stoke-on-Trent Art School, latterly under Gordon Forsyth. This strong management team had no intention of letting its new ideas go unnoticed in a competitive market. They opened new showrooms in Holborn, and enlisted the services of W. H. Smedley, a native of Stoke-on-Trent, to advertise their table and nursery wares (which are discussed in Chapter 6). They took a page every month in the *Pottery Gazette*, sometimes using full colour and sometimes two-colour images, and launched an advertising campaign in the national press, particularly in women's magazines.

Pieces from a china tea service in the Mode shape of 1930 by Shelley Potteries, decorated in dramatic black and red print and enamel geometric pattern, 1930–32. (Pages 57–8)

The most striking invention of their advertising campaign was the introduction in 1926 of the 'Shelley Girl', an elegant young woman drawn with the fine outlines of Art Deco graphics. She appeared in various guises, often draped in fox fur and with small nose peeping from under a cloche hat, always drinking tea from a delicate Shelley china cup. Sometimes she acquired a name, 'Elsie Harding', which in the 'twenties was more chic than it seems today. The implication of the advertisements was, of course, that tea-drinking was at its most fashionable out of Shelley cups.

The Shelley Girl was also modelled and produced in bone china by the company as a foot-high figure for use in the stylish window displays which they promoted for use by the retailers. They followed up their campaign with colour 'china leaflets' provided to the shops, which were in turn advertised in the *Pottery Gazette*, the covers using contemporary graphics to show discerning women admiring the quality of the tea-sets.

In 1927 they went one step further, introducing a bi-monthly magazine, the *Shelley Standard*, for retailers, which was published until 1931. The magazine gave advice, both discursive and pictorial, for the design of window displays (which became increasingly dramatic and stylized as they developed in the 1930s). In particular, the magazine contained articles giving advice on salesmanship to the retailer, with the proper approach he should take to his customer discussed at length. An essential part of this instruction was the characterization of the typical customer for Shelley's bone china tea and breakfast sets, whom they had correctly surmised to be middle-class, female and with an eye for fashion. In July 1930, for example, the *Shelley Standard* published a little essay entitled 'Good China from a Woman's Point of View' purporting to be by an anonymous 'Woman Customer' to illustrate the point to the salesman:

> Of course, my favourite china is my tea service. And here I think most other women would be in agreement with me. Women take great pride and joy in the best tea service. Mine has a rather modern pattern of brilliant hand-painted flowers in red, green, and orange.
> ... I think it an excellent plan if the china is chosen to match something in the room, such as window curtains or upholsteries, but this must be done without becoming monotonous. Breakfast in the kitchen can be quite bright and enjoyable if the breakfast service harmonizes with the colours of enamelled kitchen cabinets or the lacquered canisters on the shelves.

The 'Woman Customer' is hardly convincing as a personality, but she is a very clear indication of the market Shelley was aiming to attract. She is young, married, middle-class, and sufficiently modern and daring to suggest that breakfast might be taken in her fashionable kitchen – providing the tableware is right.

Watkins, Harvey and Senft point out in *Shelley Potteries* that the company's annual advertising budget reached a staggering £10,000, an expenditure which was not covered by profits. It did, however, ensure that they achieved an unrivalled distribution of the wares, as the *Pottery Gazette* pointed out in August 1929:

> They have a wonderful connection right through the British Isles; it would be difficult to enter a single town – industrial, residential, or purely agricultural – where the Shelley range of goods is not included in the stock of the recognized pottery vendor . . .

Shelley's Art Deco tableware designs, in fine, almost transparent bone china, were amongst the most beautiful and inventive produced in Britain. Their daring in matters of design and colour and its use on expensive bone china rather than cheap earthenware was unequalled anywhere in the industry. It was one thing to produce modern designs for very cheap earthenwares which would be abandoned and replaced by the latest fashion within a couple of years, but quite another to try to persuade the buyer to choose a dramatically modern design for her best bone china. As we shall see, most of the fine china manufacturers largely avoided producing very modern designs, relying instead on adaptations of traditional patterns which would not date. In 1931, the *Pottery Gazette* described Shelley as 'daring in their spirit', and went on to comment:

> They may, or may not, carry the public by storm; but one thing they certainly will do; they will cause people to stop and think. And if one can do that there is something to be hoped for. There are those who, for a long time past, have been agitating for a more adventurous spirit in the manufacturing circles of the pottery trade. Well, here it is!

The Shelley Girl's first sips of tea in the advertisements were taken from plain white china cups in the *Queen Anne* shape, which was registered in 1926. This was octagonal, with the sides of the cup slightly concave so that the whole appeared rather like a flower. It could hardly be described as modern, but it was relatively simple and pretty, and being in plain white, relied on the quality of the china and the potting for effect. The intentions of Shelley were clearly stated in their china leaflets:

> From the very earliest days white has been accepted as a symbol of purity. To look at and to touch any piece of Shelley White China is to realize how very beautifully this symbol has been translated.

The company was keen to emphasize the bright whiteness of their fine bone china and its delicate appeal to the buyer. However, they realized that plain china was an acquired taste, and were also to develop decorated wares to the full. In 1925 an editorial in the *Pottery Gazette* had stated:

> . . . it is generally recognized that nothing can be more acceptable, in the long run, than good printing in conjunction with good enamelling – two departments in which English pottery can hold its own in open competition with the rest of the world. On the art side, a greater recognition of this would be the trade's salvation.

Shelley employed the 'print and enamel' techniques of decorating pottery, where an outline pattern, most often in black, brown or blue, is transfer-printed onto the pottery to be filled in by hand to great effect with coloured enamel paints. During the remaining years of the 1920s, the *Queen Anne* shape was applied with a range of print and enamel patterns from traditional florals to

A selection of Shelley Potteries'
china tea-, coffee- and dinner-
ware in the Regent shape of c.
1932. The pattern (front), print
and enamel and banded, is a
fine geometric design of
graduated blocks, dating from
1933; the plate and cup and
saucer (top left) are in a print
and enamel floral design of
'Honesty', c. 1932–34; the cups
and saucers (centre) show fine
washbanding and lining, c.
1932–34. (Pages 58–60)

more restrained and formal designs. A number of 'Cottage Garden' scenes was used, depicting English flowers in a naturalistic style, always including tall varieties like hollyhocks and foxgloves to give height to the patterns. These 'chocolate box' designs proved popular, and were repeated in various colours and permutations of the same theme. By the late 'twenties, Shelley's pattern books (where designs and instructions for their painting are recorded for use in the factories) show the gardens and cottages becoming more stylized and simplified as Art Deco became a more current design language for graphic and other adaptations. In addition, the palette of colours used to paint the patterns became brighter and less naturalistic, mainly black, scarlet and sea green.

The most successful design on the *Queen Anne* shape is known as *Sunset and Tall Trees*. Introduced in 1929, it appears frequently in the pattern books in varying colour combinations, and continued to be produced up to about 1935, a relatively long period for a fashionable new design. The pattern features a central country field gate, with tall black trees towering around it, and on the horizon a yellow or red (or other colour) bursting sunset. The stylized sunset is a familiar Art Deco device and the arrangement of tall trees on either side of a central landscape a favourite motif among the Victorians and later, of Art Nouveau. The pattern proved adaptable enough to be used on some of Shelley's more conventional shapes such as *Vine* or *Doric*.

Other popular patterns on *Queen Ann* were *Blue Iris* and *Crabtree*, the latter devised as a coloured lithographic print and used on dinner-ware to match the tea-services. By 1930, numerous patterns containing combinations of black trees with coloured fruits, bursting sunsets, stylized landscapes with trees or tall flowers framing them in the foreground were produced. By 1932, the pretty *Queen Anne* shape was adapted for *Floral Dainty* wares, the octagonal shape being decorated, for example, in alternating pink and white sections to enhance the look of a flower-petal structure, and the handle re-shaped and moulded as a tulip, subsequently painted. Despite the daintiness and floral moulded handles, such vivid patterns as solid matt black ground with a gold flower were also used for the shape.

In 1928, Eric Slater (b. 1902) took over from his father much of the responsibility for design at Shelley. He was responsible for the shapes, glazes and patterns throughout the period of Shelley's dramatic productions of the late 1920s and early 1930s. Although he was the youngest of a powerful pottery dynasty dating back to the eighteenth century, he was to use tradition to its best advantage – perhaps as a result of his training under Gordon Forsyth – extending his high-quality potting principles to inventive but well-constructed new designs. By 1929, the *Pottery Gazette* was commenting favourably on his work:

> There is a freshness of spirit in the designs, a uniformly high standard of quality noticeable in the body of their wares, and apparent on all sides a desire on the part of the firm to supply the trade with a middle-class brand of both china and earthenware which will prove capable of giving universal satisfaction.

In 1930, Shelley's launched the *Vogue* tea-ware shape, the name immediately linking the radically different tea-sets with high French fashion. *Vogue* was severe, consisting of an inverted, steep-sided cone with a solid triangular handle to the tea-cups and milk jugs. It has come to typify the most elegant of the extreme Art Deco shapes produced in British tableware of the period, and what makes it even more exceptional is that this uncompromisingly modern style was used, not for transient earthenware manufacture, but for very fine bone china. The creation and production of the *Vogue* shape was a very daring response to the tough economic climate and consequent competitiveness in the Potteries (see p. 64). The youthful management team were not concerned to play safe, but instead took the risk of attracting attention to themselves for extremism in the hope of establishing themselves as the most up-to-the-minute manufacturers.

Vogue did make an impact, particularly with its Art Deco-inspired print and enamel patterns, painted with a limited but vivid palette of colours. The most striking pattern was *Sunray*, a boldly geometric sunburst covering almost the entire surface of the wares with its solid triangular 'rays'. Colour combinations were stark – black, orange and gold; red, green and gold; or blue, green and gold, for example, on the delicate pure white china. Other patterns were variations on a strict Cubist theme: rectangles and squares in various arrangements, often overlapping and in three contrasting colours such as green, black and silver (a favoured contemporary combination widely used at the time), red and black, or yellow and black. Precisely outlined diamonds and narrow triangles, reminiscent of the 'lightning flash' motif used by many European designers, were also used, as well as stylized, angular flower designs.

The *Mode* shape, with its similarly fashionable French name, was launched later in 1930. It too was of inverted conical shape with solid triangular handles, although the cone was at a less pronounced angle than *Vogue*, resulting in a wider, splayed effect. *Sunray* and Cubist patterns were used on the shape, and a greater proportion of stylized florals than are found on *Vogue*. One of the best is of stylized red tulips (combined with mauve, orange and dark green), or yellow and ochre tulips (with green and dark and light blue). Another pattern depicted a black print of peacock butterfly wings, enamelled in yellow or green. Others were produced with dramatic gold interiors to the cups, enamelled one colour on the outside. The shape was also adapted for co-ordinating dinner-ware.

Although *Vogue* and *Mode* had enormous visual impact, and did succeed in establishing Shelley as something of the 'fashion house' of fine tea-ware, they did not endure. After two or three years they were phased out, and cannot have been an overwhelming commercial success in view of the enormous amounts of money which Shelley spent to advertise them. Their short lifespan indicates the problems of introducing dramatically modern ideas to an essentially conservative market. It was difficult to persuade the buying public to tune its eye to such a new shape and to accept that a cup need not incorporate a curve and a handle need not have a hole through the middle. Even when the overall design was as exciting as Shelley's, the perceptual gap was too wide for the average buyer, particularly when the majority of wares which she was used to using and seeing on the market were still of a very traditional nature.

This problem is well illustrated, as an aside, by the fate which befell the **Greta**

Various items of earthen tea-ware in Bizarre Ware *by Clarice Cliff: the shape is* Conical, *designed in 1929, and the exotic freehand-painted pattern is* Ravel. *(Pages 68–73)*

Pottery. This small undertaking was conceived by Margaretta Marks, a German designer who arrived in Stoke-on-Trent from the Bauhaus, fresh and enthusiastic, and intent on launching her starkly modern pottery shapes in Britain. She persuaded Ridgway and Minton to produce these angular and sparsely decorated shapes for her, but they proved too radical for the British market, and she was soon forced to give up her enterprise.

It should also be said of Shelley's *Vogue* and *Mode* that however pleasing they were as objects of display they were not the most practical for taking tea. In an inverted cone the beverage will cool quickly, as the surface area of the liquid is much greater than the volume at the bottom of the cup. Also, with no hole in the handle to crook a finger through, a cup can more easily slip from the hand (particularly, as was said at the time, the larger masculine hand). Moreover, the shapes looked rather strange when decorated with the less severe banded patterns that were becoming popular and which Shelley's were interested in producing.

The shapes came in for a good deal of criticism, particularly in relation to the solid handle, so Eric Slater responded by designing the modified *Eve* shape in 1932 (this name, perhaps, deriving from ideas of a 'new woman' modern enough to buy such china shapes). *Eve* cups were similar to *Mode*, but the handles were open triangles, and accompanying teapots had curved spouts for facility in pouring, rather than straight ones at a severe angle.

Just as the shape of *Eve* was a modification of earlier designs, so were the patterns used to decorate it. The dominant geometrics were scaled down to comparatively small motifs, fairly similar to those found on the tableware of other manufacturers. They were frequently complemented by heavy coloured bands on the rims and bases of the cups, while other patterns consisted entirely of banding, for example in coral-red and silver. The shape is still found in the pattern books of 1939, by which time simple banded wares had been widely produced. *Eve* was also used for the less stylized, and sometimes virtually naturalistic, florals which once again became popular in the late 1930s. Shelley's were no exception in using the fashionable flowers of the time for decoration – for example, crocuses, gladioli, daisies and pansies. As the 1930s advanced, the colours also reflected the current modern tastes, with brown, grey and ochre replacing the vivid reds, oranges, greens and blacks of the turn of the decade.

The finest shape which Eric Slater designed for Shelley was undoubtedly *Regent*, decorations for which first appear in the pattern books in 1932. As its name suggests, the shape takes more account of tradition than its predecessors. The conical rim of the cup tapers in a curve towards the base, and inside the simple but conventional handle is a hollow ring (the whole handle has been compared to one half of a pair of scissors). This was a device unique at the time of *Regent's* introduction, but which certainly drew inspiration from nineteenth-century designs, for example by Worcester. It was the perfect design compromise: simple and modern but with traditional overtones, not high-fashion but suitably stylized. Not surprisingly it met with critical acclaim from such arbiters as the DIA and Gordon Forsyth, who praised its simplicity and the design of its handle, which was 'practical and easy to hold' in his influential

book *20th Century Ceramics*, published in 1936. By 1933, Shelley's advertisements in the *Pottery Gazette* show *Regent* alongside *Eve*, *Queen Anne*, *Vogue* and traditional *York* shapes, although a year later similar advertisements were devoted to *Regent* alone, as the company's most successful new shape.

Early *Regent* patterns include florals, very few geometrics, and many simple banded and lined patterns, for example brown band and jade-green line, green and mauve, green and blue, green and orange. Banding is a technique where a flat area of colour, wider than a mere line, is applied spirally with a brush while a piece is rotated on the wheel; shaded gradations of colour were achieved within the band by exerting varying pressures over the brushstroke. Such florals as *Anemone Bunch* and *Syringa* proved very popular. The shape seemed infinitely adaptable, looking as balanced with florals as it did with bands and with the 'Modernist' patterns of the later 1930s. *Regent* was used for many different patterns: graduated all-over designs of bands merging from shade to shade in greens, pinks, blues and yellows; a popular *Green Swirls* pattern; and a 'double' polka dot pattern. The polka dot was used extensively for tableware patterns in the later 1930s, and harks back to the 1870s, when spotted borders were a popular decorative device. Other *Regent* tea services were decorated on the outside and coloured inside the cups in a pale shade, or decorated with scattered leaves and the neat pastel florals which eventually replaced the more domineering rustic examples of earlier years. Decorating instructions in the pattern books indicate the softer colour treatments, with notes for colours with such names as Harmony Brown, Salmon Pink, Egg, Apple and Ginger. As early as October 1933, for example, directions appear for a silk-print pattern in grey, with wavy lines tinted in Meadow Green, Turkish Blue and Amber. In a number of examples of the period, lithographic printing in more than one colour was used to make up part of the pattern as well as the earlier outlines.

In the second half of the 1930s, Shelly returned to more traditional shapes, largely abandoning the designs of earlier years, and *Regent* survived alongside *Oxford*, *Princess* (an adaptation of *Queen Anne*), *York*, *Ely*, *Kent*, *Essex*, *Court*, and *Mayfair*. These names indicate the Englishness of the wares; there was no more aspiration to French fashion. Trade had settled down to some sort of equilibrium and there was less need or demand for escapist designs. In May 1937, the *Pottery Gazette* commented:

> It is definitely noticed that, both in shapes and decorations, there have been many striking changes in 'Shelley' china quite recently. The severe angular shapes are much less in evidence, as are also many of those styles of decoration which many people are apt to describe under the sweeping term 'modernistic'. In many ways, it would seem, there has been a rounding-off to conform to the public taste; there is more to be seen in floral sprays and coloured bands, and much more gold is now being employed in connection with many of the decorations. This might possibly be taken as an indication that there is more money to spend nowadays on better-class household equipment.

As a footnote to the tableware produced, it is worth noting that Eric Slater was also experimenting with designs for decorative wares – vases, jugs and chargers

– often known in the trade at the time as 'ornamentals' or 'fancies'. In 1932, Shelley's developed earthenware designs known as *Harmony Ware*, which they produced until 1935. The wares were hand decorated, banded in graduated shades of one, two or more colours. A one-colour piece, for example, might have strips of colour ranging from a dark blue at one extreme to the palest sky blue at the other, with six or seven intermediary shades. Yellows, pinks, greens and greys were colours frequently employed either singly or in combination. The resultant different shades of colour meant that the *Harmony Wares* were varied enough to suit every decorative scheme. The shapes used were simple and unpretentious. The technique was also used on some china teaware shapes, notably *Regent*.

Harmony Wares were also produced with a 'drip glaze' technique where one band of colour appears to run down into the next. Watkins, Harvey and Senft point out that Eric Slater discovered the techniques used for dripware by accident while he was producing the straightforward banded *Harmony Wares*, and decided to pursue the idea. The powder colours were mixed with turpentine and applied as bands, with the pot being decorated on a wheel. Once the glazes had dripped to form a suitable decoration, simply breathing on the mixture would dry it sufficiently to prevent further dripping.

Other earthenwares included simple jugs, preserve jars and so on, all produced in subtle and sympathetic designs, predominantly banded and lined in a limited combination of colours.

Thus we can see that during the Shelley Potteries' thirteen years of production, shapes moved from elaborate, through Art Deco geometric, to Modernist curves, with the traditional shapes co-existing in the background. Decorations moved from naturalistic florals, through brightly coloured stylized florals, daring geometrics, more modest geometrics and wash bands, to a mixture of simple modern designs and more traditional florals. In about 1932, a number of these shapes and patterns were produced and advertised alongside one another, until the more extreme fell by the wayside and the simple curves and patterns of the modern wares took over. This year, indeed, was something of a turning point for the industry as a whole, as well as an illustration of the confusion about what constituted 'modern design' – the superficial features of French Art Deco seen at the 1925 Paris *Exposition*, bright expressionistic colours, or the refined and rather strict Modernism of the German Bauhaus. It is unlikely that any one of these interpretations of the 'new style' was exactly clear in the minds of the pottery manufacturers, but in dilute form they all provided inspiration.

CHAPTER THREE

The Art Deco Style Catches On

The productions of Shelley provide a useful model for an examination of tendencies within the whole industry because the new tableware designs they produced were often first in the field and relatively unadulterated examples of a particular style. But it is easy to imagine that only a few companies and artists were responsible for the design developments of the period, and this is not strictly true. Names such as Shelley, Clarice Cliff, Foley, Susie Cooper and Keith Murray are those that immediately come to mind, and certainly they are amongst the most interesting and inventive, but in the 1930s some four hundred pottery manufacturers were operating in Stoke-on-Trent alone, and few of them were oblivious to changing tastes and fashions. The greater proportion of the factories producing tablewares tried new designs in one or more of the 'categories' which are evident from Shelley's productions, with varying degrees of success and real regard for style. Many watered down rustic floral and Art Deco themes to produce what some would see as the worst vulgarizations of the style; some produced undeniably ugly and even kitsch designs; but the vast majority produced pleasing and occasionally exceptional designs for their simple tea- and dinner-services.

A great many potteries experimented with the design obsessions of the era, copied each other, edged into something slightly different, and helped move the industry as a whole from one kind of design to another. It is very unlikely that one pottery could have developed new designs in isolation, so it would be ill advised to consider any one figure or pottery outside the wider context of the industry. Clarice Cliff, for example, is often considered a unique artist, or design eccentric, who emerged as a lone fashion figure from a moribund industry, but it will become clear that, although she did possess individualistic qualities, she was not a maverick and did not have a monopoly on originality.

Moreover, the very fashionable wares that were produced in the late 1920s and throughout the 1930s were far from constituting the industry's principal output. They were produced against a backdrop of traditional manufacture – shapes which had survived little changed for sometimes two hundred years,

A Bizarre Ware *breakfast set by Clarice Cliff in the chunky* Bon Jour *shape, painted with the* Cowslip *pattern in the mid-late 1930s. (Page 73)*

and decorations which were adapted only very slowly to suit gradually changing tastes, as we have seen with William Adams's *Titian Ware* (see Chapter 1). The larger companies in particular, producing mainly fine china for the top end of the home and export markets, launched very little which could immediately be perceived as 'modern', and when they did the results were a tiny proportion of their overall output. Export markets, particularly the important colonial ones, were often conservative, preferring dainty reminders of the roses of good old England to newfangled ideas. The same principle is at work today: for example, perhaps the best-selling bone china tableware of all time, Royal Albert's *Old Country Roses*, is still being produced by the million pieces, but could as well have been bought in the 1880s as the 1980s. The design consists of precisely the 'naturalistic rose sprays tastily displayed' that manufacturer H. J. Plant had identified in 1921 as the type of decoration much appreciated by the public, to the despair of contemporary Modernists. The Royal Albert shape is best described as 'frilly', with both eighteenth-century and Victorian overtones (and its largest market is Canada).

The top markets that such companies as Wedgwood, Mintons, Worcester and W. T. Copeland were catering for protected them against having to produce novel ideas for everyday cheap tableware, while their size provided a buffer against the economic conditions resulting from the Depression. It was rather the small and medium-sized companies who had to respond to fashion in their tablewares, which were cheap enough to be replaced within a few years and therefore could not rely on a pattern whose main attribute was that it would not date. They needed to invent something interesting enough to catch the eye and compete in the severely depressed market of the late 1920s and early 1930s, and thus economic factors were of paramount importance in persuading many a reluctant manufacturer to change his design ideas.

By July 1926, at about the same time as the fox-furred Shelley Girl appeared, at least 25,000 pottery workers in Stoke-on-Trent were unemployed. The *Pottery Gazette* commented on the situation:

> Eight weeks of coal strike have had the effect of placing the pottery industry in what might almost be termed a disastrous condition. At the time of writing there are very few potteries indeed to be found working at all and these only under the severest disabilities.

The coal stoppage continued on after the General Strike of 1926 had ended, and obviously seriously affected the industry. If the small manufacturer did not feel able to risk the expense of ambitious advertising he would perhaps be well advised to do something to attract attention to his own business rather than the next man's. In addition to facing problems in the British market, the manufacturer needed to consider conditions of trade in his foreign, export markets during these uncertain times. In the late 1920s Britain's export trade in china and earthenware was largest to Canada, followed by the British East Indies, the Argentine Republic, and then the USA and Australia. There is little evidence that the average small pottery manufacturer was at all knowledgeable about retail demand in these foreign markets (we have seen that his awareness of the home market on his doorstep was extremely limited). He may, however, have had a rudimentary idea of fashions in North America: although ceramic design in the US had begun to be influenced by the Modernism issuing from Vienna and the artists of the Wiener Werkstätte, the market in the late 1920s was sluggish and its cheaper levels open to novelty and colour as visual antidotes to harsh economic realities. The requirements of home and export markets were thus broadly perceived to be similar.

□ Hand-painted decoration

We have already seen how A. E. Gray was among the first to exploit hand-painted decoration on pottery rather than relying on badly designed lithographs. The growing fashion for hand-decoration in the Potteries was inspired by developments at the influential firm, Josiah Wedgwood. The firm had employed designers Alfred and Louise Powell in a studio in London from 1907, where they experimented with hand-painted decorations for Wedgwood's industrially-produced wares. In the ensuing years, hand-painted wares, mainly ornamentals, were increasingly produced by Wedgwood, until in 1926 the demand justified the opening of a studio at the Etruria, Stoke-on-Trent, factory. Here a number of paintresses were employed to implement the Powells' designs, which were now being applied to tablewares (see Chapter 8). Indeed, by the mid-1920s this idea had established quite a grip on the industry as a whole, and it is worth examining the pros and cons, as they were considered at the time, of this manner of decoration. It was, of course, hardly new, and as a result, those discussing its value in the 1920s were divided into those who saw it as reintroducing the possibility of fresh new patterns and those who saw it as a retrograde step, a return to craft principles rather than those of mass-production. In the former camp was the influential Gordon Forsyth, who was extensively teaching hand-painting techniques at Stoke-on-Trent School of Art. After the 1925 Paris *Exposition*, Forsyth was enthusiastically reporting:

> Another of the outstanding features of the Exhibition was the tremendous preponderance of hand-decorated ware. There was almost a total absence of mechanical processes in decoration. This, it seems to me, was a very healthy sign, and I feel sure these are the lines we ought to work upon much more in the Potteries. People seem to be getting dead-tired of the ordinary, commonplace lithographic patterns. Some of these patterns really never were alive, and they are more dead now than ever.

An opposing view was put forward at a meeting of the Art Section of the Ceramic Society in November 1925 by the chairman, F. Lambert, then Curator of Stoke-on-Trent Museums, who is reported as disagreeing:

> Mr Forsyth praised the return to almost entirely hand-decoration. Was not that . . . going rather too far back in the attempt to produce fine art? It must not be overlooked that nowadays we were living in an age of machinery. Ought we not, therefore, to make the very best possible use of this machinery, rather than revert to methods that were in force when machinery, in its present form, was unknown?

A Fantasque 'tea for one' set
by Clarice Cliff in the first
version of the Stamford shape
(the teapot spout poured badly,
and was later curved). The
freehand-painted pattern is
Melon of c. 1930–34. (Page
73)

The discussion continued with Gray defending Forsyth's position, adding that in reverting to hand-treatments the new decorations need not be elaborate. Another speaker dubbed Forsyth an 'idealist'; and yet another suggested that the good hand-work should go into the original designs which should then be used to make lithographs for mass-production (a proposition which was to be discussed and put into action in the early 1930s). In his superb study *An Inquiry into Industrial Art in England*, published in 1937, Nikolaus Pevsner comments that 'unscrupulous manufacturers feel annoyed by this human competition with their mechanical methods'.

For the time being hand-painting won the day for new patterns in decoration. The available lithographs were of a miserably poor standard of design, and hand-painting *over* the glaze, which enabled the most vivid colours to be fired at a lower temperature than was required for the glaze itself, was the best way to create the colourful wares that were becoming popular. As the 1920s progressed, hand-painted decorations and gradual changes of shapes were implemented to accommodate stylized florals and 'Cubist' designs. Companies such as A. G. Richardson (*Crown Ducal*, see pp. 112–5), E. Brain (*Foley China*, see pp. 80–5) and the Newport Pottery Co. were already beginning to produce noticeably different tableware designs with bright enamel paints and often octagonal shapes.

□ Newport Pottery Co. (*Newport Lane, Burslem*)

In 1920, the firm of A. J. Wilkinson (Royal Staffordshire Pottery, Burslem) took over the neighbouring Newport Pottery, which ten years later was to become the source of some of the most exotic earthen tableware produced during this period. Clarice Cliff, who was to make the pottery famous, was born in 1899, and joined A. J. Wilkinson at the age of 17 as a lithographer. At some point during her apprenticeship she attended classes at Burslem School of Art: this date is generally given as between 1924 and 1925, although her own biographical notes, published in conjunction with an exhibition of her work at Brighton Museum and Art Gallery in 1972, state that she attended the school at the age of 16 or 17. Certainly by the early 1920s she had become fascinated by the fashionably garish colours of the jazz age and the Russian Ballet, whose extraordinarily vivid sets were in contrast to the austerities of the simpler forms of Modernism.

Serge Diaghilev's ballet company, which first visited London in 1911, was to leave a lasting impression on modern interior designers, whose work was satirized as part of Osbert Lancaster's collection of interiors in *Home Sweet Homes*, published with amusing illustrations in 1939:

> Before one could say Nijinsky the pale pastel shades which had reigned supreme on the walls of Mayfair for almost two decades were replaced by a riot of barbaric hues – jade green, purple, every variety of crimson and scarlet, and, above all, orange.

The more modest walls of Stoke-on-Trent could be similarly transformed:

Clarice Cliff's sister Ethel has described on several occasions how Clari
painted their shared bedroom extraordinary colours. A chest-of-drawers,
example, was transformed with orange paint, toned with black between
drawers and on top.

By 1924 or 1925, Clarice Cliff was one of many young women in the Pott
with a rudimentary grasp of Cubist and colourful Art Deco ideas, which
supplemented by such events as the opening in 1922 of Tutankhamen's
which sparked a craze for Egyptiana. A glance at some of the pieces of p
painted by students at the art schools clearly shows that many
paintresses were experimenting with 'jazz' and 'Cubist' patterns in
colours. Clarice herself was not only determined enough to shock her
by painting her bedroom in wild colours, but also, it appears, to persu
Wilkinson's Sales Director, Colley Shorter, to allow her to experiment on some
left-over stock of undecorated wares at Newport Potteries. These pieces were of
predominantly Art Nouveau shapes and were probably seconds – it seems
unlikely that Newport would have accumulated a large stock of perfect
undecorated wares.

It is often suggested that Colley Shorter saw the potential in bright and
thickly applied paint for covering the imperfections in discarded wares. He
must also have been keen to dispose of this otherwise dormant stock, and the
decorations were a means of bringing old shapes right up to date. Also, as 1926
was the year of the General Strike and the extended coal stoppages, he may
well have seen it as desirable to use up existing wares when faced with the
industrial difficulties of producing new ones.

After a brief spell at the Royal College of Art in London in 1927, Clarice Cliff
returned to the Newport Pottery to continue, now with the assistance of a few
paintresses, to decorate the stock of wares with her bizarre patterns. Probably
late in 1927, Colley Shorter tested the market with the wares, and, to the
travelling salesmen's astonishment, the vivid plates and vases, with their
highly coloured bands and zigzag triangles, were snapped up by the retailers.
Bizarre Ware, at this stage consisting only of decorative rather than tableware
(with the exception of a few teapots), was launched. By March 1928, the *Pottery
Gazette* had sent its reporter round to Newport's studio, and commented of
Bizarre:

> . . . if the name is intended to convey that the designs are singular and
> capricious, then it is, indeed, thoroughly apt. In viewing this new type of
> pottery decoration one has to remember, that there is a demand, in the
> realm of modern furnishings, for, shall we say, extravagant colourings . . .

He goes on to judge rather patronizingly that the retailer should 'not succumb
to your first shock at what is undoubtedly a real blaze of colour', but should
remember that the female of a household might well be attracted by such
colour 'even though it may be simply riotous in its presentation'.

Although Clarice Cliff has since stated that the paintresses who worked in
her studio were merely filling in the guidelines of patterns she had drawn on
the wares, the *Pottery Gazette* article presents rather a different picture, and is
worth quoting at length for its detailed description of the *Bizarre* studio:

It consists for the time being of a single room, in which is to be found a group of young ladies working under the personal superintendence of a mistress instructor, who, whilst herself creating new free-hand styles of decoration, and applying these direct to pieces of ornamental pottery, simultaneously holds a watching brief over what is being done by her apprentices. It is quite a delight to watch this coterie of hand-craft decorators – for the most part, we believe, if not entirely, the product of the local art schools – giving *free expression to their artistic inclinations direct upon pottery.* [author's italics] They have no printer's guiding lines to hedge them round, no prescribed limitations; they simply brush away with colour upon pottery, producing designs which are never conventional, oft-times even whimsical, but full of life and, in the ultimate, attractive to a degree. These studio painters, if so we may describe them, seem to exhibit a real zest for producing something that is fresh, even though it may be startling in its newness.

Clarice Cliff was clearly in charge, but it is quite evident from this firsthand description (and there is no reason to think that the reporter would set out to mislead) that she was not the only artist-designer at work. This has subsequently been confirmed in interviews with the paintresses themselves, who tell of their own interpretations of the modern styles they saw on postcards and the like, which were nevertheless marketed under Clarice Cliff's name.

This was not surprising, since from a marketing point of view the name of one designer on the base of the wares is a better promotional tool than an unmemorable selection of many names. However, Clarice Cliff as she is known today is something of a composite being, representing the talents of a number of unknown pottery artists. In this respect she was a truly modern designer, designing herself but also marking out the limits of a style within which others could work on her behalf. The actual choice of the designs produced was hers, and as the 1930s progressed she scoured the local art schools for talent that would complement the Newport style.

The business brains of the enterprise belonged to the good-looking, eccentric Sales Director, Colley Shorter who, it is said, liked a drink and his Rolls Royce. He decided to market the wares under the name *Bizarre* (the word itself undoubtedly came from Clarice, although it was a much used adjective to describe the 'Jazz Modern' style), and to risk expenditure on the experiments on the old wares. In many ways, by getting her to sign the wares, he 'made' her as a marketing ploy; indeed a couple of years later he was to use his own nine-year-old daughter Joan in a similar capacity as the publicized young designer of Nursery Ware (see p. 167). Clarice had undoubted talent and daring as well as an unforgettable name and a special relationship with Colley Shorter – since Clarice's death in 1972 it has been widely reported in Stoke-on-Trent that she had a long-standing affair with him until, after the death of his first wife in 1939, she married him in 1940. It is unclear when a serious relationship might have started, but it appears that Clarice moved out of her family home into her own flat before any *Bizarre* ware was marketed.

The hand-painted *Bizarre* wares by Clarice Cliff had caught on, and advertisements for them from late 1928 onwards depicted an extraordinary creature –

A traditionally-shaped earthenware coffee service in Bizarre Ware by Clarice Cliff, dating from the late 1930s, painted up freehand with the very popular Crocus pattern. (Page 73)

the 'Bizooka', a man-sized and impossibly ugly donkey made up of items of Bizarre ware with candlesticks and candles for ears and the spout of a teapot projecting as a tail. In the advertisements 'Bizooka' was drawn, but he also existed in several incarnations of wired-together wares to be used at home and abroad for promotion and display.

Both the wares and Clarice herself were attracting more and more publicity. In 1929 newspapers reported that Bizarre 'looks like a Russian ballet master's nightmare' and 'is reminiscent of crazy paving', and by 1930 were able to describe the newly promoted Cliff as 'the only woman art director in the Potteries' and 'a brilliant young designer'. Clarice obliged by explaining that her inspiration came from such sources as watching a child make a coloured paper cut-out and listening to jazz dance music on the wireless after dinner. Her enormous appeal today relies heavily on this naive image which, it would be fair to say, is in part real and in part consciously projected. She has become a romantic figure – working-class women paintresses in the Potteries rarely became art directors, and her success was dramatic.

In fact, inspiration for Bizarre also followed what could now be called conventional Art Deco thinking, and Clarice Cliff was not alone in turning to the art of ancient civilizations. The *Pottery Gazette* reports in February 1929 on

> . . . some remarkable replicas of capitols of columns in the Temple of Luxor (date 1250 B. C.), and it would seem that the search for suitable material has extended even into the Roman period of 140 B. C., for amongst the examples is a replica of the capitol of a column of the Hypaethral Temple at Philae.

She produced some stunning blue and green decorated matt-glaze vases called *Inspiration* and *Persian*, whose sources are evident from their titles. American Indian art, most notably the 'stepped' effect of Aztec temples and pyramids, and Ancient Egyptian art were already being plundered as design sources by other enthusiasts. At the same time as these 'ancient' Bizarre wares were produced, Newport were providing retailers with special promotional material for window displays, one of which consisted of a football field whose players were pottery representations of ducklings, which could be decorated in the colours of a local football team. The mind boggles at a juxtaposition of this with pottery versions of Egyptian temples.

As she has herself said, Cliff's designs cried out for new shapes, and she was particularly keen to produce tablewares. The first new shape was *Conical*, which she designed in 1929. It was severely geometric – tea-cups had solid triangular handles, teapots triangular handles and spouts, and cruets were thin perfect cones. By December 1930, advertisements had changed from the 'Bizooka' and factory collages of earlier years to elegant graphics of plant stands of graduating height, each topped with the outline of a piece of dramatically, shaped tableware. Over the next two or three years, new shapes followed. *Odilon* was a fine streamlined shape with semi-circular handles, the vegetable dish having a niche to rest a spoon and a lid which could be upturned to rest firmly on its flat circular knob. The *Biarritz* shape included the famous rectangular plates with their round indentations. The *Stamford* shape had round plates but a vegetable dish which was made up of two halves of differing-sized spheres, the smaller for the lid, the whole resting like a globe on four protruding solid feet. The *Stamford* teapot was 'D'-shaped. Other comparatively early shapes include *Bon Jour*, *Daffodil*, *Lotus* and *Isis*. An enormous range of wares were available in several of the shapes – dinner- and tea-services, breakfast and morning sets, coffee, sandwich and fruit sets, together with additions such as bridge sets, cruets, tea-caddies and biscuit jars.

Owing to the enthusiasm of today's collectors of *Bizarre* ware, detailed research is being done into the Newport productions. A pioneering book on Clarice Cliff by Peter Wentworth-Shields and Kay Johnson, to which I am indebted, was published in 1976. There is thus neither the need nor the space to enumerate and describe all the shapes and patterns produced; it is sufficient to say that during the four or five years when the bulk of the wares appeared (between 1929 and about 1934) an enormous variety of decorations – banding, all-over geometrics and florals, stylized landscapes, one-colour glazes, drip-glazes and restrained Cubist and line patterns – were all implemented. The supplementary *Fantasque* name covered a variety of patterns, and individual pattern names such as *Ravel*, *Caprice*, *Coral Firs*, *Gayday*, *Hello*, *My Garden*, *Secrets* and *Tibetan* give an indication of the preoccupations of their creator. The most successful design of all, and the longest lived, was the well-known *Crocus*, first designed in predominantly orange but subsequently modified to add *Spring Crocus* (pastel colours), *Blue Crocus* and *Peter Pan* (where small crocuses grow at the base of a silhouetted tree and boy).

Clarice Cliff's remarkable imagination ran riot in the early 1930s, and every imaginable item – some inspired, some purely entertaining, some kitsch – hit the market. Newport products included cut-out ceramic flowers, ingenious table-centres with parts which fitted as chosen like Meccano, golliwog bookends, chicken drinking-sets (with chick-shaped teapot), puff-boxes and bases, animal and figure models, wall masks (including a black Greta Garbo), elephant napkin rings, inkwells, wall pockets, tubular vases and hippopotamus ashtrays.

Throughout these years the *Bizarre* girls, as the paintresses came to be known, enjoyed fame and status (although their wages were still low). Their smiling faces and bobbed heads shone out of shop windows where they sat demonstrating painting techniques, from carnival floats in the streets and from the pages of national newspapers. Life for them at the Potteries, however, was rigorous under Clarice's watchful eye: they worked long hours and were obliged to be strictly punctual. The Sales Director was not a man to be argued with either – a neighbour of the Shorter family in the 1930s tells the possibly apocryphal story of how he would rush furious into his garden armed with a shotgun if he spied boys stealing his apples.

Later shapes produced at Newport included embossed moulded wares like *Corncob* (clearly inspired by eighteenth-century wares), *Water Lily* and *Shell* ware, *Chestnut* and *Raffia* ware, and *Gnome* ware, where the eponymous character comprised the handles of cups and teapot. Most of these later moulded wares were by this time fairly usual in the trade and differed little from the types produced by other companies. The extraordinary *Le Bon Dieu* shape, which had the appearance of a sort of tumour (its inspiration was the burr formations

A Bizarre Ware *bachelor set by Clarice Cliff in the softer* Trieste *shape of the late 1930s, decorated with a freehand banded and leaf pattern.* (Page 76)

which are sometimes found on tree-trunks), was hard to forgive.

In the mid-1930s, Clarice Cliff was working with some of the most influential artists of the day, producing tableware in conjunction with E. Brain (Foley China) for an exhibition at Harrods in 1934 (see Chapter 7). Amongst these artists was Milner Gray, who produced designs for Cliff and for E. Brain which were displayed at the earlier 'Exhibition of British Industrial Art in Relation to the Home' held in 1933 at Dorland Hall, Lower Regent Street. In reviewing the exhibition, the *Pottery Gazette* attacked Gray's design for Clarice Cliff:

> To describe this pattern as fantastic would be to exercise a full measure of restraint. There are no doubt people who may be attracted by it, and who may even like to possess it, but if there are, we simply cannot share their taste. 'Whoopee' is the name of the pattern, and 'Whoopee' it certainly is. It is a pattern barbaric in its crudity, but perhaps it has been incorrectly described as a morning set and is intended for the nursery.

So much for trade reactions to the artist working in the pottery industry!

By the late 1930s Newport designs were influenced by both the shift forward to simpler Modernist designs and the shift back to more traditional floral decorations. Shapes such as *Trieste* were rounded rather than angular, the three-cornered plates having soft curves rather than straight lines, and were treated to patterns of small floral motifs and polka dots. Such restrained flowers, spots, crosses and banding were even now applied to such uncompromisingly 'Cubist' shapes as *Biarritz*. A new shape, the prosaically named *Windsor*, displayed nothing but elegant and softened curves, and the pretty banded and floral decorations were treated with a gentle honey glaze. Wares with Chinese-inspired coloured glazes in grey, green and oatmeal, pioneered by such companies as Wedgwood, were produced under the series names *Kang* and *Yuan*. By this time, Clarice herself was more in evidence as a director than as a 'hands-on' designer.

No one could deny the liveliness and simple appeal of Clarice Cliff's work or the effect she had on rival potteries' designs, but because of her extremism she rouses strong emotion. Some will pay thousands of pounds today for a vase which would have sold for a few shillings when first made, while others are fiercely critical of both the designs and the standard of potting of *Bizarre* ware. When Clarice's name is mentioned in Stoke-on-Trent today, the word 'lump' is muttered by many in response – the dismissive term applied to discarded wares which are not even seconds or thirds, but worse. Many in the Potteries are still disturbed by the publicity that Clarice Cliff has attracted, which has overshadowed the finer work of other designers and manufacturers.

□ A. J. Wilkinson (*Royal Staffordshire Pottery, Burslem*)

After taking over the Newport Pottery, the parent firm continued production though its products were less keenly in the public eye. A. J. Wilkinson's medium-priced earthenwares were marketed under the name *Royal Staffordshire*, and included full ranges of tableware, toilet-ware and ornamental lines. While

Clarice Cliff was experimenting with hand-painting over the glaze, A. J. Wilkinson were developing techniques of under-glaze lithographic decorations – in the 1920s attention had to be paid to glazes which would withstand the new detergents now coming onto the market.

The firm had already established a reputation for experimentation with 'artistic' wares, and one of their most successful ornamental lines was *Oriflamme*, which had beautiful bright glaze effects. This, although produced before 1920, was exhibited at the British Empire Exhibition of 1924. In about 1923 A. J. Wilkinson brought out a very successful honey glaze, as William Adams had already done with the *Titian* glaze (see Chapter 1). This paradoxically had the effect of mellowing the bright colours used for the decorations, in contrast to Newport's deliberate displays of vivid colours.

The speciality of the house, which continued throughout the period, was lithographed and gilt tableware, now complemented by the honey glaze. By the late 1930s, these effects were again the order of the day, and some fine tableware was produced with the additional advantage of some of the later, rounded modern shapes designed at Newport. The *Lynton* shape, which had a ribbed appearance to emulate hand-thrown ware, was used to good effect with moderately stylized floral patterns such as *Daphne* combined with the mellow glaze.

□ Shorter and Sons   (*Stoke*)

A. J. Wilkinson and Newport also had a close working relationship with Shorter and Sons, a company run by the same family, where Colley Shorter of A. J. Wilkinson was also a director. The firm, established in the early 1870s, was best known for its coloured majolica, and specialized mainly in 'fancies' – vases, bulb bowls, fern and flower pots and so on – and novelty wares. Their most important design development of the inter-war period, the production of coloured matt-glaze earthenwares, started in the late 1920s and continued into the 1930s. Matt-glaze wares, another important facet of pottery design during the period, were mainly ornamental, but some successful plain matt-glaze tablewares were also made. The glaze was used both on Art Deco and Modernist shapes, most notably for those produced by architect-designer Keith Murray for Wedgwood (see Chapter 8).

Shorter's wares were available either plain or with lithographic or hand-painted decorations. Their shape books (where the actual configurations of the factory's wares are recorded) of about 1934 show matt glaze vases, bulb bowls (including some incorporating modelled rabbits and squirrels) and coffee- and dinner-services with open triangular-shaped handles.

In the 1930s they were also producing novelty embossed wares (see Chapter 6). Shorter's leaf-shaped salad wares were less true to life than Carlton's, with pointed, angular leaves, producing a strange semi-naturalistic, semi-stylized appearance. Preserve jars were shaped and decorated as a tomato, strawberry, pear, apple, lemon and pineapple. Advertising material promotes these wares as: 'Quick selling lines of table novelties in rich self-coloured glazes'. The

Tulip shape china coffee service
by John Aynsley and Sons, with
embossed petals and enamel
painting in green, with black
and orange detailing, 1931.
(Page 96)

fashionable motifs of the era were adapted for wall masks, Scottie-dog bookends, ashtrays with flying ducks and ranges of vases and wall-pockets. Shell-shaped wares, animal models, angular vases, cigarette boxes and table centres made up a highly fashionable and unsophisticated stock for the inexpensive end of the market.

The products of Shorter and Son have little to do with fine design, but they do help to illustrate the determination with which the Shorter family, through its collective concerns in earthenware manufacture, endeavoured to capture a profitable chunk of a depressed market. Together the three companies, Shorter and Sons, A. J. Wilkinson and Newport could provide almost any type of earthenware the retailer might want for his stock – conventional and extremely modern table and ornamental wares, table and other novelties, in an astonishing range of shapes, decorations and glazes.

□ E. Brain & Co. (*Foley China Works, Fenton*)

It hardly comes as a surprise to learn that Clarice Cliff's early designs were not readily admired by Gordon Forsyth or the DIA: in no way did they represent the economical shapes and restrained decorations that the serious design pundits required.

What better company to produce modern tableware that was nearer this design ideal than one which had long prided itself on the utilitarian rather than decorative qualities of its products? E. Brain and Co. took over the Foley China Works in Longton in 1903, and during the early years of the century produced wares which were noted for their plain, simple designs and extremely restrained decorations. Such tablewares, particularly in the post-World War I period, were produced in conscious response to the recommendations of the DIA, and intended to be easy to clean and in 'good taste'. Patterns of self-coloured sprays, festoons, wreaths, bands and simple edge linings were all that was allowed by way of decoration. In terms of shape, nothing ornate or embossed was to be found in the company's range.

By 1927–8, however, the firm was confronted with the economic results of the General Strike and the vogue for bright colours which the pottery industry had generally accepted as the dominant factor in what the public wanted to buy. In consequence, *Foley China*, as the company's wares were known, took up an artist's bright palette. In October 1928, the *Pottery Gazette* commented:

> E. Brain & Co. Ltd, would have been out of step had they not recognized this new demand, and whilst they have certainly catered for it, one observes that there is still the same distinctiveness about the ware in general; there is still something about the productions that is essentially 'Foley' in spirit – the principles remain, although changes in fashion have brought about modifications and compromises in regard to colours.

Accordingly, several ranges of simply shaped but brightly decorated wares were brought out, and one tea-service used the Cube Teapot, carrying through the design to square cups with recessed handles and square saucers. Decorations had such contemporary and self-explanatory names as *Cubist Landscape* and *Cubist Sunflower*, painted colour combinations like black and wine, blue and orange, and blue and red. However, the designs were not splashed across the whole body of the wares with the gay abandon of the Newport Potteries, but restricted; for example, the *Cubist Landscape* occurred only within the confines of a border decoration around the rims, leaving the rest of the surface undecorated. The *Pottery Gazette* editorials are full of praise for such a compromise. The journal reflected the conservatism of the industry, but was equally at pains to give the new a chance and avoid accusations of unresponsiveness to new ideas. While editorials about the qualities of Clarice Cliff's designs are uneven in their search for an acceptable opinion that could cautiously admire such extreme innovation, only gaining confidence as *Bizarre* began to sell, the journal's position was clear with Foley in 1929:

> Although colour is now in demand, and plenty of it, there is still room for the exercise of discretionary thought as to how colour shall be applied; it is not sufficient merely to dab colour upon a plate or a cup and saucer with the sole object of masking the body of the china and giving people plenty of colour for their money. Viewing the matter from the other extreme, studied formality and strict conventionality exert little or no appeal nowadays to the buyer of a tea or breakfast set; something less stiff and rigid is required than many of the 'Foley' patterns which were immensely popular ten years ago ... the pendulum, having swung back, Brain & Co. Ltd., are now having to compromise. The public want colour, and they will see that they get it, but one of the aims of the manufacturers of 'Foley' china is to present their patterns – colourful though they be – in a form which will not offend the susceptibilities of the person of cultured taste.

Although there was evidence, as we have seen, that the public did indeed demand colourful ceramics, the *Pottery Gazette* throughout the 1920s and 1930s was perhaps guilty of exaggerating the real demand. The above description contains typical echoes of the journal's reflection of the Potteries' resentment of the DIA strictures after World War I, and a clear and understandable determination that the decorating side of the industry should remain strong and its workers protected from the threat of unemployment implied by a fashion for completely plain tablewares. E. Brain & Co could keep utilitarian tastes happy, but even they were taking to modern decorations, and the *Pottery Gazette*, although doubtless having a real admiration for the wares, must have seen in this some sort of vindication of its difficult editorial position.

At this time (1929), Foley were producing restrained Modernist decorations, generally applied to very simple, streamlined, curved forms – stylized oriental landscapes, small scattered landscape motifs and linings, stripes and polka dots. For the Christmas 1930 trade, they brought out a striking Modernist shape, *Pallas*, with a curved body which continued round in a curved handle, rejoining the body in a straight horizontal line. The shape bore more similarities to those being produced in Germany than to the products of Stoke-on-Trent.

Advertisements for *Pallas* emphasized the quality and modern spirit of the

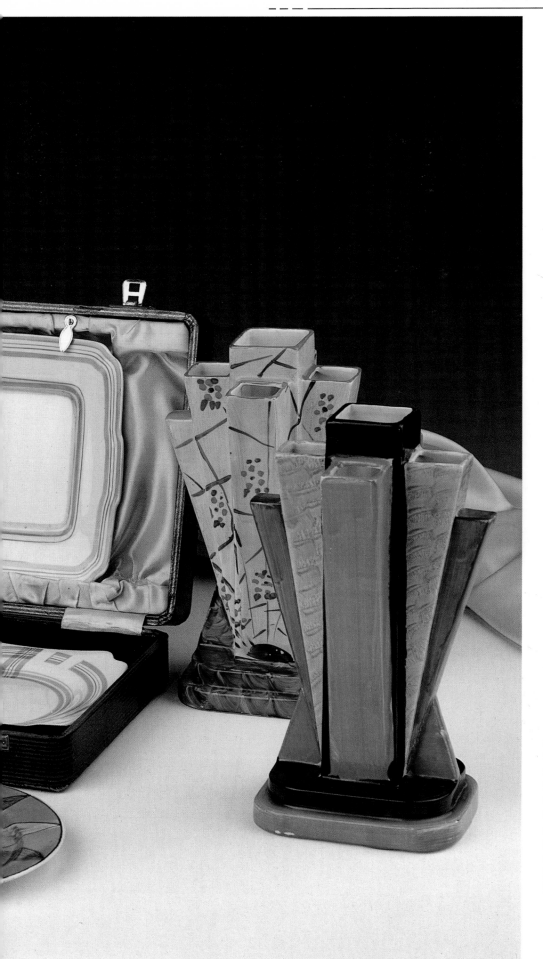

A selection of hand-painted
earthenwares: jug and fan-
shaped vase (left) and pyramid-
shaped vases (right) by Myott
and Son, 1934–38 (page 120);
boxed sandwich set by Myott
and Son, c. 1935 (page 120);
and two plates by Barker Bros.,
designed in the Moulin Rouge
pattern by John Guildford,
1929. (pages 96–7)

shape: 'The new "Pallas" is a rational design, properly so-called . . .'; and it was praised as much for its practicality as for its modernity. Instead of jumping one way or another for decorations, the shape was given both vividly coloured and pastel patterns: one had heavy and unrelieved dark bands, another stylized but not geometric flowers and wavy lines in greys, blues and pale green. More conventional shapes, such as *Perth*, *Devon* and *Avon*, carried simple landscapes and florals. Decorations such as *Purple Clover* and *Clovelly* resembled those pioneered by Truda Carter at the Poole Pottery (see Chapter 1). Some decorations were achieved by the print and enamel hand-painted technique, but others employed newly designed lithographs. *Clovelly* was exhibited both at the British Industries Fair and the 'British Art in Relation to the Home' exhibition at Dorland Hall (see p. 180) in 1933, and was much admired. The design featured an early-Victorian embroidery treatment in four colours – green, blue, yellow and pink.

Foley's principal market was middle-class or upper middle-class and, like Shelley's, their tablewares, predominantly tea-services and breakfast sets, were made in fine bone china, not earthenware. In 1932 Thomas Acland Fennemore (1902–1955) joined E. Brain as Managing Director, having worked for a few years previously as Sales Manager of Paragon China (see p. 111). From 1919–26 he had worked in advertising, and brought to the company useful experience of the retail trade. There are obvious parallels between E. Brain and Shelley – both were catering for modern tastes in the medium-priced, middle-class china market, and both had the advantage of directors who were energetically in touch with modern commercial practice. Although E. Brain did not adopt a vigorous advertising campaign, with the arrival of Fennemore they did plan to make an impact on the market.

In 1932 twelve patterns of an uncompromisingly stark design were produced for a series titled *Mayfair* – leaving no doubt about the middle-class market at which it was aimed. The designs consisted of groupings of varying widths of graduating black lines and bands on bright white china, with one colour introduced in the form of a square, spot or triangle. The *Pottery Gazette* ventured outside its usual vocabulary to describe them as 'very chic', whilst the *Manchester Guardian* described them thus in December 1932:

> The modern note is largely summed up in the single word 'speed', and the idea of speed is ably suggested by the straight line . . . The effect is both charming and out of the ordinary . . . Besides the usual sets of tableware an assortment of handy gift articles, such as cigarette boxes, ashtrays, match boxes, bon-bon dishes, and milk horns [beakers with handles], are made.

Mayfair plates were strictly octagonal, and cups were tall, straight-sided and with open triangular handles similar to Shelley's *Eve* shape. The series received acclaim as an example of good modern ceramic design in such influential art journals as *The Studio*, and by adopting an almost Continental simplicity of design, avoided the excesses of some Art Deco wares. Indeed, one rather arch report describes the designs as 'simple in the extreme'. The firm's own claim for *Mayfair*, that 'careful balance and admirable restraint combine to invest this design with a character and smartness peculiarly its own', was generally upheld after the series was exhibited at the 'Exhibition of Industrial Art in Relation to the Home' at Dorland Hall in 1933.

With characteristic concern to cater for all modern tastes, Foley produced six new floral patterns for tea-ware by 'a celebrated designer of interior furnishings' shortly after *Mayfair*. They were issued on the new *Langham* shape, which consisted of a gentle conical-shaped cup with open angled handle containing an open diamond (rather as Shelley's *Regent* contained an open circle). The bread-and-butter plate had three solid semi-circular handles, the intention being again one of practicality, as the plate could thus be easily passed around for serving. The florals were pretty and stylized, and the range was extended using English flowers such as primroses, forget-me-knots, asters, gladioli, cornflowers, sweet williams and bluebells. The shape was also used for a variety of other decorations: polka dots, leaf motifs, simple geometrics positioned at the rim and a very striking design of radiating dancing figures. All bear comparison with Shelley's designs for similar shapes, and the two firms must have watched and copied each other very closely in order to compete in the same market. Patterns such as Foley's *Ritz*, featuring lines and blocked coloured rectangles, are clearly influenced by Shelley designs, and also illustrate such designs' popularity, albeit transient, in the market.

E. Brain were reaching further down market as well, and in 1933 they produced Foley *Spot* china, decorated with large coloured polka dots, of which a 15-piece coffee set would sell for a modest 15s. 9d. Foley took part in an ingenious exhibition held in Liverpool in 1933, entitled 'The Guinea Tea Shop', displaying 21 china tea-services for six people, all at 21 shillings.

Between 1932 and 1934, Fennemore was pursuing the idea of using contemporary artists to design for ceramics. Together with Milner Gray, the designer, and artist Graham Sutherland, and in conjunction with A. J. Wilkinson and Clarice Cliff, he commissioned leading artists to design ceramics for an exhibition in London in 1934 (see Chapter 7). In the meantime, Milner Gray had already produced designs for Foley, including *Convolvulus* – a plain brownish-black printed tea-ware pattern that was rather better received at Dorland Hall than his *Whoopee* design for Clarice Cliff (see p. 76).

Foley China presents a remarkable aspect of design in the 1920s and 1930s, particularly in the way it gave great variety and resisted extremes in spite of offering new and daring tablewares. The company never forgot the utilitarian nature of crockery, yet were able to produce both streamlined Modernist shapes and the most practical geometrics – they were amongst the first to lease the Cube shape. They never moved as far away from 'fitness for purpose' as Shelley's *Vogue* and *Mode*, yet they produced some of the most minimal and demanding patterns of all in the *Mayfair* series. Although keen to experiment with colour, their wares were never garish, and pastel-shade alternatives were always available. At the time that they produced some of the hardest-outline geometric patterns ever seen in the British pottery industry, they were careful to supplement their stock with easily digestible florals. Although pioneering the use of fine artists as ceramic designers, they were in the vanguard of good new lithographic prints, indeed in many ways Foley's wares represent a commendable balance between the abilities of man and those of the machine.

Three embossed and hand-painted earthenware animal character jugs in Burleigh Ware by Burgess and Leigh (rabbit, kingfisher and parrot), dating from the early 1930s. (Page 103)

CHAPTER FOUR

Colour and Commercial Success

□ The paintresses

As an introduction to the great number of hand-painted wares produced throughout the Potteries by the 1930s, it is important to look at the role of the paintresses whose talents were so essential in the production of the tablewares of the period. Although written some years earlier, in 1902, Arnold Bennett's description of the lives and working conditions of the paintresses at Henry Mynor's works in his novel *Anna of the Five Towns* presents a picture which was little changed by the 1930s:

> The paintresses form the *noblesse* of the banks [an abbreviation of 'pot banks', the local name for the manufacturing factories]. Their task is a light one, demanding deftness first of all; they have delicate fingers, and enjoy a general reputation for beauty: the wages they earn may be estimated from their finery on Sundays. They come to business in cloth jackets, carry dinner in little satchels; in the shop they wear white aprons, and look startlingly neat and tidy. Across the benches over which they bend their coquettish heads gossip flies and returns like a shuttle; they are the source of a thousand intrigues, and one or other of them is continually getting married or omitting to get married. On the bank they constitute 'the sex'. An infinitesimal proportion of them, from among the branch known as ground-layers, die of lead-poisoning – a fact which adds pathos to their frivolous charm. In a subsidiary room off the painting-shop a single girl was seated at a revolving table actuated by a treadle. She was doing the 'band-and-line' on the rims of saucers. Mynors and Anna watched her as with her left hand she flicked saucer after saucer into the exact centre of the table, moved the treadle, and, holding a brush firmly against the rim of the piece, produced with infallible exactitude the band and the line. She was a brunette, about twenty-eight: she had a calm, vacuously contemplative face; but God alone knew whether she thought. Her work represented the summit of monotony . . .

Although the paintresses did represent something of an 'artistic' élite in the pottery industry, their earnings were not high, and for the most part considerably lower than those for men doing similarly demanding jobs. The British Pottery Manufacturers Federation published a figure for 1929 of £1 11s. 5d. as the average weekly earnings of a paintress in a general earthenware section for a 42 ¾ hour week. Although women and girls had been employed as paintresses at least since the mid-nineteenth century, the numbers in the industry increased of necessity during World War I, and had remained high since. As we have seen, this comparatively cheap labour force meant that the production of hand-painted wares was economic from the manufacturer's point of view in the two decades following the war.

The art schools taught paintresses from the age of 14 or 15, so that by the time they reached 18 they were extremely skilled. Nevertheless, they remained apprentices until the age of 21, and part of their wages was deducted for training and for brushes. From a very low starting salary, the girls would eventually graduate to piece work, where if sufficiently competent they could double or even treble their weekly earnings immediately. They worked often in very dirty conditions, under the strict supervision of a decorating manager (almost invariably male) who would provide them with the patterns to paint onto the wares.

On most of the hand-painted wares of this period the decoration was applied over the glaze to enable it to be fired to a lower temperature than that required for the glaze itself. This was necessary to achieve the brightest enamel colours, which were oxides of various metals, each producing different ranges of colour – uranium, for example (subsequently banned), was used to yield the characteristically very bright yellows. The powdered colours were mixed with turpentine and oils to produce the correct consistency of pigment.

Lead was used both in enamel colours and glazes, so both the paintresses and glaze 'dippers' were particularly at risk of poisoning through ingestion or skin absorption. Almost every month, the *Pottery Gazette* carried reports of one or more recorded death; the following, from 1925, is a typical example:

An inquiry which took place in Burslem of December 16 into the circumstances concerning the death of a married woman who was formerly employed as a majolica paintress at the works of H. & R. Johnson Ltd., led up to a verdict of 'Death from lead poisoning'. It was stated that the deceased had not worked since October 1921, when she went to the North Staffordshire Infirmary and was certified as suffering from lead poisoning. She subsequently received a lump sum in settlement of compensation. Altogether, before becoming incapacitated, she had worked as a paintress for fourteen years. The medical evidence, as the result of a post-mortem, was that death was due to chronic nephritis [inflammation of the kidneys].

Generally speaking, the various hand-painting tasks were broken down so that one paintress would specialize in only one part of the decoration, passing the wares on to another for the next specialist stage. Different brushes were used for the various techniques – a very fine angled brush for thin lines and a broader brush for wide bands of colour, both of which were done with the wares

Pieces from a 'semi-porcelain' earthenware tea service in Solian Ware by the Soho Pottery; the print and enamel pattern is Melody *of c. 1935. (Pages 116–7)*

revolving on a wheel. Paintresses would either fill in an outline-printed pattern with enamel colours (print and enamel) or work on the wares entirely freehand to produce a pattern as close as possible to the original drawn design of the pattern books. Enormous skill in brushwork was required to achieve the correct and varied intensity of paint on the wares, and shades in the petals of a flower or leaf were made with a single deft stroke. Much of the attraction of the wares is that it is possible to see every confident brushstroke which was applied to make up the pattern.

□ The middle market

The influential pottery manufacturers discussed in the preceding chapters constitute only a tiny percentage of the hundreds of firms competing in the depressed market of the late 1920s and early 1930s, under pressure from imported earthenwares from countries such as Germany, Czechoslovakia and Japan. As we have noted, the products of Continental firms were generally more advanced in design than those that had issued from comparable British firms. This was the case even at the cheaper levels of the market: for example, Czechoslavakian 'rustic' floral designs, lustred wares and modest angular tea-and dinner-wares were available at low prices.

By 1930 an enormous number of British factories, particularly the earthen-ware manufacturers, were producing colourful, fashionable and novelty designs with varying degrees of aesthetic success. The vast majority of their wares were hand-painted, following a lead set by the trail-blazers, and a taste that the Potteries believed the consumers had acquired. They also produced anything novel and in tune with whatever current enthusiasms might give them a lead over their competitors – be it Winnie-the-Pooh, Mickey Mouse, or the 1937 Coronation.

The factories were, of course, competing first and foremost for the eye of the stock buyer of the shops – the immediate problem of selling to the public being encountered at retail level, where the decisions about what items would catch the customers' imaginations and purses were made. Thus the potteries aimed to appeal to various levels of retail outlet – from Harrods, Heal's, and Waring and Gillow to the more modest Barker's, Lawley's or Woolworth's, and even, for some, seaside shops and fairgrounds, where tablewares were awarded as prizes. Large pottery manufacturers were in a position to appeal to a wide range of such outlets, by producing both china and various earthenwares, whilst smaller firms were restricted by their size to trying to capture specific areas of the market.

It is interesting to look at the typical products of a number of middle-market and medium-sized manufacturers in the late 1920s and 1930s. Some are inventive, designed under the auspices of lively art directors, while others are more pedestrian, produced under the control of decoration managers, whose role was more managerial than artistic. Decoration managers rarely had a sophisticated art education and were often subject to the design prejudices of the companies for which they worked.

The tablewares discussed here include both those which achieved modest and attractive designs and those which failed to be much more than ordinary. All the companies described were producing tablewares in china or earthenware for a middle market (the products of the larger, top-market firms like Doulton and W. T. Copeland will be discussed in Chapter 5). These tablewares appeal to some, principally for their colour, freshness, naivety or even comedy, while others agree with Pevsner, who found the majority 'thoughtless in design' because of a 'conscious application of art' which ignored utiliarian principles. Wherever one's sympathies lie, it is important to record this period of industrial design history and to consider the wares in the context of the calamitous economic conditions that prevailed during their production (see p. 64) and the changing social habits of the period. One aspect of the latter was described in an editorial in the June 1932 issue of *Homes and Gardens*:

> Today there are fewer formal occasions, large dinner-parties, or stiff 'at homes' than there used to be, and table appointments have altered with the changing times. We no longer have 'best china' to be used only on state occasions, but, much more sensibly, make the best possible effect every day with simple but charmingly coloured services . . .

Most important of all, when seen in the context of the stale lithographed patterns produced during previous years, these hand-painted tablewares are artistically progressive. Their design may not always be consummate, but they nevertheless demonstrate a willingness in the pottery industry to implement new ideas which was at times to result in a very competent Modernism in the late 1930s.

□ Adderleys (*Daisy Bank Pottery, Longton*)

'Handcraft decorations, of more than ordinary merit, appear to have invaded, of late, every department of the Daisy Bank Pottery' announced the *Pottery Gazette* in September 1931. Adderleys was a well-established firm, manufacturing both expensive china and cheaper earthenware products and providing a full range from practical kitchen-ware and toilet-ware to expensive china dinner services. They were noted for the sound quality of their potting and, repeatedly in the *Pottery Gazette* in the 1930s, for their originality: 'There are some firms which elect to copy and adapt; but Adderleys, Ltd., evidently prefer to create and evolve.'

By 1928, Adderleys announced their *New Octagon* shape, a development that many potteries were making at precisely this time. By 1929, they had adopted modern graphics for their advertisements, and by 1930 were producing brightly coloured stylized landscape patterns for tea-services, albeit on conventional shapes. *Bourton*, *Watteau* and *Orchard* were the most frequently promoted patterns. About 1931, tea-, coffee- and breakfast-wares were designed with semi-geometric patterns, in colour combinations such as blue and green with platinum, amongst them *Madeira* and *Jewel*, which appeared to have an Islamic influence. During the 1930s, some very pretty and brightly coloured floral

tea-and coffee-sets were backstamped with their designers' names.

The extant earthenware pattern books provide a picture of a company anxious to be up-to-date, but unwilling to really grasp the nettle. The results were often very mixed design concepts, which fail because there is not enough consistent design integrity: geometric shapes are decorated with naturalistic patterns; semi-stylized flowers are painted with realistic centres; colours are muted rather than vivid. The books nevertheless show some inventive designs for toilet-ware – neat colourful squares, enormous splashes of yellow daisies and beautiful wash-banded examples including graduated colour combinations of yellow, coral and brown. Some have sculpted handles – flowers, birds, even an elephant's head with the trunk curving down for the handle (here the designer was unfortunately unable to resist adding an eye and a tusk when the head would have looked better unadorned). Banding was also used very successfully on tea-ware, sometimes inside the cups, and on lemonade beakers.

By the end of the 1930s, Adderleys had largely returned, one can sense with a certain relief, to traditional decorations on its more expensive wares. In January 1939, the *Pottery Gazette* explains:

> . . . as in the case of many of their competitors, Adderleys, Ltd., have been compelled, through the sheer force of economics, to make compromises during recent years, and to embark on the manufacture of certain cheaper lines in order to satisfy the insistent demand for goods of that type, and at the same time to keep their factory busy, they have certainly never failed to maintain a close touch with those better-class productions which were at one time their main forte, and for which they are still hoping and believing there will be a return of demand ere long.

The company did, however, produce *Glade Green* ware in 1938, which had a coloured body (that is, the pottery itself, rather than the glaze, was tinted), which was uniform from piece to piece, and successfully decorated with simple lines around the wares and gold borders.

□ Allertons   (*Park Works, Longton*)

New patterns in Allertons bone-china tea-ware were noted by the *Pottery Gazette* as early as 1925: 'There is an altogether different spirit about the tea-ware decorations . . . [which] have been suddenly invested with a sense of liveliness and modernity.' Bright groundlay colours were used in conjunction with semi-stylized patterns, some of which showed an oriental influence, others using fruit motifs and even silhouetted landscape patterns. The company was also noted at this time for developing new shapes: the *Kensington*, for example, included plates angled off into ten sides, providing scope for alternate panels of decoration. Hand-painted wares of the 1930s included good banding and an unusual *Pebble* border design, in grey overpainted with linear floral designs. Plain white earthen tea-ware, with touches of silver on the handles and knobs, was exhibited at Dorland Hall in 1933. The company was owned from 1912 by Cauldon Potteries.

Three pieces of A. G. Richardson's Crown Ducal earthen tableware, decorated with the two-colour Red Tree (also now known as Orange Tree) print and enamel pattern, introduced in 1925. (Pages 112–3)

□ John Aynsley & Sons *(Portland Works, Longton)*

Aynsley was first founded in 1775, and was at the Portland Works in 1864, where the firm became well known for bone-china tablewares. New designs of the late 1920s and early 1930s are best characterized by the very dainty shapes formed and painted as flowers, such as *Tulip*, with handles as butterflies, used for tea-ware. These were based on earlier precedents and paid little attention to contemporary vogues. Nevertheless, the clear colours of the painting of the flower shapes mean that they have become easily recognizable as products of the period.

In 1933 a new octagonal shape was introduced, and in 1934 an extremely plain new shape, *Boston*, which successfully combined straight tapering lines for cups with gracefully curved handles. It was praised as both practical and delicate, and used for tea-, coffee- and morning-sets. It was treated with understated modern designs such as *Arta*, consisting of horizontal bands and small motifs of vertical lines in contrasting colours, finished off with gold or silver. Other patterns included *Elaine*, where flowers were panelled on the wares with geometric ornaments, and *Ascot*, which the *Pottery Gazette* described thus:

> This is very sweet in its simplicity. It consists of nothing more than an edging effect in green grass brushwork, relieved by a few touches, at intervals below the edging, of choice enamelling. For the person of discrimitative taste, who desires something that is not expensive, this would appear to be ideal.

□ Barker Bros. *(Meir Works, Longton)*

From the evidence provided by the *Pottery Gazette* and extant examples of tableware it would seem that Barker Bros. excelled in their ability to copy the best new ideas on the market quickly and efficiently. This is not to say that they did not also produce some entirely original ideas, and on occasion it might be claimed that their patterns simply coincided, in the same climate, with better-known productions.

In December 1926, the *Pottery Gazette* illustrates semi-porcelain dinner-ware which is an almost exact copy of William Adams' *Titian Ware* design of fruit, which dates at least from 1920. Extant examples show the pattern less subtle, produced lithographically rather than by hand, the potting and glazing inferior. Semi-porcelain is a high-quality earthenware, which the company decided to concentrate on producing for specialist lines from about 1925, cutting out the manufacture of china. Some hand-painted wares bore a striking resemblance to the products of Poole Potteries, but most interestingly, Barker Bros. were either quick to copy – or even possibly predate – Clarice Cliff. In April 1929, the *Pottery Gazette* reports:

> A new artistic era seems to have been embarked upon, and it would be difficult to point to anything more striking, novel and courageous in the decoration of domestic pottery than this firm's 'Storm' pattern, hand-painted by John Guildford. One's attention was arrested also by a number of

> patterns of the strongly coloured bizarre type, such as the 'Autocrat' and the 'Moulin Rouge'. Whilst such designs as these may, perhaps, do no more than pander to a passing craze, they do, at least, indicate that the house is not unmindful of the present-day leanings of the public.

The article illustrates a striking plate, with vivid bands of green and blue on bright orange radiating like a catherine wheel (*Moulin Rouge*). Although the editorial post-dates the earliest Newport *Bizarre* ware, Barker Bros. employed as designer John Guildford, who as we have seen had been creating original handcraft patterns as early as 1920 for A. E. Gray. It is reasonable to assume that ten years later he was equally inventive. All-over geometric and floral patterns such as *Arabesque*, signed by Guildford, could at first glance be mistaken for the work of the better-known Clarice Cliff, although the application of colour is generally cruder. It is impossible to judge now who was looking through whose painting-shop window – the truth is probably that everyone was guilty of the practice, and Clarice Cliff was certainly not averse in later years to blurring the exact dates of the actual conception of her designs.

To be fair to Barker Bros., if they are guilty in this respect, they were not alone; the practice of copying becomes evident time and time again. Shelley's *Eve* shape is an easily recognizable case: we have already seen that E. Brain produced a very similar shape for the *Mayfair* series, and many other firms followed suit. By the mid-1930s the problem was widespread, raising considerable comment and condemnation. For example, at the United Commercial Travellers' Association annual dinner (North Staffs. Branch) in 1934, a speaker said:

> Another point I should like to raise tonight is the growing practice of copying shapes, designs and ideas. Should a manufacturer introduce a new feature in shape, within a few months half a dozen people have something almost identical. Should another manufacturer strike a new idea in decorations, very little time elapses before a host of makers have very similar styles. Some people may say this is not a new matter; and it is not; but, probably owing to the lean times through which we have been passing, it has been growing, and I feel the time has come when a strong protest should be made against this reprehensible and dishonest system.

Barker Bros. were certainly resourceful and alive to the responses that were needed to battle their way through hard times. In early 1928 they advertised *Triumph Ware* for hotels, dinner-ware which featured detachable metal knobs for vegetable dishes so that when removed the lids could be stacked like plates. By 1929 they were already marketing a considerable range of stylized/rustic hand-painted designs *under* the glaze, which was uncommon in view of the difficulty of achieving the intense colours by this method. These under-glaze colours were used in such patterns as *Harvest*, *Garden*, *Fantasie* and *Tripoli* (it is interesting to note that these names of about 1928–9 were probably issued before Clarice Cliff's *Harvest*, *My Garden*, *Fantasque* and *Trieste* pattern and shape names of 1929–30 onwards). Shapes were similarly inventive: the *Pottery Gazette* referred in November 1929 to *Mentone* as having 'new square-shaped hollow-ware'.

A selection of earthenwares: hand-painted tea-wares by Myott and Son, early 1930s (left) (page 120); bright freehand-painted jug by S. Hancock and Sons, early 1930s (centre) (page 119), printed and enamelled jar by Booths in the Fruit or Bowl of Fruit pattern, early 1920s (top right) (page 100); and tube-lined and painted bowl designed for A. G. Richardson's Crown Ducal ware by Charlotte Rhead, c. 1933. (page 113)

□ Barkers and Kent (*Foley Pottery, Fenton*)

Hand-painted floral and landscape patterns were produced in the 1930s, such as *Silver Tree*. The company produced a number of tablewares with novel features: they claimed to be the first to produce a fruit set with concave rim to prevent stones falling back into the fruit juice, and in 1934 manufactured 'fruit and cream' or 'salad and cream' sets, with dishes provided with a recess in the rims for the individual cream jugs which were also provided as part of the sets.

□ Booths (*Church Bank Pottery, Tunstall*)

This earthenware company was particularly known for its semi-porcelain 'Silicon China', a high-quality earthenware manufactured from the late nineteenth century. Early print and enamel patterns included *Fruit*, or *Bowl of Fruit*, with the motifs painted in clear colours on a bright white glaze. This tableware pattern was marketed by Heal's in the early 1920s (where a 70-piece dinner set in the pattern cost £12 19s. 6d. in 1925). In the late 1920s some novelty moulded wares – for example, a dressed-crab dish with a crab-shell lid on which the legs dangled down the pot – were produced. The firm was also credited for introducing the concept of breakfast-in-bed sets in the 'twenties. Embossed floral ornamental pieces were marketed as *Cornucopia* ware from about 1930.

Booths capitalized on the market for supplementary tablewares, producing bridge sets decorated as playing cards and such items as small hors d'oeuvres dishes 'specially modelled with a view to the requirements of a smaller, modern home, where space conservation is a necessity'. In about 1933 they introduced *Ribstone* ware, with a ribbed surface which gave the appearance of having been thrown on the wheel. At first used for ornamental wares, it was developed for tablewares by 1934. *Ribstone* was decorated with coloured bandings and lines in either bright or subdued tones; with elegant hand-painted florals; with simple Cubist designs; and with stitch patterns (a development for the fashion for patterns derived from embroidery). Subdued and Modernist colour schemes such as dark green, fawn, helio and black were treated with a dark ivory glaze, known colloquially in the potteries as 'toffee'. Booths did not produce angular floral patterns, so by making modifications to their earlier type of floral decorations they were producing by the mid-1930s simple florals that now appeared fresh and modern once again.

□ Bourne and Leigh (*Albion and Leighton Potteries, Burslem*)

The firm's earthenware table products of the early 1930s were typified by the *Cottage Window* pattern – semi-stylized herbaceous plants in strong colours around a vine-clad cottage window were printed and enamelled on ivory ware, treated with a rich honey glaze. Tablewares were marked under the trade name *Leighton Ware* and extended to a range of sixty tableware items. By 1936 the

Pottery Gazette reports a 'drastic overhaul' of their designs, which were now characterized by simple bandings in such colours as green and coral finished with gold or silver, and washbanding combined with simple handcraft designs. A good modern, softened angular shape called *Radio* was introduced, with some excellent modern patterns. The *Silver Grey* pattern, for example, had five fine green lines with a silver band and green shading beneath. Other lined and banded patterns incorporated very simple leaf motifs. The ranges of dinner- tea-, coffee- and breakfast-wares were extended to include fruit and egg sets, cruets, honey-pots, biscuit jars, cress trays, covered jugs and similar table paraphernalia.

□ Burgess and Leigh   (*Burleigh Ware — Middleport Pottery, Burslem*)

The table and ornamental earthenwares produced by this company are known by the name *Burleigh Ware*, and recognized as amongst the most important British wares produced in Art Deco style.

In 1926 the company secured the services of the accomplished pottery designer Charlotte Rhead, who was to remain with the firm until 1931, when she moved to A. G. Richardson (Crown Ducal). Her father, the pottery designer Frederick Rhead, who trained under Léon V. Solon at Mintons, was Art Director of Wood and Sons, where he taught his daughter pottery decorating techniques. The one for which Charlotte Rhead is now well known is that of tube-lining, which had been used to good advantage for the curvaceous decorations on Art Nouveau pottery and tiles from the 1890s. A raised, linear design was achieved by piping slip (liquid clay) onto the surface of the fired but undecorated wares with a rubber bag and glass nozzle, as though icing a cake. Charlotte Rhead trained a team of tube-liners at Burgess and Leigh to carry out work to her designs, and her influence is also evident in designs produced by the company after her departure in 1931, when her team of tube-liners continued using the technique.

The largest proportion of the company's turnover was from tablewares, then supplemented by the ornamental wares that Charlotte Rhead designed in some quantity. *Burleigh Ware* was noted particularly for the fact that numerous tableware patterns were produced *en suite* so that tableware could be collected which included not only dinner-, tea-, and morning-sets, but also egg sets, sandwich sets, fruit and salad sets, all in the same pattern.

An early successful design for tableware was the *Paisley* pattern, produced from 1928, which carried under-glaze blue printed swirls which were touched in with red and yellow enamels for flower motifs. The shapes used were fairly traditional, but the decoration was new and individualistic. The *Richmond* shape sandwich set of about 1928 consisted of rounded-off triangular plates which stacked into the two sides of the fan-shaped serving tray which had a handle at the centre – a relatively new innovation. Decorations for the sandwich set were designed by Charlotte Rhead, tube-lined and painted black, with vivid apples, leaves and polka dots painted under the glaze in orange, fawn and green.

Dinner-ware was produced in the striking new shape *Sheraton* about 1930, the

vegetable dishes of which the *Pottery Gazette* described as 'a form that has a square exterior, in conformity with modern taste, but a round inside fitting which renders easy the clean extraction of the vegetables'. The shape was decorated both with lithographed (mostly floral) and hand-painted patterns, the latter in such vivid colours as red, green and yellow on an ivory-coloured body. The colours used on *Burleigh Ware* were characteristically bright and clear, while the stylized flowers used in patterns were among the period favourites – hollyhocks, tulips and poppies, for example. Earthenware shapes like *Zenith* of the early 'thirties combined both straight lines and curves to produce a typically English derivation of Art Deco. The shape was decorated with patterns such as the very popular *Dawn*, which depicted a very slender black stylized tree, an orange sun (without the more dramatic rays of a sunset) and suggestions of green foliage. In April 1932, the *Pottery Gazette* commented that the *Dawn* pattern 'undoubtedly portrays a very effective modern style of treatment . . . based on the surest foundations, the ruling trend of refined public taste'.

All these features, but particularly *Dawn* on the *Zenith* shape, are examples of Art Deco ceramics in their most English realization: stylized but not extreme, bright but not garish, the patterns simplified but still pretty. Pattern names were resolutely English, not pretentiously French, and included *Shirley*, *Tranquil*, *Laburnum* and *Fragrance*.

Later tablewares, produced in the mid-1930s, adopted more rounded and modern shapes, some ribbed as though hand-thrown, although all still retained traditional overtones. They were decorated with simple stylized flowers or bands and lines. Shapes like *Belvedere* were treated with patterns like the gently stylized outlines of tulips, filled with red, yellow and grey. The *Pottery Gazette* describes the pattern as '. . . restful . . . neither so bright as to be aggressive nor so restrained as to be cheerless'; and, indeed, the pattern, particularly with its use of soft grey, could pass as a design of the 1970s, when similar comment could be made to describe numerous tableware designs.

Many of the most striking Art Deco *Burleigh Wares* are ornamental. A range of the late 'twenties, *Sylvan*, was hand-decorated under a dull glaze to give a slightly matt finish. In 1930 Charlotte Rhead designed the very successful *Florentine* ornamental range, with mellow colours, often incorporating subdued mauves, greens, yellows, blues and browns. Later ornamental patterns inspired by Rhead successfully incorporated tube-lining and tinges of lustre.

In addition, Burleigh produced in the early 'thirties some strikingly geometric, solidly earthenware jugs, vases and flower 'holders' – for example, double holders of superimposed squared diamond shapes. They were often embossed, with elaborate moulded handles, and decorated with large and rather crude landscape patterns. Another range featured moulded animal handles – parrots clenching the rims of jugs in their beaks, fanciful dragons with colourful, scaly tails, squirrels with paws over the rims and diving kingfishers, for example. Larger jugs had character handles in the form of, for instance, a cricketer, golfer or tennis player, although these were made in smaller quantities. The *Pottery Gazette* dubbed many of these ornamental wares 'pretentious' and was glad to see them abandoned in the mid-'thirties in favour of more austere shapes.

A Doulton advertisement which appeared in the Pottery Gazette *in April 1930. Before Doulton's more dramatic shapes were produced in the 1930s, the traditional* Lincoln *was decorated with simple, hand-painted patterns such as* Eden. *(Page 129)*

□ T. G. Green & Co. (*Church Gresley,*
Nr Burton-on-Trent, Derbyshire)

T. G. Green were outside the 'agglomeration' of Stoke-on-Trent, one of the manufacturers scattered in nearby Derbyshire. The company was founded in the 1860s to produce earthenware and stonewares. In the 1930s they were most frequently praised by the design fraternities for their solid, unpretentious, utilitarian kitchen- and tablewares. The most famous of their productions is probably the familiar *Cornish Kitchen Ware*, put into production in the early 1920s, comprising simple shapes and bold alternating bands of blue and white. This decoration comprised bands of blue slip (liquid clay) applied to the white wares as they were turned on a lathe. The white strip on the kitchen jar carried the name of its contents – coffee, flour, butter and so on – where appropriate, and the range was expanded in later years to include tablewares. Green's successful tableware pattern introduced in the mid-1930s, used predominantly for breakfast sets, was *Blue Domino* where the blue background was achieved by dipping the white wares in coloured slip, and the spots were subsequently cut through the slip to expose areas of the white body. Such coloured decorations in the actual body of the wares, incorporated in the clay slip, were very durable, and thus eminently suitable for kitchen and everyday use (**Tooth and Co**, formerly the Bretby Art Pottery, were producing a similar kitchen range, called KK *Ware*, in blue with three white bands, until 1933).

It is interesting to view these wares in the context of the more dramatic productions of the period, as they were constantly referred to by pottery commentators. Alongside Moorcroft's *Powder Blue* and Joseph Bourne's similar and enormously successful *Denby Ware* (which continued in production into the mid-1980s), Green's wares were invoked as examples of how simple, basic and cheap designs could be popular and satisfying. They were used to emphasize the point that elaborate shapes and patterns were unnecessary – although it was of course difficult to persuade the cheap china manufacturer that his fancy tea-sets should in fact emulate the utilitarian kitchenware of a company that was well known also for 'hospital wares'. A report in the *Pottery Gazette* of exhibits at the 'Exhibition of Industrial Art in Relation to the Home' at Dorland Hall in 1933 is typical of the sort of praise T. G. Green's wares received:

> This firm showed some very interesting creations in domestic earthenware intended to fit the requirements and aspirations of middle-class families. The wares included plain Rockingham teapots, simple wares for the kitchen and table, and notably the famous 'Cornish Blue' kitchen and pantry wares. These were much admired. Many commendatory references to them were overheard.
>
> This was an exhibit which emphasised very clearly how good taste can be preserved even in the humbler and very competitive branches of ordinary household pottery.

T. G. Green even found their designs of spots becoming very fashionable in the mid-1930s. About 1936 they launched their *Polka Dot* tableware, more delicately potted than *Blue Domino*, and with smaller spots applied by hand to the white ware. Their advertisements explained that *Polka Dot* had been launched 'in order to perpetuate the modern vogue and trend in fashion and the use of spots'. The shape used for this and other patterns – simple fruit and florals – was very similar to Shelley's *Regent* with its familiar ring handle. By 1938 they had launched *Polo* tea-ware, with cups one plain colour on the exteriors and white inside, and a teapot with white handles and spout contrasting with the coloured pot; lids had completely spherical knobs.

In spite of the applause they consistently received for their simpler wares, T. G. Green did not remain aloof from less utilitarian wares. In about 1930, they designed a heavy earthenware cuboid shape called *Oblique*, which was hand-painted with rather crude bright geometric patterns such as *Alpha* and *Pharos* (giving an indication of the ancient art inspiration for the designs).

Other T. G. Green productions of the period included fine stylized florals and fruit patterns such as a simple rustic apple design called *Pomona* applied *under* the glaze to fairly modern shapes; cane-coloured *Gresley Ware* decorated in simple coloured bands; geometric bulb bowls and flower jugs; and other supplementary tableware items like honey-pots, cruets, salad bowls and servers.

□ Hollinshead and Kirkham   (*Unicorn Pottery, Tunstall*)

In the early 1930s the firm was interesting for its translation of shapes normally reserved for china to high quality 'semi-porcelain' earthenware production. Octagonal and well-potted tea services of the *Varsity* shape, similar to Shelley's *Queen Anne*, were decorated with brightly coloured naturalistic cottage-garden scenes. The same sort of patterns were even used on a *Vogue*-like solid triangular-handled shape of about 1933. These wares were aimed at a country and suburban market, but by 1935 Hollinshead and Kirkham were reported as making a bid for the city and West-End trade. New shapes and patterns were added to the range accordingly. An ovoid streamlined modern shape, *Atlanta*, was introduced for tea-, coffee-, dinner-ware and 'fancies', and was decorated with stylish bandings in such colours as blue, grey and ivory or green, ivory and platinum. The bandings were sometimes used in conjunction with simple leaf sprays of the pretty herbacious plants, delphiniums and hollyhocks, already familiar in the firm's patterns.

□ Johnson Bros.   (*Hanley Pottery, Hanley*)

T. G. Green may have been admired, but Johnson Brothers were the darlings of the design pundits, their extremely plain, often completely undecorated, wares appearing with glowing praise in almost every serious article or book about modern ceramic design. Sadly, almost no records of the company in the 1920s and 1930s exist, and to make tracking their wares yet more difficult, they are hardly ever mentioned in trade journals of the period. This would seem to underline the fact that the trade journals were anxious to promote highly

decorated, fashionable wares rather than devoting editorial space to the simply practical. Johnson Bros. were not involved with hand-painting wares, and may well have been seen in certain quarters of the trade as part of a design conspiracy which would put paintresses out of work.

In an important survey of the pottery industry, published in *The Studio* in 1936 (by which the time enthusiasm for hand-painting was waning), Maurice Rena describes the wares made under Earnest Johnson of Johnson Bros:

> The productions of his firm are directed in price to the largest section of the buying public, and many of them are excellent examples of beautiful utility.
>
> Though competition is keen, Johnsons, in common with the best firms, experiment continually. Their aim is to produce earthenware bodies of fine texture and colour and to encourage decoration in printing, lithography and stamping which will show a real appreciation of these more mechanized techniques and enable the artist to produce honest work in the particular idiom and not the 'mass production' travesties of hand-painting to which one is accustomed. With his organization behind him, he actually finds it cheaper in the long run . . . to pay well for a really good design of this type and would welcome the work of leading designers ready to give of their best in an attempt to interpret the taste of his public in the most progressive manner possible.

In the same year, more praise was poured on the company by Gordon Forsyth in his *20th Century Ceramics*, a favourable entry in which was the highest design seal of approval:

> Dinner-ware made in the Potteries today, from the many first-grade firms, is unbelievably cheap and good. The firm of Johnson Brothers may be mentioned as an outstanding example of excellent cheap production.

Contrary to their expressed preference for lithography in the late 1930s, Johnson Bros. nevertheless supplied white ware to decorating firms to be hand-painted. Most important amongst these was A. E. Gray, and it is no accident that this design-conscious managing director should choose the shapes produced by Johnson.

Extant examples and illustrations of Johnson's wares show simple, often ovoid, hollow-ware shapes and very little interruption to the clean lines. Their modernism was derived from simplicity rather than from any indulgence in contemporary fashion. Ultra-modern shapes appear European besides other British productions, sometimes with gently curved bodies and open, square handles. Many pieces, those frequently illustrated by Forsyth and like-minded critics, were completely undecorated, relying for effect on a thick and even cream-coloured glaze. Johnson Bros. provided proof that good design could rely on shape alone, standing on its own merits.

Brightly hand-painted earthen tablewares by Mintons: tobacco jar, probably 1920s (or possibly earlier); embossed preserve jar with pansies and butterfly handle, 1930s; and orange-shaped (marmalade) preserve jar, 1930s. (Page 137)

□ E. Hughes *(Paladin China — Opal Works, Fenton)*

No greater contrast with Johnson Bros. can be imagined than Paladin, where imaginative decoration dominated any reliance on shape. E. Hughes and Co. was established in 1899 for the production of earthenware and bone china, and the Paladin China of the 'thirties concentrated largely on tea- and breakfast-wares. The Paladin pattern books of the early 'thirties illustrate handcraft Art Deco designs which are amongst the most vivid and exciting of any conceived in the Potteries, showing a confidence in brilliant colour which puts the most extreme *Bizarre* ware in the shade by comparison.

The problem with the pattern books is that although very talented artists were at work and hundreds of patterns were designed, there is little evidence either in contemporary literature or extant examples that more than a very few of the patterns were actually produced. Some were undoubtedly applied to sample wares, as the patterns themselves are annotated with such remarks as 'tried out' or 'done on plate and vegetable dish', while others, often the most exotic, are marked 'too much wiping out and measuring – not practical'. Nevertheless, the pattern books are so exceptional that they are worth describing as examples of the willingness of artists to design imaginatively for industrially produced pottery, even if in business terms the patterns were found impractical. They are also interesting in that they occasionally give written instructions to copy shapes produced by other companies.

It is safe to assume that the majority of the patterns were the work of one designer, who was obsessed with Art Deco stylization and motifs and had an individualistic sense of colour. His favourites were a brilliant peacock blue and a luminous uranium yellow; a frequent combination was the yellow used with bright sea-green and liquid silver on a white china body. Primary colours predominate, and orange, much used by comparable designers, is rarely incorporated in the patterns. The designer clearly had an idiosyncratic sense of humour in adapting fashionable motifs – a sunburst becomes a web, parrots' wings are flashes of lightning and so on – and the books are a wonderful demonstration of how the pastiche of Art Deco motifs can be added to from even more sources.

Except for banding and lining, curves are very rarely to be found in the patterns – everything is translated into straight lines and sharp angles. Parrots are used as a motif which would adapt easily to this sort of stylization, but even bunches of grapes are triangular, not only in their overall form but in every single grape. Art Deco motifs are adapted, so that one plate adopts the sunburst idea for a black spider's web radiating out from one point at the rim with an off-centre fat red spider sitting in the bowl of the plates. Other designs feature tulips, crocuses, daffodils, lightning flashes, butterflies, dramatic landscapes and sunbursts. One or two go badly wrong, such as a pattern with looped half circles at the rim – a popular device – which are oddly supplied with tassels as though part of a festooned curtain. One page turns over to the now chilling sight of a large silver swastika, centred on a brilliant yellow ground and surrounded by edge lines in grey, yellow and black.

Later patterns show extensive use of polka dots and spots, one a pattern using white, yellow and green to depict a gaggle of geese, and entitled *Gossip*. Shape outlines show, for example, square plates, cuboid tea- and coffee-pots with triangular handles and spouts, and instructions such as 'As Doulton

(*Pottery Gazette*)'. Most of the patterns are marked 'all freehand', and would have demanded considerable skills on the part of the paintresses.

The *Pottery Gazette* does give some evidence of pieces actually produced in Paladin China, although none of these very dramatic designs appear in its pages. The November 1931 issue illustrates an 'Ovaltine' set with a restrained composition of black and red diamonds as a border; the pattern, *Dorset*, had been used for tea-ware the previous year. In June 1933 the journal comments on the adoption of the name Paladin as 'suggestive of courtly qualities' (Paladin was one of the 12 famous warriors of Charlemagne's court and by extension had come to mean a knightly hero or knight-errant). The firm's slogan in the 1930s ran: 'Quality, selection and design'. The article refers to a new shape, *Castle* (appropriately enough), a softened octagonal, which was applied with an Art Deco leaf, line and zigzag pattern in black, green and platinum; another pattern for the shape combined yellow, green and coral. Paladin was noted frequently for its high-quality, delicate china potting. A later editorial refers to a pattern called *Allandale*, and very original designs using under-glaze crayoning, a technique which will be examined in relation to Susie Cooper (see p. 190).

Sadly, the evidence points to the fact that the greater proportion of tablewares produced by E. Hughes in the 1930s were of an entirely traditional nature, probably, as we have seen with other firms, because they were selling to the expensive end of the middle market. However, this company is one that richly deserves further research.

□ J. & G. Meakin   (*Sol Ware — Eagle Pottery, Hanley*)

Meakins were one of the largest manufacturers of earthenwares in the Potteries. In the late 1920s they produced a new shape, *Moderne*, under the trade name of *Sol Ware*, which was elongated and streamlined but basically traditional in appearance, with the addition of a rectangular open knob to hollow-ware lids. Bright floral lithographs were judged of high quality, producing smooth and glossy effects on the shape. A version of the shape was decorated with grey shaded borders which gave the impression of fluting, and with single scarlet Modernist roses. This design was exhibited at Dorland Hall in 1933.

□ New Pearl Pottery   (*Royal Bourbon — Brook Street Potteries, Hanley*)

The company was so named from about 1935, previously working as Pearl Pottery and producing tablewares under the trade name *Royal Bourbon*. The change of name heralded new modern shapes and treatments in earthenwares, many hand-painted with large, bright rustic daisies. The *Cuba* tea- and coffee-ware series of about 1935 was a heavy cube and triangular shape similar to Clarice Cliff's earlier *Conical*. More traditional, slightly octagonal shapes were decorated with fresh hand-painted florals such as *Primrose*.

Striking a Modern Note!

● *At left:* "SYREN." *This unique shape is typically British—the conventional flowers are in gorgeous colours—the fine earthenware permits a silky finish reminiscent of sunshine.*

● *Below:* "MECCA." *When the public see Doulton "Mecca" they live in hopes of buying it. So jolly in shape, so merry in its dashing colours and so modest in cost, that when they learn its price—hope becomes undeferred and satisfied.*

TWO Modern Doulton designs in fine earthenware, with shapes that win by a smiling robustness.

The sunny ground has a cheery effect, and the very quaint designs are vividly coloured.

Ready for hard wear and at prices which sell quantities in the hardest times— Two good lines for to-day's needs.

Doulton Figures continue to expand sales. Have you seen the new models and new miniatures? If not, you have a pleasure in store.

TABLE CLOTHS. One reason why the new, modest-priced Doulton Sets are selling, is the charming new Table Cloths which match the Doulton designs and colourings (guaranteed fast). There are now seven different cloths to choose from, to exactly match the Table Ware at a price unbelievably modest. Table Cloths available matching "Syren," "Eden," "Norfolk," "Dubarry," "Rosslyn," "Leeds Spray" and "Arvon."
Why not see them?

Royal Doulton

DOULTON & CO. LTD., THE ROYAL DOULTON POTTERIES, BURSLEM, STOKE-ON-TRENT.

G

□ Paragon China   (*Atlas Works, Longton*)

Paragon is another company which has not received the attention which its 1930s designs warrant. From about 1903, it operated under the title Star China (although backstamps incorporate the name Paragon), becoming Paragon China in 1919. As with Paladin, the name adopted deliberately alludes to the excellence of manufacture. The Paragon pattern books are either inaccessible or have been destroyed, but there is sufficient evidence elsewhere to chart some of the notable shape and pattern designs of the period. Paragon was famous for its nursery wares, which are discussed in Chapter 6, and in the early 1920s for gold-printed patterns (a technique which they applied to some striking cocktail sets around 1930). In 1929 T. A. Fennemore, later to be influential at E. Brain, was appointed Sales Manager. Fresh from London and the retail trade, he assisted the Managing Director Hugh Irving in the establishment of a close relationship between Paragon and the retail shops, advising on displays and loaning window-dressing schemes to mount imposing arrangements of Paragon China. His arrival was commented upon by the *Pottery Gazette*: 'This is, we believe, a portent of what the company intends to do in the direction of creating, by scientific means, an increasing demand for their own particular productions.'

The firm's output, initially predominantly for export, was of tea- and breakfast-wares, expanded in the 1930s to include dinner services as the home market became more important. Paragon recognized that their main competitors were Aynsley and Shelley, producers of china to a similar top-middle market, and were among the companies producing Art Deco shapes to compete with Shelley in the early 1930s. Their technique was the same – a high-grade delicate china body and print and enamel decoration – and their commercial aims were clear, the caption to an early 1931 trade advertisement running:

> Paragon possesses the rare ability of interpreting the public's taste in china and creating designs which are pleasingly familiar yet distinctively modern.

By 1931 they had a distinctive tea-ware shape – cups conical like Shelley's but with stepped ribs; handles like an open triangle with the point straightened off; solid triangular teapot spout; diamond-shaped knob; and octagonal plates – the serving plate extending into triangular handles. The shape, called *Duchess*, seemed somehow to involve all possible fashionable attributes, but none-theless appeared well balanced. It was decorated with pretty print and enamel stylized florals of the now familiar species – tulips, poppies, crocuses, nasturtiums – or left plain with simple pastel-coloured edges.

Paragon did not rely on decorating managers, but engaged designers like Ceri Clayton (who had studied under Forsyth at Burslem School of Art) in the 1920s and 1930s, and most notably, Agnes Pinder Davis, who also designed for other firms, including W.T. Copeland. A dinner-service for six by Agnes Pinder Davis was not cheap – retailing at £10 15s. 0d. in 1935.

Very early on in the 1930s, at least by 1932, Paragon were producing

A Doulton advertisement which appeared in the Pottery Gazette *of September* 1932. *The two patterns,* Syren *and* Mecca, *were launched for the Christmas 1931 trade, decorating a solid earthenware shape. The advertisement also promotes matching tablecloths available in the same patterns.* (Page 129)

Modernist designs of a more rounded shape than *Duchess*. The most successful appears to have been an oval-bodied shape and rounded handles with the hollows filled in at top and/or bottom with solid ribbed triangles. Spouts were either traditional or solid and hooked, reminiscent of Susie Cooper productions, and knobs were of a stepped 'Aztec' effect seen in all sorts of productions of the Art Deco period (particularly radios and clocks). Tea-, coffee- and bridge-sets appear to have been produced, and the DIA's Harry Trethowan commented: 'The bulbous shape of the teapot seems to be good in that it should retain the heat of the tea, but the handles are not very convincing.'

Examples were produced in one-colour glazes – white, duck egg blue, pink, green and peach, and in some beautiful patterns like the much admired *Hydrangea*, where a blotched and stippled pink and green application of colour created an all-over effect of these shrubby flowers. Other very simple lined pieces were produced, some with understated flower and leaf motifs, which could be harmonized with matching table linen – a growing fashion in the 1930s.

Paragon was appointed with a Royal Warrant from Queen Mary in 1933, largely as a result of their royal successes with nursery ware designed for the Duchess of York's children – the young Princesses Elizabeth and Margaret Rose (see Chapter 6). In 1933, some stunning tea-ware patterns, closer in effect to Foley's *Mayfair* than anything else in the trade, were supplied to Queen Mary, a keen buyer of contemporary ceramics. (The Queen purchased such a quantity of wares from Stoke-on-Trent manufacturers over the years that Royal Warrants were granted frequently, and one wonders how even a palace could use and store so many tea-sets!) The plates had undecorated bowls and rims treated with bold ground colours and stripes, chequer sections and sunbeams.

Paragon was another company which experimented to the utmost throughout the 1920s and 1930s, making successful Art Deco, Modernist and nursery designs, marketing them vigorously, and surviving by keeping in the vanguard of both fashion and contemporary 'good taste'.

□ A. G. Richardson (*Crown Ducal — Gordon Pottery, Tunstall; Britannia Pottery, Cobridge from 1934*)

The decorative device of a black silhouetted tree, the upper branches spreading out at the edge of a plate or rim of a cup, is found in numerous interpretations in patterns produced by various manufacturers – Shelley's *Crabtree* is just one example. There is little doubt that A. G. Richardson's *Red Tree* (also known today as *Orange Tree*) was the precedent for such patterns: launched in 1925, it took the trade by storm and proved so popular that it continued in production for many years.

In May 1925 the *Pottery Gazette* greeted with justified enthusiasm a 'two-colour pattern of outstanding interest'. The pattern consisted of printed black trees grouped in pairs in a wide border and stretching out at the rim, with an outline landscape extending between the trees, dotted with enamelled red fruit.

> Both in the matter of spacing and colouring this pattern is quite unlike anything we remember having seen previously in English pottery, and it seems to stand proof, if proof be needed, that the manufacturers of 'Crown Ducal Ware' are alive to the necessity of keeping in intimate touch with the modern trend of design, and are even desirous of educating the public up to something different in the matter of pottery decoration by actually giving a lead.

The shape used was fairly traditional and rounded, although vegetable dishes had concave octagonal rims. By 1932 *Red Tree* had become 'that good old design' and was still in demand.

A. G. Richardson were manufacturers solely of high-quality earthenwares – tea-, breakfast- and dinner-services and ornamental wares. In the first half of the 1920s they had introduced plain-coloured aerographed (see p. 190) tea-wares, mainly for the export trade, which were produced in such bright colours as orange; they also manufactured striking lustred wares. Their use of vivid colour was so advanced that as early as 1925 the *Pottery Gazette* was commenting:

> . . . they have done as much as any firm in the Staffordshire Potteries to illustrate the possibilities of strong colour treatments in relation to pottery decoration, and how much this has meant towards the enlivenment of the drab surroundings of some people whose habitations are perforce situated in industrial neighbourhoods one can only imagine.

By 1929, new print and enamel patterns were being produced as alternatives to *Red Tree*, such as *Acacia*, *Blackthorn*, and subsequently, the very popular *Red Poppy*. Ornamental ware in a new range, named *Arcadian Glazes*, with glaze effects of several broken and variegated colours, was launched at this time. In 1931, Charlotte Rhead joined the company, and her artistic and technical influence is to be seen in subsequent productions.

By early 1933 about 90 per cent of the wares produced at the factory made use of new patterns. Many were applied to the new hollow-ware shape, *Cotswold*, whose vegetable dish had solid Modernist handles and stood on four feet, with the body of the dish cut away in between in gentle curves. Early patterns such as *Sunburst*, in orange and black, were succeeded by more subtle, modern designs conceived by Charlotte Rhead. In 1934, her *Stitch* pattern appeared, based, as the name suggests, on embroidery, with the stitch pattern tube-lined under the glaze to emulate raised threads at the edge of the wares. Simple banding and lining were the only other additions to the pattern. Tea-ware in the *Cotswold* shape was mainly decorated with print and enamel florals, some stylized, such as *Daffodil*, while others, like *Linden*, simplified traditional treatments.

In the mid-1930s, quantities of simple lined and wash-banded wares were produced – a typical example being a lemonade set, banded in graduated beige shades and over-painted with lines in blue, green and yellow. Simple wavy lines were used in *Trilby*, and by the late 'thirties sophisticated patterns like *Trellis and Dot*, where polka dots are placed seemingly at random rather than evenly spaced, are typical. Charlotte Rhead produced a large number of patterns for ornamental pieces, marketed as *Rhodian Ware*. Her terms of reference for the

Roc
Ivory all over
Green band
printed in Y298 brown
Coloured in
   Yellow green
   3303 yellow
   Blue
   Rose C.
   Coral.
   Redredge

B.1216.

lines to be printed

April 1930

designs were largely Byzantine and Chinese art, and have been discussed in some depth by Bernard Bumpus in his books and articles about Charlotte Rhead (see Bibliography).

Manufacturers of china tea-ware

Many companies capitalized on the growing market for pretty china tea-wares of medium price. Between them they produced hundreds of the brightly painted print and enamel floral tea- and breakfast-services, either in traditional, octagonal, or very slightly angular shapes that immediately spring to mind as typical of 1930s china. None of the tablewares of these companies could reasonably be called Art Deco, but they do show how fashionable trends influenced even the most traditional manufacturers. All remained utterly 'English', but palettes brightened and then dulled again, rounded shapes were angled a little, and hand-painting ensured pretty and fresh tea-sets which are still found in quantity today. Although not aiming at an expensive market, these established china manufacturers had no need for the more extreme novelty appeal which dogged the earthenware potters.

Shore and Coggins (Bell China – Edensor Works, Longton) are pre-eminent amongst the medium-priced 'china-tea-set' houses of the period. By 1930, they were producing *Bell China* both in traditional border transfer patterns and in coloured print and enamels such as *Crocus*, *Tulip* and *Nasturtium*. *Rambler Rose*, *May Blossom* and *Autumn Leaves* followed, all on fairly ordinary shapes. The most stylized shape they designed was *Tudor*, with conical and ribbed cups, which was decorated, for example, with stylish chequerboard patterns in various colour combinations. The *Bute* shape, also fairly angular, was decorated with pretty geometrics.

The company's pattern books of the period, crammed with hundreds of tea-ware patterns, reflect an overall impression of prettiness and of Art Deco motifs toned down to their least dramatic. By the late 'thirties, very attractive polka dots and banded wares in more pastel shades make their entrance into the pattern books as expected.

The Colclough (Royal Vale China — Longton) story is very similar: tulips and harebells and other very English flowers, painted with a palette predominantly black, coral, yellow and green, appear on a wide range of traditional tea-shapes, although an *Octagon* shape was produced by 1930 and a *Tulip* shape with a double link open circle handle was produced in about 1933 – again probably in response to Shelley and other up-market china companies who were setting the style. Colclough's china potting was comparatively cheap, but delicate in keeping with the floral decorations.

Blyth Porcelain (Longton) were the producers of *Diamond China*, particularly tea- and breakfast-ware. Simple, restrained print and enamel floral patterns such as *Honesty* and *Tulip*, and stylized tree designs such as *Solitude* were produced throughout the 'thirties. Some gentle angular tea-ware shapes were introduced, notably *Coral*, with a squared-off handle. In the later 'thirties shapes reminiscent of Shelley's later productions were manufactured: for

Page from a Mintons pattern book of c. 1930–34, showing one of Reginald Haggar's designs for his Landscape tableware series. (Page 133)

example, a tulip-shaped tea-cup with double ring handle, decorated with restrained polka dot patterns.

Crown Staffordshire Porcelain (Minerva Works, Fenton) were in the same league, although slightly more adventurous. The names of special patterns were incorporated in the backstamps, and extant patent registration documents provide an interesting picture of some shapes and patterns they were keen to protect in the 'twenties: in 1924 a teapot lid moulded as a bunch of primroses and another in the shape of a parrot; a 1927 cruet in the shape of Brussel's sprouts; a 1929 plate decorated with stylized gold and red narcissi with grey printed leaves. Tea-cup handles were sometimes moulded in the shapes of flowers, like Aynsley's, and mildly 'geometric' shapes were almost identical to Shore and Coggins's. The same progression through tulips, daisies, hollyhocks, buttercups and zinnias, banding and polka dots can easily be traced.

One of the company's most unusual patterns was the highly successful *Shadow*, created in 1931 and described thus by the *Pottery Gazette*: '. . . the border . . . is a three-toned effect grading from a well-defined colour at the edge to a faint or shadow colouring which seems to lose itself at the shoulder of the plate.' Another concurrent departure from the floral norm was a plaid design used for an after-dinner coffee-set.

New Chelsea Porcelain (Longton) were another company producing fashionable china tea-ware for the middle market. Advertisements from 1930, demonstrating hand-painting of the wares, claimed to accommodate the 'craze . . . for brighter things . . . expressed with a Frenchy [sic] accent . . .' Tulip shapes like *Nouvelle* were painted with English garden scenes such as *Woodland*, Chinese-inspired florals such as *Maytime* or *Mandarin* and modernistic pretty geometrics like *La Belle*. These wares were also advertised as: 'The china that will stand boiling water'. A faintly angular *Nile* shape was introduced about 1933, decorated most successfully with a diamond geometric border similar to the earlier Paladin design (see p. 109), purporting to be 'a dignified treatment for upper-class trade'.

The china tablewares of **Thomas Wild and Sons (Longton)** were manufactured under the trade name *Royal Albert*, a name still famous today as part of the Royal Doulton Group. In the early 1930s china tea-services were treated with gently modern shapes and restrained Art Deco patterns. In 1934 *Royal Albert* launched one of the most stunning Art Deco tea- and coffee-ware shapes of the period, *Apex*, which had daffodil-shaped cups with rounded handles broken in the middle by a zigzagged lightning-flash shape, and serving plates with handles emerging from the round, stepped Aztec form. A very inventive Art Deco pattern was applied to the shape, consisting of horizontal and vertical bandings crossing in one corner, overlaid with octagonal daisy flowerheads whose sides abutted each other irregularly like linked gearcogs. All the best elements of Art Deco were used to advantage, particularly with the steps and lightning flashes used in the shape itself rather than as painted motifs.

Although the **Soho Pottery (Elder Works, Cobridge)** was devoted entirely to earthenware, Soho's 'semi-porcelain' productions were of a high-enough grade to retail at a reasonable price to the middle market. A 1925 advertising booklet describes *Solian Ware* as 'almost as thin as China, and equally brilliant in finish, it is much stronger and more durable'. The company produced tea-, breakfast-, coffee and dinner-wares as well as ornamental items. *Solian Wares* were followed by *Ambassador Wares* which boasted an ivory body of exceptional strength, treated with a brilliant glaze.

Decorations on Soho's tablewares thus imitated the quality of those used by china manufactures. Simple florals like *Briar Rose* and cottage garden landscapes like *Marie*, on fairly traditional shapes, were gradually augmented by about 1932 with more modern shapes and decorations. Dramatic angular tea-sets, hand-painted with vivid stylized flowers and geometrics, and under-glaze banded wares such as the popular *Queen's Green*, were successfully marketed by the middle of the decade. In 1933 a *Chequers* border pattern was launched, with a tartan effect in blue, green and orange; at the 1935 British Industries Fair a geometric *Sunray* pattern in brown and yellow for tea-ware in the *Burlington* shape was exhibited (yet another inspired by Shelley's *Eve*, although this time produced by an earthenware manufacturer). Later patterns included severe Art Deco treatments such as *Melody* and florals such as *Hydrangea*. Other patterns for *Burlington* simplified out into fine border-line decorations, arranged like a sunburst reduced to the merest suggestion of the motif in *Unique*, designed in about 1935. Simple and accomplished coffee-services were produced, for example with green and silver banding.

□ Other noteworthy manufacturers of modern china and earthenware

George L. Ashworth and Bros. (Hanley) exhibited wares at the Dorland Hall exhibition in 1933 which were admired, particularly banded wares and simple Art Deco designs of zigzags and small Cubist motifs which were described as 'striking a note in the development of design which rings true both in form and utility'. The firm was famous for its manufacture of Mason's 'Patent Ironstone'.

Bakewell Bros. (Brittanic Works, Hanley) had a reputation in the early 1930s for moderately priced earthenware dinner- and tea-ware, supplemented by fruit and sandwich sets. Pretty floral treatments were either lithographs or print and enamel decorations. Two new earthenware bodies, one ivory and one amber, were introduced for hand-decoration with bright enamel colours.

Baker and Co. (Fenton) developed striking, brightly coloured floral earthen-wares in the late 1920s, which developed from their hand-decorated sponge-wares of earlier years. They also experimented with striking geometrics: pattern books show designs for bursting stars and lightning flashes, in such colour combinations as chrome yellow, white and brilliant blue. Decorative wares in more muted colours bore similarities to the products of Poole Pottery.

Cartwright and Edwards (Borough Pottery, Longton) produced both earthenwares and china. Octagonal earthenwares were produced from about 1930, and some embossed wares, such as *Honeyglazed Wicker*, for sardine boxes, covered butter dishes and ornamental wares. In the mid-1930s a china tea-ware shape, *York*, in imitation of Shelley's wares, was produced, decorated with

patterns such as *Mayfair*, with a border of overlapping blue, fawn and yellow 'balloons' and Art Deco patterns.

James Cope (Wellington China) produced utilitarian bone china with neat print and enamel garden scenes in bright colours. In 1931 geometric patterns were introduced. By 1933 they had china tea-services moulded in relief florals with floral cup handles; in 1935 they produced a tea-cup with circular handles called *Queen* shape, an imitation of Shelly's *Regent*.

Elijah Cotton (Nelson Pottery, Hanley) advertised *Nelson Ware* tea-services from the late 1920s with illustrations of fashionable flapper girls drinking out of cups with handcraft over-glaze patterns. By 1930 heavy floral Art Deco patterns were applied to equally heavy earthenware shapes by paintresses who worked by eye and not by printed or sketched outlines. Their concerns were utilitarian and 'no time is spent in the production of trifles and bric-a-brac'. In the mid-1930s some of these chunky shapes were left undecorated, treated simply with ivory glaze.

Furnivals (Cobridge) produced similar earthenwares with heavy, bright free-hand florals, as did **S. Hancock and Sons (Hanley)**, with unpretentiously named patterns such as *Gaiety*. **Grimwades (Stoke)** produced a number of good floral patterns from 1930 on *Royal Winston Ivory* earthenware, notably *Poppy* and *Beverly*. An Art Deco pattern, *Persian*, consisting of sunburst, clouds and abstract geometrics in strong colours, was used for tea- and breakfast-sets from 1930 by the company. **Albert E. Jones (Palissy Pottery, Longton)** produced bold Art Deco tablewares of the Clarice Cliff type, for example in 1932 a bright geometric pattern called *Futuresque* and a stylized *Landscape* with naive clouds and Lombardy poplars were hand-painted onto a heavy cuboid shape. These designs were again 'left to the hand and eye of the paintresses'.

George Jones (Crescent Pottery, Stoke) manufactured china and earthenwares, continuing with pretty floral lithographs into the 1930s. Some good print and enamel patterns for china, such as *Country Bunch*, exhibited at Dorland Hall in 1933, were executed under the glaze. Their banded earthen tablewares were sold by Heal's in the mid-'thirties, and at about the same time they produced novelty and ornamental earthenwares, such as a jug in the shape of a squirrel and children's beakers with modelled nursery-rhyme character handles.

John Maddock and Sons (Newcastle Street Pottery, Burslem) produced earthen tablewares on gently fashionable shapes. The rounded *Minerva* octagonal shape was printed and enamelled in simple, still quite naturalistic floral patterns such as *Summertime*. The *Earl* and *Venice* shapes, with tea-cup handles in open triangular and diamond shapes respectively, were launched from 1932, treated with simpler, modern floral patterns. **Mayer and Sherrat (Longton)** manufactured similar floral patterned china tea-ware under the trade name *Melba China*.

W. R. Midwinter (Burslem) are worth noting for designs of the late 1930s which heralded their more famous wares of the 1950s. In 1936, a very geometric tea-service shape was decorated with *The Flower Shop* pattern, a stylized design of flowers displayed inside a shop, which was very unusual for the period: exterior landscapes were used for decorations but rarely interiors.

Two striking Art Deco designs of the latter 1930s, signed by John Wadsworth for Mintons: bone china vase with stylized lotus pattern in matt black, burnished gold and green enamel, printed and painted over the glaze, together with its original art work; and silver lustre earthenware ashtray. (Pages 133–6)

Myott and Son (Stoke, Corbridge and Hanley) produced earthenware traditional and stylized tableware shapes with modern wash-banded and print and enamel patterns and in the 1930s a number of Art Deco freehand-painted ornamental wares, such as fan-shaped and pyramid vases.

R. H. & S. L. Plant (Tuscan Works, Longton) manufactured *Tuscan China*, which was heavily advertised in the trade press from the 1920s, and from 1929 *Tuscan* hand-paintresses were staging public demonstrations of their artistic skills. By the mid-1930s, tablewares were supplemented by novelty wares, painted in pastel shades of green and turquoise as well as the more vibrant colours.

Pountney and Co (Bristol) produced good-quality earthenwares, and perhaps because they operated outside the intense atmosphere of Stoke-on-Trent they continued to produce lithographed decorations rather than following the fashion for hand-painting. As a result, the firm was noted for exhibiting some of the very few modern lithographs on modern shapes – of simple leaves and grasses – at the exhibition of 'British Art in Industry' at the Royal Academy in 1935.

Wedgwood and Co (a separate firm from Josiah Wedgwood and Sons), were producers of general domestic earthenware, and in 1932 they launched a new shape called *Farnol* for tea-ware. This was an almost exact copy, in cheaper earthenware, of Shelley's *Eve* shape, and was treated to similar banded, stylized floral and small Art Deco patterns. These were print and enamel, in such fashionable colour combinations as black, green and platinum. By 1935, the range was extended so that practically all tablewares were available in the *Farnol* shape. Wedgwood and Co also produced good modern ornamental wares – embossed vases and bowls decorated with glossy green, matt marbled and matt white glazes.

From the mid-1930s **H. J. Wood (Alexandra Pottery, Burslem)** produced floral earthenwares with the signature 'E. Radford' incorporated in the backstamp. These wares were designed by and under Edward Radford, who worked for H. J. Wood on a freelance basis (although they have been erroneously attributed to 'Elizabeth' Radford). Many of the pieces were hand-thrown, and all were hand-painted with decorations under the glaze, featuring softly outlined pastel-coloured flowers, particularly anemones. Special glazes, coloured honey, pink, turquoise and blue, produced a sponged, matt effect. The range of wares was mainly ornamental but included cruets, jugs and cheese dishes.

The enormous variety of wares produced by these companies illustrates the range of responses to both modern design and economic conditions in the Potteries during the 1920s and 1930s. Heavy cuboid earthenwares, bright rustic florals and geometric designs coexisted with pretty china floral tea-wares, some streamlined Modernist shapes and a very few utilitarian wares that relied on shape alone for their modern effect. Some of the resultant tablewares were daring and successful, others daring but ill judged. Whatever specific criticisms could be made, it was clear at least that the industry was developing its design ideas.

CHAPTER FIVE

The Grand Old Potteries

The great variety of tablewares produced by the middle-market china and earthenware manufacturers clearly shows that no one genre of new pattern predominated. With characteristic thoroughness, in his *An Inquiry Into Industrial Art in England*, Pevsner considered the various patterns of wares in the categories referred to by the manufacturers and retailers, and researched the percentages sold in each:

> The statements of retailers were especially useful with regard to the order of popularity as between the various types of pottery decoration in the English market. Manufacturers and distributors classify these as a rule under All-over Prints, Period Floral, Modern Floral and Banded. The terms 'All-over Prints' means any design of the 'Willow Pattern' or 'Blue Italian' or 'Cottage View' etc. 'Period Floral' are those old-fashioned floral borders, spray borders, broken borders, etc., which are to be found in most eighteenth-century porcelain. 'Modern Floral' signifies two different types, either hand-painted rustic designs or lithographed (or hand-painted) flowers of a modern commercial character, often intermixed with some cubistic elements. The term 'Banded' needs no explanation.

Pevsner found, as we have already noted, that the percentages of each sold by various retailers depended upon the level of the market to which their shops were selling, and correspondingly whether their stock was mainly of earthenware or bone china. He found that above a certain level of price modern floral decreased rapidly in importance, but that by 1936 it still comprised an important portion of the earthenware market, although the rustic examples were by now considered old-fashioned. Banded ware he saw as typical of medium-priced wares, and gaining ground: it had been produced by some manufacturers since 1930, and increasingly by many factories since 1933. Period floral, and particularly all-over prints, were of comparatively little importance to this market, and he found English earthenware as a whole 'modernistic' in appearance.

CASINO

by ROYAL DOULTON

This robust design, with quiet colourings will create a new interest and increase sales. Simple modern lines and unusual handling devices give the whole a pleasing effect.

"MARQUIS" DESIGN

MODERN WARE

"Casino" offers a choice of three distinctive effects, "Marquis" and "Radiance" (illustrated) being in bands and hair lines; "Envoy," a frieze of blue curves of soft shades. *Why not write for full particulars ?*

"RADIANCE" DESIGN

DOULTON & CO., LIMITED, THE ROYAL DOULTON POTTERIES, BURSLEM, STOKE-ON-TRENT

L.*

Pevsner's findings precisely reflect the designs and changes in design we have seen amongst the earthenware and china discussed in the previous chapter. At the top end of the market, he found a very different situation: with the porcelain firms little had changed during the previous twenty years. All-over prints might make up as much as 50 per cent of the wares produced, with period floral at 30 per cent and banded at 20 per cent, leaving no room at all for the modern floral category. The explanation given by one manufacturer was that porcelain sold only to the older age groups, the young preferring to spend their disposable income on new modern pursuits like cars and 'weekending'.

When we turn to the actual products of the great names of English pottery manufacture – Doulton, Minton, W.T. Copeland, Wedgwood and Worcester – these conclusions are demonstrated. With some exceptions of modern designs produced in china, these firms restricted their 'modernistic' tablewares largely to earthenware, with the added complication that they felt they should resist any design excesses which would detract from their wider, traditional reputations.

In discussing these large and historic companies in the context of new tableware designs of the 'twenties and 'thirties, it is unrealistic to try to give a very much wider impression of the companies in question. There is room only for brief historical detail and passing references to some of the great products of the firms. In particular, this chapter will concentrate almost exclusively on tablewares, thus omitting detailed discussion of ornamental and art wares, which are for the most part well documented in the histories listed in the Bibliography.

□ Doulton and Co. (*Royal Doulton Potteries, Nile Street, Burslem*)

The history of Doulton and Company as it exists today begins prosaically with drains – more specifically with stoneware drainpipes and conduits, pioneered in London by Henry Doulton in the mid-nineteenth century in response to the need to sanitize Britain's cities. From these beginnings, the famous Lambeth Studio developed, producing art wares. Subsequently Doulton and Co. were established in Staffordshire at Nile Street, Burslem (where they remain today) by 1882, by the determined but rather unwelcome southener Henry Doulton. After World War I, production at Lambeth was on a reduced scale, and the pieces produced up to World War II were predominantly ornamental stonewares and garden-wares ranging from important sculptures to garden gnomes. The London business was overshadowed by expansion in Burslem, and the Lambeth works closed in 1956. The products which are relevant to the study of interwar tableware were manufactured at the Nile Street factory.

In the late 1890s Art Director John Slater and then Charles Noke, who succeeded Slater in 1914, in collaboration with the artist-potter Bernard Moore, began experiments with high-temperature glazes which resulted in the colourful, Chinese-inspired *Flambé* wares that were much admired in the early twentieth century. From 1919, these transmutation glazes were also produced under the name *Sung*. The glowing colour effects, typically dark red or streaked

A Doulton *advertisement which appeared in the* Pottery Gazette *of September* 1934 *for the elegant Art Deco* Casino *shape, introduced* c. 1932. *These two decorations on earthenware,* Marquis *and* Radiance, *were produced from* 1933. (*Pages* 125–8)

blue, often under-glaze painted with decorations in black, won the highest acclaim from Gordon Forsyth in his summary of British exhibits at the 1925 Paris *Exposition*: 'No firm deserves greater praise than Messrs. Doulton's for their constant endeavour to produce pottery of a high artistic order.' Very few items of tableware were made with flambé glaze because of the problem in maintaining an even consistency of the glaze in matching sets, and the effect was reserved for ornamental pieces.

The earliest stirrings of Art Deco design at Doulton can perhaps be seen in some ornamental pieces of *Titanian* ware, a lustrously glazed pottery noted for pastel colours which Noke had devised, and Doulton's artist Harry Tittensor painted and designed. In 1923, after the opening of Tutankhamen's tomb the previous year, pieces were decorated with Egyptian designs. However, the backbone of Doulton's Burslem business was not such ornamental 'art' wares but mass-produced tablewares and ornaments, and by the 1930s the company was producing Art Deco tablewares in both china and earthenware, and experimenting with using contemporary artists for mass-produced designs.

Frank Brangwyn (1867–1956) had been employed by William Morris back in the early 1880s to decorate pottery, but by 1930 he had become a distinguished designer of murals, stained glass and furniture. He, like so many others, was dissatisfied with the gulf between artists and industry, and in consequence undertook to design a range of household commodities including furniture, carpets, textiles and pottery for an exhibition held in October 1930 at the galleries of the furniture firm E. Pollard and Co. He approached Doulton for the pottery, and easily won the collaboration of Charles Noke, under whose auspices a number of new shape and pattern designs were produced from 1930.

A publicity leaflet which accompanied the launch of Brangwyn's wares makes clear the artist's intention to supply new designs for industry as well as pin-pointing a reaction against some of the garish wares that had hit the market during the preceding couple of years:

> The collection and study of old English china has in measure led to the retention and in some cases the re-adoption of old designs. This worship of the antique has had a retarding influence upon the growth and development of design in ceramic art . . .
>
> Nor has the only sin been that of ill-conceived shapes, a more prevalent departure from ceramic cannons has been the amateur's easy glide into misplaced and misused colour.

The earthenware shapes which Brangwyn designed were rounded, simple, but with a heavy, uneven appearance which deliberately imitated hand-thrown wares. The body of the wares was buff-coloured, with soft greens, blues, reds, pinks and lemon yellows used for patterns which were moulded and incised by hand very slightly into the body. The intention was that the patterns should not be sharply defined or heavily outlined, and the colours are described as 'woven' upon the background, so that no colour, either of the body or the decoration, appeared uppermost. The whole was treated with a 'limpid' glaze. These hand-crafted wares were not intended to appear consistent, and marketing blurbs even emphasized the fact that no two pieces were exactly alike. They were enthusiastically received by design commentators, and the *Pottery Gazette* described their introduction as marking 'another epoch in the development of industrial art'. The designs were used for dinner-, tea- and coffee-services, vases, ashtrays, beakers, lamp bases, biscuit barrels, candlesticks, plaques and sandwich boxes.

The most successful design was called *Harvest*, the softly outlined pattern suggesting a scattered arrangement of fruit and flowers on a muted greeny-beige ground. In 1930 tea-sets for 12 people retailed at £3 3s. Od. and dinner-sets for 12 at just over £8. Despite these very modest prices, the Brangwyn wares were not a commercial success: they did not sell as intended to people on low incomes, but instead appealed in a modest way to middle-class buyers who had a collector's interest in art pottery. It is possible that the irregularity of the pieces and the fact that they appeared hand-thrown dissuaded the ordinary buyers from treating them seriously, accustomed as they were to the clean-cut lines and uniform patterns of traditional and other modern tablewares. They may even have been seen as potentially unreliable. However, the fact that the wares were so widely admired and written about by contemporary critics and the artist/industry experiment so applauded did Doulton's reputation nothing but good. *The Studio* responded to the exhibition at E. Pollard and Co. by saying:

> It is true there is only one Brangwyn – in himself not enough to go round the whole industry of Great Britain – but, apply the principle of what Brangwyn stands for, and a better-looking and more comfortable Britain is assured.

Charles Noke and his son Jack worked together during the 'thirties. Jack had been with Doulton since World War I, trained at the Burslem Art School and finally took over from his father as Art Director in 1936. He was keenly aware of contemporary tableware fashions, and throughout the 'thirties a number of Art Deco and modern earthen and china tablewares was produced from the designs, and under the direction of, father and son – always alongside, rather than in preference to, Doulton's traditional manufactures. In particular, throughout this period Doulton produced a number of 'olde English' patterns on tableware – hunting scenes, thatched cottages and the like in completely naturalistic colourings, as well as Charles Noke's very successful moulded *Dickens Ware*.

The *Casino* shape was introduced in the early 1930s (probably 1932), and was produced in both earthenware and china. The shape boasted 'simple, modern lines', and was remarkably advanced, combining Art Deco ideas and stream-lined, practical shapes. Vegetable dishes, for example, were rounded and flattened, moulded to produce a gentle and elegant 'stepped' effect, like a graduated pyramid. Designs used for the china ranges included the beautiful and understated *Tango*, which used simple rim-banding with a single edge motif of a semi-circular form made up of lines, crossed by another set of straight lines. This very refined Art Deco decoration appears to have been based on a sunburst, severely stylized, and was available in black, gold and red, or black, gold and green on the white china. The *Lynn* pattern consisted of a stylized paisley effect in black and green, while *Glamis*, *Bella* and *Stella* were stylized leaf and floral designs using combinations of green, yellow, black, gold

Earthen tablewares and vase
designed for Doulton by Frank
Brangwyn from 1930, and
decorated by hand. The
dinnerware shapes are described
in advertisements as 'moresque',
and are intended to harmonize
with Tudor furniture. The teapot
is decorated with Brangwyn's
Harvest pattern. (Pages
124–5)

and blue. All these patterns were produced on *Casino* in 1932. More conventional florals, using a brighter palette with reds, oranges and yellows, were also devised for the shape, including *Rosea*, *Poppy* and *Leonora*.

Many of these patterns were also produced on a gentle, triangular shape called *Fairy*, which was much closer to Shelley's Art Deco shapes: it boasted an open triangular cup handle and simple cuboid bases to sugar bowl and milk jug. As the name suggests, tea-services in the *Fairy* shape were intended to be delicate, and in consequence were sometimes decorated with over-fussy geometric patterns. Other Art Deco china patterns included the stunning *De Luxe* of 1932, where a black and platinum diagonal across the wares divided areas of white and green, and *Zodiac* of 1934, which consisted simply of platinum banding. These were also applied to simple, tall tea- and coffee-ware of rounded overall shape. When *De Luxe* was exhibited at Dorland Hall in 1933 it prompted a thoughtful response in a *Pottery Gazette* report of the exhibition:

> The designs of this house sounded a powerful note as regards freshness of impulse, and they clearly indicated that the old-established houses in the manufacturing circles of the pottery trade are not necessarily hide-bound by conservatism.

Doulton's preference for simple lines and bands produced some very stylish hotel-wares about 1935 – for example, for Claridges, the Savoy and the Waldorf. 'C', 'S' and 'W' respectively were incorporated typographically in the edging lines.

Casino was later produced in an even wider range of earthenware patterns which were characterized by a finely balanced use of banding and lines. *Marquis*, orange and brown bands and lines, and *Radiance*, green and black bands and lines, were both produced from 1933 on wares of a cream-coloured body. *Envoy*, in the same year, was a transfer-printed blue and white pattern. *Athlone*, a printed pattern in browns and greens, with the motifs a collection of fine lines made to look like stylized leaves, was produced on *Casino* from about 1935.

Earthenware shapes and patterns, as expected, were more extreme and daring than those applied to china. Bold Art Deco shapes and heavily coloured and outlined decorations of wares produced by Doulton in the early 'thirties are in complete contrast to the principles behind Brangwyn's contemporaneous tablewares for the company.

The Christmas 1931 trade was greeted by a solid, curved-off cuboid tea- and coffee-ware shape, decorated with vivid blocks of colour. *Syren*, for example, was a strong paisley-shaped loop pattern in orange, green, yellow, blue and fawn. *Mecca* had a large and rather grotesque Islamic flower design, described thus in a trade advertisement:

> . . . we illustrate a few pieces from the new 'MECCA' – inspired by Omar Khayyam – golden sunshine tempered with a formal flower culled in some Persian Oasis – gay colours and laughingly robust shapes. Mecca is a good seller – and prices are very moderate. The Public are quickly learning that Doulton is no dearer than mediocre pottery, but ever so much nicer.

This last sentence makes it clear that Doulton, for reasons of commerce but perhaps also with a touch of idealism on Noke's part, were making an enthusiastic attempt to reach the lower end of the earthenware market. An early-morning tea-set of this ware, for example, retailed at 11s. 9d.

Other designs for the shape, all in fairly abstract and floral treatments in strong applications of colour, included *Dubarry* (green semi-circles with coral-coloured flowers), *Arcady*, *Sylvan* (a large stylized floral spray), *Eden* (a modernized 'Chinese' tree pattern), *Fenland* and *Rosslyn* – the names aiming to describe the designs as exotic and even primitive. Some of these patterns were also applied to the *Embassy* shape, which incorporated a mish-mash of Art Deco stylistics – triangular handles for cups and teapots, semi-circular solid handles for serving plates and squared-off bases to hollow-wares. In addition, some traditional shapes, such as *Lincoln*, were decorated with some of the modern patterns, and some modern shapes were decorated with traditional patterns – sometimes producing incongruous mixes of shape and decoration, such as naturalistic pheasants winging across Cubist-shaped tableware.

By 1932, some of these patterns were matched to designs in tablecloths, a practice which was to become quite widespread later in the 'thirties. Doulton's advertisements coyly announced the marriage of 'Miss Dainty Tablecloth' to her tableware partners of the *Dubarry*, *Syren*, *Arvon* and *Leeds Spray* variety. This marketing device highlights the fact that cheap Doulton earthenwares were competing in the fashion market, and that the designs were not intended to be permanent fixtures in the company's range. The combining of textiles and ceramics also shows a conscious desire to integrate tableware with room furnishings and decorations, a way of perceiving design which was being discussed and promoted at the time.

Two other very striking and colourful designs applied to *Embassy* and other shapes such as *Dandy* were *Gaylee* and *Caprice* – the former an abstract pattern of cloud shapes in green, yellow, blue, red and brown, the latter predominantly red and green with stylized flowers. *Embassy* continued into the late 'thirties with designs such as *Sunset* of 1938. Earthenware tea-, coffee-and dinner-sets were augmented with sandwich sets, lunch trays, sweet trays, biscuit barrels, ashtrays, smoker's companions, candlesticks, boudoir sets, trinket boxes and vases – all the accoutrements of modern domestic living.

An even more extreme Art Deco earthenware shape was the appropriately-named *Pillar*. The hollow-ware teapots, coffee-pots and jugs were tall, with four feet extending in squared-off 'stepped' form. Patterns such as *Bell Flower*, which were heavy and colourful, again demonstrate an Islamic influence.

This 'stepped' form, an Art Deco device derived from the shapes of Aztec architecture, was a favourite detail in Doulton's wares of the period. It is incorporated into feet, knobs and handles, and purely decoratively moulded into the body of some of the wares. Even when the shapes were simplified into more rounded, Modernist designs in the second half of the 'thirties, the stepped effect is still found appearing in the body of the wares.

By the second half of the decade, the elaborate and weighty Art Deco shapes had given way to simpler, less angular modern shapes. *Saville*, for example, which was produced about 1938, appears as a simplified and more rounded adaptation of *Casino*. Designs used lines – plain, dotted, wavy – polka dots and

Tablewares designed in the 1930s for W. T. Copeland. The meat plate, dinner plate and covered vegetable dish in Request pattern, and the two-handled cup and cover and saucer in Mimosa pattern are signed by Thomas Hassall; the teapot and stand are in modified 'Chinese' Kymono pattern. All three patterns are printed and painted. (Page 137)

very simple outline leaf or flower motifs, often printed in one or two colours, such as red and black, blue and gold and a favourite and unusual combination of brown and green (as in the polka-dotted *Astra* pattern). Advertisements of the period, for example for the polka dot and banded *Radio* pattern of 1935, point out that the patterns are 'intended to be harmonious with modern and period interiors'. A 1936 advertisement for an angular line and dot pattern called *Rialto* claims that 'The delicate moulding and the significant lines both speak of an artist expressing himself through restraint. It is very "Royal Doulton".' Another successful design launched in the same year was the *Saxe* pattern – a combination of polka and trefoil dots in blue and gold.

Over the whole decade, then, Doulton produced an extraordinary range of china and earthenware, hand-painted and printed, in shapes and patterns ranging from Islamic and severe Art Deco to modern and very restrained. Traditional wares, *Sung* flambé, Brangwyn wares and nursery wares (see Chapter 6) were produced concurrently. This breadth of tableware production is unique among manufacturers of the period. Although such a range is only possible from a large factory, it is nevertheless a testament to the imaginations of Charles and Jack Noke, who showed themselves willing to experiment in all directions. On occasions the experiments caused trouble: a number of flapper-girl figures were launched from 1924 onwards, including some nude bathers that were felt to be quite beyond the pale and were rapidly overpainted with modest bathing suits in the mid-1930s.

□ Mintons (*Stoke*)

Thomas Minton, in partnership with William Pownall and Joseph Poulson, bought some land in Stoke in 1793 and built a small pottery factory. Throughout the company's history, earthenwares and bone china were produced both alternately and concurrently in both table- and ornamental wares, with tablewares providing the most important part of the business. By the late nineteenth century, Minton was producing spectacular majolica glazes, notable for their vivid blues, greens and reds; and wares of finely painted flowers, figures and birds in eighteenth-century Sèvres style. In 1902, Léon V. Solon and John W. Wadsworth introduced *Secessionist Ware*, based on Viennese Art Nouveau styles; some such wares were produced into the 1920s.

The designer John Wadsworth became Art Director of Minton in 1909, leaving in 1914 to become Art Director at Worcester, only to return to Minton in 1935 until his death in 1955. Few strikingly modern tablewares seem to have been produced in the 1920s, but from the arrival of Art Director Reginald Haggar in 1930, modern wares were increasingly noticeable. The *Pottery Gazette* does not comment on any deviations from traditional productions until June 1932, when it reported a new pattern:

> The pattern is the B1241, and it consists of a simple, modernistic spray in conjunction with a fine border and edge line, the last mentioned being in enamel blue. Such patterns as these are not expected to replace such

well-known traditional designs as the 'Cockatrice' or the old 'Cuckoo' and 'Indian Tree' . . . but they will support them and appeal from a new angle.

Preserved artwork from the early 1930s shows that Haggar was busy designing new tableware designs but it appears that very few of his conceptions were actually put into production. Haggar and Mintons did not see eye to eye, hence his departure from the firm after only five years as Art Director.

The pattern described above in the *Pottery Gazette* is almost certainly Haggar's work, and was probably designed in 1931. Another pattern he certainly produced by 1934 was entitled *Landscape*: the decoration, depicted central motifs of stylized landscape views, including hills, trees, churches and houses, and edge patterns, banding and lining. It was applied to an ovoid modern shape beneath a grey glaze. Haggar's artwork shows that he was experimenting with such landscape scenes as early as 1930. *Landscape* was exhibited both at the Victoria and Albert Museum's 'Exhibition of English Pottery Old and New' and the Royal Academy's 'British Art in Industry', both in 1935. The latter exhibition also notes other designs by Haggar: a tea-set decorated with silver stars and bands on a celadon (pale willow green) ground, and china dinner-ware with print and enamel pastoral decoration.

These restrained designs, in limited colours and with tinted glazes, are more characteristic of late 1930s modern style than of Art Deco derivations. However, Haggar's artwork shows a number of very colourful designs which would fit the Art Deco category. Geometric motifs and stylized flowers in apple green, tomato red, yellow and black; highly-coloured banding; red, yellow and orange nasturtiums; cuboid vases; bright crocus designs all appear, but with little evidence of their ever having been produced. A modern floral pattern called *Daisy* in greens, reds and yellows for china tea-services was made and advertised in 1932/3. None of Haggar's patterns are extreme, and many were intended for a mildly geometric earthen dinner-ware shape which Haggar called *Alpha*. Certainly by the early 'thirties Mintons were already concentrating attention on earthenware productions for the middle market.

With the return of John Wadsworth in 1935, production of modern earthenwares began to flourish on the basis of the changes Haggar had started to introduce. In August 1935, the *Pottery Gazette* reported enthusiastically:

> . . . for some years yet one of the things which the public will doubtless demand, through the sheer force of social economics, if for no other reason, is pottery that is reasonably priced, and whether it be 'Minton' or any other make, due regard will have to be paid to the price factor.
>
> . . . It would not be too much to say that that impressive-looking factory [Mintons'] which has long constituted one of the chief landmarks of Stoke-on-Trent has been veritably turned inside out during the last few years with the single-minded purpose of endeavouring to keep abreast of the times.

The article goes on to report that Wadsworth is intending to produce new designs in both earthenware and medium-priced china, although they are most impressed with the 'wonderful contribution which Mintons, Ltd. are bent upon making in regard to earthenware'.

Two tableware patterns still in production today, designed by Harold Holdway for W. T. Copeland in the late 1930s: Queen's Bird, executed in print and enamel over the glaze on stoneware Lowestoft shape, 1937; and Christmas Tree, print and enamel, of 1938. (Page 141)

Wadsworth's earliest designs included modern border patterns, some centred by stylized leaf motifs, for earthen dinner-ware. The first patterns for his *Solano Ware* appear in 1937. The name probably refers to a special coloured opaque glaze which was used on these wares. Some examples were produced perfectly plain, some decorated, but all incorporate one or more coloured glaze. The original colours were pastel shades – powder pink, pale blue, celadon, pale yellow, grey and a golden sand colour – although darker colours were added – brown, dark green and even black. Many pieces were designed with one of the pastel colours combined with the plain ivory body-colour of the wares, for example, alternate segments of the body of a cup or teapot, coloured cups with ivory handles and bases. Such treatments were applied to the *Titania* tea and coffee shape, a ribbed body, combined with a short and streamlined spout for the teapot; or to the *Duchess* modern shape, which was very rounded. These two-colour effects were probably achieved with a stencil or template masking the areas of the ware to be kept free of the *Solano* glaze. This could be done with great precision: a typical plate had an ivory-coloured dish area, a *Solano* green rim area, and a pattern of semi-circles (as many as 48 round) biting into the edge of the plate and left ivory coloured.

Complete with coloured glazes, many *Solano Wares* were subsequently decorated with enamels over the glaze, to produce very striking wares which were altogether different from designs being produced elsewhere in the trade. The combinations of colours used for these designs were quite unique. Enamel patterns applied often consisted of vivid polka dots, lines and bandings. Stunning examples in Mintons' pattern books show black and pale yellow *Solano* glazes combined on different areas of the wares, decorated with terracotta-coloured enamel spots. Another quite beautiful combination was pale yellow and mushroom glazes decorated with crimson spots.

From 1937 the *Solano* glazes and decorations were applied to a very unusual new earthenware shape, *Isis*. This was used for tea- and coffee-services, and was characterized by an elongated egg shape for the hollow-ware, with tapering-in pot lids which were topped by oblique-shaped scrolled knobs rather like birds' crests. The bases of the wares were ribbed into three layers. The shape is slightly awkward, but unusual and memorable, and its bird-like appearance has elements in common with Susie Cooper's wares (see p. 189). Applied decorations to the *Isis* shape ranged from simple polka dots to squared trellis patterns combined with stylized flowers. Sometimes trellis and polka dot decorations were combined in one pattern. The *Isis* shape range was extended to include mugs, jugs and beakers.

Mintons' range of new earthenwares extended into subsidiary tableware, novelties and ornamental pieces. In 1938 John Wadsworth designed the *Byzantine* range, with colourful decorations befitting its name under the glaze on one of four ground colourings – blue, green, pink and hazel. Bowls, cigarette boxes, powder bowls, ashtrays, trinket trays, dessert dishes, sweet dishes and flower holders were all available in *Byzantine*. Other striking Art Deco ornamental wares were signed by Wadsworth, and from 1939 and into the 'forties he designed a series of 'athlete' vases – with, for example, three nude female figures running or throwing a javelin.

Novelty tablewares very similar to Carlton wares (see p. 152) were produced in the late 'thirties, as were preserve jars, either simply banded, or painted with bright flowers and moulded butterfly or bee handles, or in the shape of fruits. Cube-stacking teapots were made for Cunard; geometric ashtrays and dressing-table sets; and some Art Deco figures of hikers, Yum Yum from the *Mikado* (even by this time Mintons were still keen on things Japanese), waiters and policemen.

In 1939, production of earthenware ceased at Mintons, and the company's energies were once more concentrated on high-quality bone-china tablewares, such as the famous floral *Haddon Hall* pattern, first produced in 1949 and still in production today.

□ W. T. Copeland (*Spode Works, Stoke*)

The names Copeland and Spode have been linked together in business since the early nineteenth century. In 1833, William Taylor Copeland bought out Spode, and although the Copeland name is perhaps less familiar, it was used for trading from 1847 through to 1970, when Spode was again adopted. Backstamps of the first half of the twentieth century incorporate both the Spode and Copeland names. This has always caused confusion, to the extent that during the period with which we are concerned other companies attempted to use the name Spode in conjunction with copied designs. Copeland were forced to take a page in the *Pottery Gazette* in August 1928 to make a formal statement condemning this practice, and commenting: 'The hard, cold fact is that trade in North Staffordshire is bad; the manufacturers know it, the workers know it too; and the conditions apply now to practically all sections of the pottery trade and to all the world's markets.'

No company provides a better example of traditional designs for the top of the market than Copeland. Old patterns, particularly oriental and floral ones, were reissued, adapted, re-coloured, simplified and designed from scratch throughout the 'twenties and 'thirties. The Chinese influence on Spode was particularly strong, dating back to their perfecting blue underglaze transfers of Chinese patterns. Floral patterns like *Lauriston*, produced in 1939, brightly coloured but basically traditional, were applied to conventional 'Chinese' shapes, while florals like *Kymono* were simplified, and produced in pastel shades. Advertisements in the 'thirties often carried such words as 'a delightful design true to the Spode tradition'. In keeping with companies like William Adams, whose *Titian Ware* is discussed in some detail in Chapter 1, Copeland used a soft yellow glaze called *Jasmine* for traditional wares.

However, the company were also involved with modern times, and produced a number of successful Art Deco and Modernist patterns. The pattern books show such designs scattered, albeit rather thinly, amongst the traditionals, and it is likely that all the patterns entered in the books were actually produced – although it is usually impossible to say whether they were made in any quantity or when they were discontinued.

It is interesting to note first of all that Art Deco patterns appear from 1928,

Overleaf. *Four printed and hand-painted plates illustrating dinner-ware patterns for* W. T. Copeland: Anemone (top left) *by Thomas Hassall,* c. 1935; Reindeer (top right) *by* Harold Holdway, 1936; Country Souvenir (centre) *by Agnes Pinder Davis,* c. 1936; *and* Shepherd's Hey (bottom) *by Agnes Pinder Davis,* c. 1937. (*Page 141*)

placing Copeland with the most speculative factories, who investigated the style before 1930. It would be impossible to catalogue all the new designs here, but this representative selection gives an impression of how design developed during the 'twenties and 'thirties.

1928 patterns favoured the use of zigzag motifs – outlines like lightning flashes, stepped Aztec effects, blocked borders of triangles and diamonds. The decorative influences were more clearly French than is generally the case in the British potteries, and there are no entries of rustic florals or overstated Cubist patterns: Copeland's Art Deco devices are relatively refined. Bone-china patterns such as *Jazz* were printed and then coloured with groundlay overall in black and coral red; others used more modest colour combinations, primrose yellow and pale blue, for example. A 1928 china coffee-service is designed with moulded cats as handles, the curve formed by the cat stretching and holding onto the rim with its front paws: cups with plain fawn groundlay had tortoiseshell cat handles; pink cups had black cats.

Stop and Go was a Deco pattern used both for china and earthenwares (although predominantly the latter), and was definitely produced in some quantity. Edge lines were interrupted by a Deco line motif – the segment of a circle arranged with crossing lines of a 'reduced half sunburst' – and next to it, within the border lines, three squares were aligned, painted red, orange and green to emulate Cubist traffic lights, as the pattern name suggests. In this pattern, the lines were done in green and silver.

By the early 'thirties subtly banded wares and Modernist decoration are already in evidence – wavy lines, polka dots, 'flirts' (a hand-painted dash like an elongated teardrop), geometric landscapes, people and animals on nursery ware, large overlapping dots, and very simplified flowers, leaves and grasses. In some patterns flowers were reduced to a circle with a dot in the centre, with one straight line to suggest the stem. A *Melba* earthenware tea-service with *Jasmine* glaze of 1933, for example, depicts very simple long grass and leaf sprays, incorporated with a line trellis pattern, printed and enamelled in grey, red and black or pale blue, pink and coral. Banding in primrose and two shades of grey with edging lines in terracotta is representative of the beautiful patterns and colour combinations of the 'thirties.

Shapes like *Empire* of about 1933, with a ribbed body, were designed specifically for the modern decorations. Others remained fairly traditional, as one might expect from a firm with the history and tradition of Copeland; for example, *Marlborough* and *Florence*, which were characteristically decorated with polka dots and flowers. Contemporary sales catalogues advertising these wares do so in measured tone:

> Spode table ware has always been favoured on the Continent and 'Polka Dot' breathes the atmosphere of France. It succeeds in combining modern ideas with the vogue of 1810 in a pattern of delicate blue with an ornamental spray of red, blue and green. A design to suit every taste.

Thomas Hassall joined Spode in 1892 at the age of 14, became Art Director in 1910 and continued in the position until 1940, when he was replaced by Harold Holdway. All these designs were produced under his auspices. By the mid to late thirties shapes were leaning towards Modernism rather than Art Deco geometrics. Successful wares designed by Tom Hassall, some of which are signed by him, were characterized by simple line and band decorations, often incorporating silver and green, and central stylized floral transfer prints in muted shades such as grey, over-painted in one enamel colour such as turquoise, as in the *Request* pattern. Other patterns, such as *Leaf and Berry*, were hand-painted. Many were treated with the *Jasmine* glaze.

As we have already seen, it is often difficult to ascertain who was actually responsible for a design. Harold Holdway joined Hassall's department in 1934 and became Chief Designer on Hassall's death in 1940. Holdway was certainly responsible in the 'thirties for the *Reindeer* tableware pattern of 1936, which incorporated panels of leaping reindeer with grass and bows, printed in black and delicately painted in soft brown. Two other Holdway designs of the late 'thirties, *Queen's Bird* and *Christmas Tree*, are still in production today. The former, a colourful print and enamel pattern inspired by the birds on Dutch tiles, was made in stoneware on a curvaceous *Lowestoft* shape. *Queen's Bird* is so named because at the 1937 British Industries Fair the young Queen Elizabeth (now the Queen Mother) requested a set of the wares, and Holdway produced a complete range of tableware for her with a different bird for every piece.

The *Christmas Tree* pattern of 1938 provides an excellent example of a successful response to market trends. In May 1938, Copeland's US agent arrived saying he badly needed something special for the Christmas trade. Holdway was dispatched to produce a design, and returned with a Christmas tree festooned with presents. The agent pointed out that the presents would normally be collected at the bottom of the tree, with only decorations on the tree itself. Holdway's family had never had a Christmas tree, so he took the agent's word for it and revised his design from imagination. One piece, an ornamental ten-inch plate, was produced, with the caption 'Wishing you a Merry Christmas 1938' on the reverse. The agent was worried that the design was sentimental, and Holdway was worried about a heavy triangular design in the centre of a round plate, but the US salesmen were inundated with orders.

Over the following years *Christmas Tree* developed into whole services – with green border lines, holly and ivy for saucers, stumpy trees on cups. It was so successful that Copeland did not have enough paintresses to keep pace with demand. It was used as ballast in ships returning to the US during the war, adapted as a lithographic print in 1962, and has sold consistently ever since, with the pattern even adapted for ceramic knife handles. More *Christmas Tree* pieces are now sold every year than any other Copeland pattern.

Designers from outside the industry were also employed at Copeland. From 1938, the Norwegian Eric Olsen, who had previously worked for Wedgwood (see p. 204) had his own studio at Copeland. He designed beautiful tablewares such as *Seagulls*, in which the outstretched wings of the birds joined to form circular border decorations. Olsen also designed figure models and animals, notably *Bison* and *Polar Bear* in stylized Art Deco form in about 1938. Agnes Pinder Davis, who was also employed at Copeland from about 1936, designed *Country Souvenir*, which depicted stylized grasses in brown and grey, and *Shepherd's Hey*. She was the first to be allowed to break the company rule and sign her work.

Pages from a Worcester Royal Porcelain Co. china pattern book of the 1920s with instructions for a pattern of grasses showing Japanese influence. The dramatic black groundlay is over-printed with gold and finished in enamelled red; a variation with terracotta groundlay is also depicted. (Pages 142–5)

Copeland's factory was extensively modernized in the mid-'thirties, including the introduction of a gas-fired kiln in 1934. In the following years, the output of traditional wares increased to meet the renewed demand of the end of the decade. New, simple ornamental wares were also produced, similar in style to Keith Murray's designs for Wedgwood (see p. 197). A plain grey earthenware body, treated with a clear glaze and incised or moulded with ridges, was called *Onyx*; a matt-glazed treatment of an ivory earthenware was titled *Velamour*, and used for ornamentals and modelled animals, ashtrays, jugs, bookends and wall brackets. *Royal Jade* was an ivory earthenware with a matt-green glaze.

Art Director Hassall certainly carried the weight of tradition behind him: he was the second generation of his family to work for Copeland, by the 'thirties was on the board of directors, and was on occasion accused of holding ideals which remained contrary to mass-production design. Nevertheless, under his direction Copeland produced an enormous variety of different bodies, glazes and decorations for their new designs: earthenware, bone china, a 'stone china' made to an eighteenth-century Josiah Spode recipe; transfer prints, hand-painting, print and enamel, banding and lining, with decorations done both over and under the glaze. However modern and varied, all the wares could be said to be in the best Copeland/Spode tradition.

□ Worcester Royal Porcelain Co.

The Worcester Porcelain Company was established in 1751, and early on specialized in the production of tea- and dessert-wares. The city of Worcester became a centre of porcelain making. By the start of the twentieth century the company was under the chairmanship of C. W. Dyson Perrins, a collector and benefactor who provided considerable financial support for Worcester's fine china productions.

In 1915 John Wadsworth (earlier and later of Mintons) was appointed Art Director, and it is fascinating to look first at some of the tea-services and 'mocha'-services (small, straight-sided coffee cups) he was responsible for at least by the early 1920s. The wares are exceptional for their very early use of geometric patterns, and interesting also because they appear in pattern books alongside Neo-classical designs. One style informed the other, and on occasion the two were mixed together in one pattern.

Often the wares, particularly the coffee services, were decorated with very bright, solid groundlay colours of yellow, orange, blue, red or pink, and the patterns were limited to wide borders at the edges of saucers or rims of cups. The border designs included overlapping 'balloon' dots in combinations of colours; stylized trees and grasses demonstrating some Japanese influence; and black and white stripes, checks or zigzags, some augmented with classical swags, contrasting vividly with the groundlay colours. In 1921, a border combination of black and white checks and swags edging brilliant yellow, blue, red or pink groundlay was used for tea- and coffee-services of Art Deco appearance. The teapots were angular, flattened into a horizontal shape.

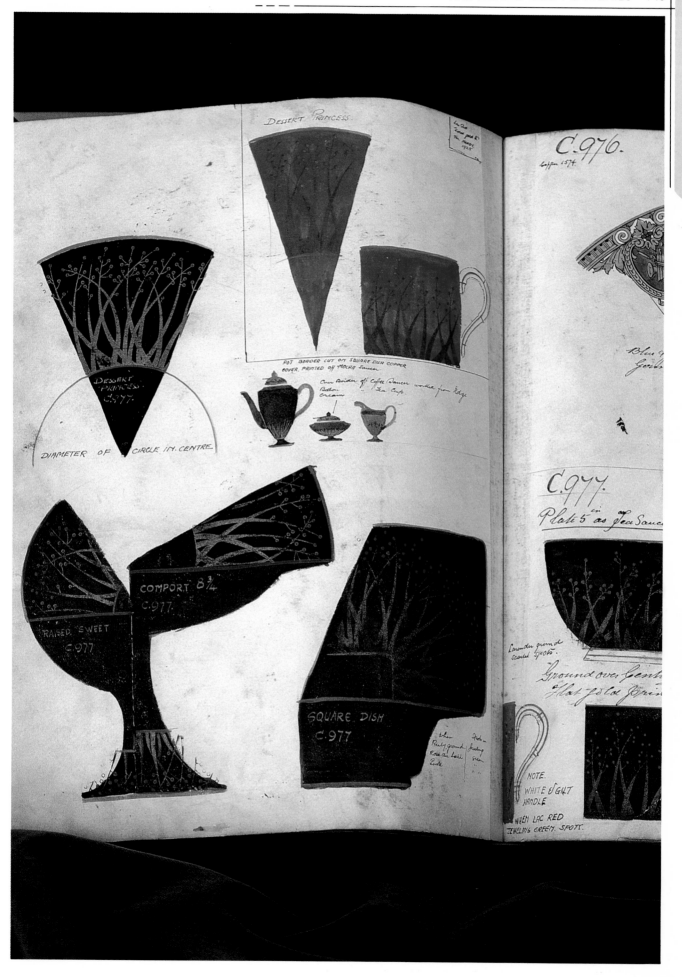

One of the most striking new designs of these very early years had a simplified and stylized landscape pattern of hills, fields and trees used for the wide border. The colours chosen for the pattern were very subtle, from a palette which only became commonplace in the pottery trade in the late 'thirties: tomato red groundlay was edged with the landscape in brown, beige and white; pale sky blue groundlay had the pattern in pale yellow, grey and black. The basic pattern here and with most of the other designs was printed, and it is likely that Wadsworth had bought the lithographs from abroad, as they are so different in style from the prints available at the time from British manufacturers.

It is interesting to consider these lovely and unique tea-and coffee-services in the context of the British Art Deco pottery style because of the number of discernible influences they show. Geometric patterns appear to emerge out of Neo-classical motifs, Victorian colours are adopted in combination with Modernist pastel shades, and Japanese influences in shape and stylization of tree motifs are also evident. They clearly demonstrate the important point that no designs are created in isolation, but are informed by a variety of influences, many of them of familiar past styles. These wares are also a testament to an early response to fashion and a willingness to make design changes.

China pattern books of the 'thirties show a range of new designs (in amongst the traditional ones) which were applied to simple but largely traditional shapes. Almost all the patterns were lithographic prints, the few that were hand-painted carrying special instructions as to which painter from Worcester's studio should undertake the work.

The following selection of patterns provides an idea of Worcester's more inventive creations of the period. Firstly, the colours used for tea- and coffee-wares were particularly dramatic: matt black groundlays decorated with primrose yellow and coral red; peacock blue groundlays with solid silver or gold inside cups and for their handles; dark blue and green with gold. Patterns include a cloud border – a subtle sky effect which would not look out of place in a 1960s pattern book – leaping deer, seascapes and stylized otters (a unique motif of the period!). There are very few rustic or stylized florals (normally reserved for earthenwares), until patterns of the late 'thirties, where floral printed motifs are understated and used in two-colour combinations.

Many of these excellent patterns feature fine line and banding, polka dots and asterisk stars. A breakfast set, for example, was ivory coloured, with brown banding, bright blue lines and coloured asterisks scattered all over the wares. By the later 'thirties, this scattered polka dot effect was employed for tiny leaf and flower sprigs.

The books also contain patterns by outside designers. A series featuring conch shells was done by Joan Topham, and exhibited at the Victoria and Albert Museum's 'Exhibition of English Pottery Old and New' in 1935. The wares were edged, for example, with lines in yellow, blue and green, and a conch shell in the same colours formed a simple, central motif. These, together with simple line patterns by René Crevel (which are strikingly French), are evidence that Worcester were employing artists to work on lithographs rather than on less mechanistic hand-painted designs. Other extremely simple lined patterns were designed by Wadsworth to decorate classical Worcester shapes. These were admired by the critics, as shown by this extract from a critique of the 'British Art in Industry' exhibition at the Royal Academy in 1935:

> This [a dinner service] is executed in bone china, and it has a series of wavy lines in platinum, the design being attributed to Mr. J. W. Wadsworth, a designer of wide experience in connection with the highest classes of china and earthenware. Both shapes and decoration – and particularly the two in combination – portray a sense of real refinement.

The most geometric and Art Deco inspired designs done by Worcester were reserved for special commissions, usually for hotels. Sunbursts, Cubist motifs, a 'machine-age' pattern of a cogged wheel interlocking with opposing diagonal lines, a Cubist tartan border with geometric thistle for the Caledonian Hotel in Edinburgh, all appear in 'specials' pattern books. Most satisfying of all is the use of Art Deco graphics for the initials of hotels incorporated in designs.

The combination of traditional and modern production did not save even Worcester from the disastrous markets of the late 'twenties. In 1929 the company was put into the hands of the Receiver, proving that even manufacturers of high-price wares were struggling for survival. Worcester did survive, and was bought by Dyson Perrins in 1934. His passionate interest in traditional eighteenth-century design encouraged the production of reproduction wares. John Wadsworth moved back to Minton in 1935, and many of Worcester's modern designs were discontinued.

Worcester was also active in the production of ornamental wares throughout the period. In about 1924 lustre earthenwares were produced, with vases decorated with under-glaze paintings of castles, imitative of Wedgwood's earlier 'Fairyland Lustre' (see p. 194). Hand-painting over the glaze was employed on earthenware *Crown Ware*, used for powder bowls (some modelled with satyr figures as handles) and figures. Eminent figure modellers were employed in the 'thirties, many female. Doris Lindner was an animal modeller associated with Worcester for over 40 years; Stella Crofts studied animals at London Zoo to inform her models, and Phoebe Stabler of Poole Potteries also worked for Worcester. Art Deco figures were in production for only a short period and are amongst Worcester's rarest wares.

As we might expect, these long-established firms at the top end of the tableware market produced the majority of their most interesting modern designs during the mid- to late 'thirties, when more subdued shapes, motifs and colours predominated over the earlier fashion for Art Deco. This more restrained and sophisticated brand of Modernism was more in keeping with the tastes and traditions which the great potteries were keen to maintain. In addition, the 'thirties saw them experimenting, with serious intent, with designs produced by artists working with industry – who had the added advantage of working with well-trained art directors rather than the purely managerial decoration managers more common to the smaller firms discussed in the previous chapter. (Experimentation with new designs for the top of the market was carried out extensively by Josiah Wedgwood and Sons, who,

China teapot and stand, tea cup and saucer and coffee cup and saucer by Worcester Royal Porcelain Co. The pattern, of black and white checks and classical swags bordering brilliant yellow groundlay, dates from 1921. (Pages 142–5)

because of the special nature of their achievements in this field, are discussed in a separate section in Chapter 8.)

Most important of all, none of these large firms became dominated by handcraft patterns alone. In retaining a predominance of traditional designs, they also retained the means to produce them, and were thus in a strong position to lead the way with the crucial development of good new lithograph patterns. As we have seen, some such experiments were tried in the 'thirties. Furthermore, the expense of producing the moulds for new shapes was less daunting to large firms. These two factors, vital to healthy design development in the industry, are discussed in greater depth in Chapter 7.

CHAPTER SIX

Novelty and Kitsch

It is significant that the old English fondness for disguising everything as something else now attained dimensions of a serious pathological affliction. Gramophones masquerade as cocktail cabinets; cocktail cabinets as bookcases; radios lurk in tea-caddies and bronze nudes burst asunder at the waist-line to reveal cigarette lighters; and nothing is what it seems.

Osbert Lancaster on the 'Modernistic' interior in *Homes Sweet Homes, 1939.*

. . . a change of material or the use of inappropriate materials, the disguising of an object's function or . . . the contrast between the form which it often assumes of a different but easily recognized object and its own essential form . . .

Part of Gillo Dorfles definition of his subject in *Kitsch: An anthology of bad taste,* 1968.

The extremes described by Osbert Lancaster as part of the 'Modernistic' style informed later definitions of kitsch, a term which is even vaguer than Art Deco. Very briefly, kitsch indicates bad taste, and as such can be seen as the central accusation levelled by the DIA against the pottery industry. As we have seen, such criticism implies superiority, an assumption that members of the DIA were in a position to pronounce on design in Stoke-on-Trent which was rejected by the manufacturers themselves. In his book *Kitsch*, Jacques Sternberg quotes Baudelaire, who wrote: 'What's so intoxicating about bad taste is the aristocratic pleasure of being displeased.' Many contemporary critics certainly appeared to relish their displeasure in 1920s and 1930s pottery.

Kitsch, like Art Deco, is also defined as having no stylistic independence but instead vulgarizing whatever styles it happens upon, which implies both extremism and a lack of proper understanding of the styles in question. We can thus suggest that when the more excessive and ill-conceived of Art Deco designs (which adopted the style of other art and cultures) borrow even more

Embossed tablewares in Carlton Ware *by Wiltshaw and Robinson: cup and saucer and cruet in the shape of foxglove leaves and flowers, mid-1930s; other pieces in the* Apple Blossom *shape, with green or honey coloured glaze, late 1930s. (Pages 152–3)*

inappropriate styles and disguises, they are better defined as kitsch. In addition, in *The Spirit and Splendour of Art Deco*, Alain Lesieutre says:

> It |kitsch| is also, often, the result of trying to achieve an 'exclusive' effect through the methods of mass-production – the conflict between ends and means produces the discord we recognize as kitsch.

Again, we have already noted that manufacturers recognized an economic necessity of producing 'exclusive' designs to attract trade. If all these definitions and associations of kitsch are looked at together – articles appearing in the guise of something else, bad taste, extremism, the vulgarization and misunderstanding of other styles, and the mass-production of something 'exclusive' – we arrive at a reasonable late twentieth-century definition of the term, useful for looking at some of the novelty and ornamental wares produced by the potteries between the two World Wars.

However, other commentators have suggested that *good* taste is, conversely, an enemy of art, or that there are elements of kitsch in all art, and that art itself necessarily relies for effect on both selection of styles and exaggeration. The pottery manufacturers might have preferred to see their wares in that light. At the time they considered their novelty tablewares as useful, decorative and amusing, and were reluctant to examine them in more abstract terms. The most important factors of these wares were their 'exclusivity' and novelty value, which, if good enough, would attract buyers in a depressed market. The manufacturers were also aware that in a flagging market buyers could only afford useful wares, and would economize by resisting the purely ornamental. In novelty productions the functions of utility and ornament were both present – in effect, two for the price of one. Besides which, they were of course making no attempt to produce high art: Harold Rosenberg said in *The Tradition of the New* in 1959, 'Kitsch is the daily art of our time, as the vase or the hymn was for earlier generations.'

The pottery companies discussed on the following pages specialized in the production of novelty items, and of supplementary items of tableware which could be bought as 'one offs' and were thus open to decorative extravagance: for example, cheese-stands, lemonade sets, biscuit barrels, preserve jars and cruet sets. Many of these items were aimed at the gift market as small presents that might be bought for Christmas or weddings, and as such had in-built qualities of frivolity and originality. Many offer clearer interpretations than more ordinary wares of the modern preoccupations of the age – racing car teapots, tennis sets, picnic sets and inessential luxuries like grapefruit dishes. Many also testify to middle-class dining habits and entertaining, for example, the plethora of inessential salad wares that would be used and displayed at a respectable high tea. Dishes specifically designed for serving tomatoes, or for draining and serving cress, for example, were prevalent during the period. A number of the companies discussed also produced regular tablewares, although often limited to the coffee/breakfast in bed varieties, and others produced superb ornamental wares, which often represented the finest of the Art Deco style. Some description of these latter productions is also included.

□ Wiltshaw and Robinson (*Carlton Ware — Carlton Works, Stoke*)

Wiltshaw and Robinson was established in about 1890, specializing in ornamental wares. By 1920 the firm was well known for lustre decorations, which they developed into a range of 12 colours, characterized by dark shades such as *Rouge Royale*, *Bleu Royale* and *Noir Royale*. Although the firm's style is perhaps most strongly linked with its novelty tableware designs of the 1930s, during the mid to late 1920s the company produced some very fine Art Deco ornamental wares. Brilliantly coloured lustred and enamelled vases, ginger jars, bowls and plaques were decorated with sunburst, lightning flashes and shooting stars, and Byzantine, Aztec and Egyptian influences were apparent in fantasy designs. A ginger jar, for example, was designed in Egyptian style with the lid in the form of Tutankhamen's mask. By the end of the decade they were also producing ornamental wares with coloured matt glazes.

From 1925 onwards, however, the Carlton Works produced novelty earthenware pieces for the table. Advertisements from the *Pottery Gazette* in 1926 show an orange marmalade dish shaped like an orange and resting on a leaf saucer; novelty cruet sets in the form of a hen and chickens or a toy drum-major; and a one-piece grapefruit holder incorporating a saucer for spoon and pips.

The Carlton Works were limited mainly to the production of earthenwares, so by about 1928 Wiltshaw and Robinson had taken over the china firm of Birks, Rawlins and Co. in order to expand their production in the china market. Modern, but not very geometric, shapes were produced for tea-, coffee-, and breakfast-services, which were decorated with colourful print and enamel stylized landscape and 'cottage garden' patterns such as *Springtime*, *Delphinium* and *Sunshine*. *Springtime* was a pattern of a tree and flying swallows over an orange-lustred ground. Many of the sets were sold in conjunction with wicker trays on which to serve them.

The business was further expanded with 'Carlton Ovenware' which, reported the *Pottery Gazette* in August 1929, satisfied 'a growing need of the household in these days for a type of pottey which can be pressed into service as being both utilitarian and ornamental'. The ovenware was of a fire-resistant white ware, decorated very strikingly with edge banding, and with a series of wide abutting wavy lines in three colours. It was intended to be attractive enough to bring straight from oven to table, a concept familiar today but new at the time. Wiltshaw and Robinson had great confidence in the ovenware's durability: the range was guaranteed for one year, and they claimed that it could withstand being plunged into cold water direct from the oven.

One of the most successful and enduring of the novelty designs, launched before 1930, was of embossed salad ware, shaped and brilliantly painted in green and red to represent lettuce leaves garnished with tomatoes. Matching salad bowls, cruets and salad servers were made, whilst other salad sets took the form of lobsters, with their claws holding the bowls from below. Jam pots, sweetmeat dishes, toast racks, cheese stands, cups and saucers, jugs, sugar bowls, sugar shakers, powder bowls and ashtrays were amongst the embossed relief novelty wares produced in the 1930s and through into the 1940s and 1950s. Such embossed wares, with their brilliantly-coloured painting, and shiny glazes, harked back to the bright, tin-enamel glazed majolica wares introduced in Mintons in 1851. A great variety of decorative items were made in majolica by the Victorians.

Flowers were frequently employed for the embossed shapes, for example foxglove, rose and primrose leaves, with the flowers raised as motifs, or jam dishes and ashtrays in the form of large daisy heads. Brilliant colours of painted decoration gave way to pastel shades in later productions. Embossed *Buttercup* and *Apple Blossom* wares were introduced in the late 'thirties.

□ S. Fielding and Co. (*Crown Devon — Devon Pottery, Stoke*)

The Carlton Works were by no means alone in the production of such novelty wares. From 1911, S. Fielding and Co. operated from the Devon Pottery, manufacturing ornamental and tablewares. By the late 1920s, the *Crown Devon* range included embossed salad wares in both green and straw-coloured glazes in the form of Savoy lettuce leaves. The range included salad bowls, lobster bowls and tomato trays, again naturalistically decorated with bright red tomatoes. Other novelty wares available by 1930 included a Jaffa marmalade jar, a beehive honey pot and a breakfast cruet set with the figure of a cockerel as its handle. Some designs, such as a novelty egg set, consisting of a tray centred by a duckling handle and surrounded by four egg cups and a salt and a pepper shaker, were simply amusing (Clarice Cliff later produced a very similar design at the Newport Potteries.)

Other novelty designs were certainly kitsch, such as an elaborately embossed 'village' cruet set. The tray to the cruet set was decorated with grass and paths leading to each of its three pieces, and the handles of the tray were painted up as field gates. The salt took the form of a crudely designed windmill, the pepper appeared to be a dovecote, barn or well, and the mustard was a half-timbered house. The whole effect is ugly and almost entirely lacking in charm. Similar patterns were moulded for the *Old Inn* range, used for a cheese stand, biscuit box and preserve pot. In 1930s, new heights or depths were attained with the launch of musical novelties. Tankards, jugs, cigarette boxes and even salad bowls were designed, which, when lifted, played popular tunes such as 'John Peel' or 'Daisy Bell'. A 'Musical Baby Grand Piano' cigarette box was subsequently made in a cream matt glaze, finished with 'best burnished gold'. Whether in bad taste or not, they were heavily in demand and still in production in the late 1950s.

Crown Devon also specialized in more straightforward supplementary items of tableware. In the late 1920s they manufactured an octagonal shape, called *Era* to demonstrate its modernity, which was decorated with semi-stylized floral print and enamels such as *Poppy* and *Iris*. The *en suite* range included such items as covered toast dish, cress drainer and plate, a teapot with ceramic stand, a toast rack (available with five or three bars), a honey-pot and stand, and a tennis set. The tennis set was a piece of tableware (or, rather, when-not-at-tableware) designed for outdoor occasions such as a tennis party. It consisted of a plate, often oval in shape, with an indentation at one side forming a

A selection of embossed novelty tablewares of the 1930s: butterfly and cottage hand-painted plates by S. Hancock and Sons (page 119); hand-painted peony-shaped dish and long dish decorated with wild roses by Shorter and Son (pages 77–80); 'Olde England' cottage-ware cruet in Rubian Art Pottery by Grimwades (page 160); and Buttercup sandwich set with plain green glaze and leaf-shaped sugar sifter in Carlton Ware by Wiltshaw and Robinson (pages 152–3)

'saucer' for the accompanying cup or beaker. The idea was that both food and drink could be held in one receptacle, leaving the other hand free for its consumption, and originates from the late nineteenth century when similar pieces were made as 'afternoon' or 'croquet' sets. Tennis sets were made by a number of earthenware factories, and in the late 1930s and 1940s the Newport Pottery designed some notable pieces, some shaped like artists' palettes. Later incarnations saw the design adapted for use when watching television.

Embossed dinner, tea and breakfast wares were produced in floral patterns from 1930, treated with a light primrose-coloured glaze. By 1932, the *Belle Fleur* range of relief-moulded wares, painted and primrose-glazed, consisted of embossments in the shapes of poppies, pansies, snapdragons and other flowers. The glaze, combined with red relief decoration, was also used for salad ware.

The company also produced some superb Art Deco morning-, coffee- and lemonade-sets. Some were sold with wicker trays, and many were decorated with striking patterns. A coffee-set in the *Orient* pattern of about 1930 was decorated in vivid black, gold, green and red, with stylized flowers within alternate triangles reaching the full height of the straight-sided cups. The coffee-pot lid was painted with a large black star, and the whole set for six was presented on a wicker tray with a looped handle like a basket. At about the same time, the pencilled one-colour lines of the striking *Checks* tableware could be supplied with tablecloths to match.

Crown Devon's pattern books, dated 1925 onwards, show sophisticated patterns for this 'Best Coffee Ware'. Some were 'swilled' (dipped into liquid paints) with gold interiors and aerographed blue, Sèvres green or brick red on the outside; many incorporated black and gold in Cubist designs, sunbursts, stylized florals, 'broken' circular bandings, zigzags and lightning flashes. In these bold designs there is no indication that *Crown Devon* were looking for an anglicized style: their interpretation of Art Deco is exotic.

Such uncompromising patterns, adapted for these tablewares, were employed in their full glory for ornamental wares – vases, jugs, dishes and covered jars in both traditional and geometric shapes. The names of the patterns often give a direct indication of their stylistic source. *Aztec* had a decorative border of zigzags with fish swimming over the rest of the ware; *Espanol* was vividly banded with diagonal stripes in yellow, sea green, brown and purple; *Moresque* was striped in Islamic blue; and the stylized florals of *Mattajade* indicate an Indian influence. Oriental sources are found in florals, patterns incorporating Chinese dragons, and in *Sylvan Butterflies*, where a powder-blue background was decorated with painted and gilt butterflies. This plundering of decorative sources, particularly ancient ones, was central to Art Deco design, and frequently seen as here in its most refined form in ornamental wares. In the 1930s the firm also produced some tube-lined ornamental wares, mostly in the form of floral and geometric vases and jugs.

Matt glazes, pastel shades, lamp bases and figurines were added to this enormous range of earthenwares, which illustrate the very varied skills of its design department. *Crown Devon* had made considerable efforts to achieve this output, and to survive in the competitive earthenware market of the late 1920s and early 1930s. They were consistently applauded by the *Pottery Gazette*, which in February 1932 told the trade:

> If the dealer is on the lookout for something which is topical and 'snappy,' something that will at once arrest attention because it is dainty and appealing, yet capable of reaching the hands of the final purchaser at a modest price, then he can be recommended to get into touch with the 'Crown Devon' productions, for there is nothing that one can think of, from the tiny cruet to the most imposing ornament, which is unprovided for, and particularly impressive is the range of goods of illimitable variety which have the merit of being both useful and decorative.

□ John Beswick   (*Gold Street, Longton*)

John Beswick was left in charge of the firm of J. W. Beswick from 1920, and began to change its character, paying less attention to the utilitarian wares of earlier years, and concentrating on ornamental wares. Many of the new designs were overseen by Jim Hayward, who had studied under Gordon Forsyth at the Burslem Art School, and joined Beswick's design department in 1926. He became Decorations Manager in 1934, at the age of only 24.

By the early 1930s, Beswick were producing lettuce wares very similar to those designed by Carlton, but retailing at lower prices. John Beswick was keen that competitively priced wares would retain high quality potting and decoration. Embossed and painted, the lettuce wares included salad bowls and servers, cucumber trays, tomato trays and celery trays. *Gardena* ware was produced from about 1931, embossed in the form of flowers and painted in pastel shades. It was immediately successful, and the range of supplementary tablewares was impressive – fruit sets, sandwich sets, egg sets, cruets, cheese dishes, covered muffin dishes, jugs in four sizes, biscuit jar, teapot, hot-water jug, preserve pots.

Beswick's success with such embossed wares is demonstrated by the large number of designs which were produced during the first five years of the 1930s – dishes in the shape of pansies or butterflies, beehive honey-pots, orange squeezer with accompanying cup shaped as the orange and basket-work embossed wares, number but a few. Other productions were yet more exotic or sentimental: napkin rings in the shape of frog, rabbit or duck; cruet sets in the form of a mosque, rowing boat, chess set, soldiers and Shakespeare's house; Scottie-dog (the fashionable canine shape of the age) bookends; and bunny ashtrays.

In addition, inexpensive earthen tablewares were produced with hand-painted rustic florals in delicate colours on a straw-coloured glaze. Wild rose, hollyhock and marigold were flowers used for three different designs.

Beswick's now well-known *Cottage Ware* was introduced in 1934 (the idea itself dates from the early nineteenth century, when the first cottage wares were produced) for jugs, teapots, cheese shoes, biscuit barrels, covered muffin dishes, preserve jars, sugar bowls and other adaptations. The 'cottages' depicted ranged from thatched stone cottages and half-timbered manor

James Sadler and Sons' Motor (or Racing) Car *teapot,* designed by 1934, with its registration plate 'OKT42'. This example is in yellow-glazed earthenware with black and silver detailing. (Page 162)

houses to simple log cabins. The series was not withdrawn until 1971, an indication of the continuing market for such nostalgic novelties.

Cottage Ware was augmented from 1937 with the extraordinary *Sundial Ware.* An Art Deco motif was used in a most inappropriate and anglicized form: the stepped effect of Aztec architecture was incorporated, for example, in a cheese shoe's shape as a flight of steps, liberally decorated with flowers with a sundial at the top. A teapot handle zigzagged down in steps towards the base of an octagonal body, with a sundial lid. This motif, seen in so many guises during the previous ten years, was appropriated in *Sundial Ware* for an English cottage garden scene filled with naturalistic standard roses and hollyhocks. Even toast racks were somehow adapted for the style, which was successful enough to be produced into the 1950s. To its credit, *Sundial Ware* did at least use the stepped effect as part of its shape rather than applying the structural element merely as a decorative motif.

Throughout the 1930s Beswick were also producing the animal models and figurines for which they are best known – appealing horses and dogs, wild animals and the most sentimental of cartoon-like creatures. These purely decorative items (and those produced by Shaw and Copestake under the trade name *Sylvac,* including the famous matt-glazed bunnies) are of only marginal interest in a discussion of tableware. However, some of the plain matt glazes used by Beswick for their animal models were, from 1934, also used for hundreds of simple vases and jugs. Some were embossed with stylized and angular flowers, some had indented spouts, others had very simple incised banding lines. These stylish and inexpensive ornamental wares were matt-glazed in turquoise blue, pale green or oatmeal, for example. The matt-glazed wares were popular enough for fifty women to be employed to apply the glazes, and were the most modern and stylish of Beswick's productions, the designs carrying suitably 'artistic' names such as *Moderne, Shadows* and *Sylvan.*

□ Soho Pottery   *(Solian Ware — Cobridge)*

Soho's tablewares are discussed in Chapter 4, but in addition, as earthenware manufacturers, the company also had an interest in novelty items – ashtrays, smoker's companions, and an Edward VIII wall mask for the Coronation which never took place. In 1935 they hit upon an idea which they hoped would appeal to 'modern young folk': *Swallow Flight,* a collection of four ceramic birds to be attached diagonally across a wall. Judging by the detailed explanation given by the *Pottery Gazette,* these were probably among the first of the generations of birds that fulfilled such a decorative function:

> . . . each [is] mounted upon a steel pin, the purpose of which is to affix the swallows to the wall of a hall or living room to yield a pictorial effect. The pins are not intended to be thrust right home, but to be inserted in the wall only sufficiently deeply to secure the swallows firmly; the fact that the birds are allowed to stand away from the wall causes an interesting shadow to be thrown, which assists materially in the general effect . . .

> . . . whether it be an idea which will continue to live or not, there is likely to be a special run of business for it until some other idea replaces it . . .

Although there have recently been suggestions that ceramic birds to hang on the wall were made as early as the 1870s, the *Pottery Gazette* went on to say:

> We believe it is the first time that this idea has been carried out in porcelain, although it is not unknown that it has been put into force in such countries as Switzerland, where the birds have been carved in wood, and painted.

The run-on business was such that by 1939 Soho were advertising flying ceramic pheasants, seagulls, love birds, parrots, ducks, fairies, butterflies, bonnets (sic) and doves. The ducks were perhaps singled out by popular demand as the birds most likely to fly in such strict formation, and they flapped their wings across living room walls well into the 1950s.

▢ Other manufacturers of novelty wares

A number of other potteries produced notable novelty and embossed tablewares in the 'twenties and 'thirties. **Grimwades (Stoke)** marketed leaf-embossed tablewares from about 1932. They were followed in about 1933 with *Regina* ware, a moulded water-lily shape in four groundlay colours – green, old gold, mauve and pale blue; and in 1934, *Gera* ware, the mould based on a geranium, with flower and leaves against a wickerwork background, to be produced both decorated and in plain ivory wares. Grimwades' novelties for 1936 included the *Chanticleer* series, the moulded body of a cockerel used for teapot, jugs, marmalade jar, cheese cover and stand, mint boat and stand, and even cruets and toast racks. Their range of *Rubian Art Pottery*, launched c. 1934, included novelty 'Olde English' cottage wares. In 1938, moulded supplementary tablewares took the form of *Peony*.

Thomas Poole (Longton) had already found success with embossed tomato dishes by 1926. **Cooper and Co (Hanley)** made fancies to compete with cheap continental imports for fairs and seaside shops – tomato-shaped preserve jars and chicken cruet sets, for example. **John Steventon and Sons (Burslem)** launched their moulded floral tablewares, *Floretta*, in 1932, decorated in pastel shades and with a brilliant glaze. The company's more conventional tablewares were marketed under the trade name *Royal Venton Ware*. **Bishop and Stonier (Hanley)** produced tablewares in china and earthenwares, and some interesting 'combined' pieces in 1932. A moulded plate combined toast rack, egg cup, cruet, preserve dish and butter dish in one piece for the use of a serious breakfast eater. There were a number of variations on this breakfast theme, together with smokers' companions moulded to combine cigarette container, ashtray and matchbox holder. **Shaw and Copestake (Sylvac, Longton)** produced matt-glaze earthenware embossed vases and bowls, and amusing ashtrays, jugs, etc with accompanying animals – rabbit, mouse, fawn, for example – again decorated in one-colour matt glazes. **Shorter and Sons (Stoke)** are discussed on pp. 77–80.

□ Teapots

Ode to a Teapot

Oh, loveliness incarnate, especially
round the spout,
Divinest thing that ever poured
afternoon tea out!
Thy form embodies beauty, yet thy
base is balanced, too,
Small wonder that my heart is
caught and held by your brew!
You did not cost my savings and
undoubtedly you're good;
Your children, too, the cups
and plates, I welcome as I should!
There's breed, my dear, about you,
flush of colour I adore,
And yet, you know, I picked you up
in a famous store!
Each time we part I pray, sweet,
as your countenance is hid,
That never shall I hear those words,
'Please mum, I've smashed the lid!'
The Shelley Standard, March 1930

In the discussion of the Cube Teapot in Chapter 1, we saw how anxious manufacturers were to capitalize on the novelty or utilitarian aspects of their teapot inventions. The beauty of a teapot was that it did not have to be marketed in conjunction with a tea- or breakfast-service, but could be sold independently for its special attributes. And, as the *Shelly Standard*'s ditty implies, teapots are frequently broken and need to be replaced.

The utilitarian appeals of teapots centred around their ability to pour, the security of the lid, and methods of incorporating strainers in the body of the pot. Numerous companies, some specializing solely in the manufacture of teapots, produced designs from the beginning of the century onwards with special features, for which they made extravagant claims. The title of 'perfect pourer' was claimed for the Cube, but also for straight projecting spouts, curved and lipped spouts, small stumpy spouts or even just lipped holes in the side of the body of the teapots. Lids were designed to fit under deep flanges or with special locking devices fitting over a ceramic or metal pin to prevent them from falling off. Strainers were incorporated behind spouts, or in special sections inside the pots into which the leaves were spooned. An early example was devised by Wedgwood in the early 1900s. The 'Simple Yet Perfect' (SYP) was designed to lie on its side while the tea was brewing, and when turned upright it isolated the tea leaves in a special section.

The teapot also offered great scope to the designer concerned with its aesthetic or comic appeal. Of all items of tableware, the teapot perhaps offers

*Pieces from Shelley Potteries'
nursery range designed by
Mabel Lucie Attwell in 1926:
toadstool house teapot, toadstool
sugar basin and saluting 'Boo
Boo' character milk jug. (Page
165)*

the most sculptural potential. In Art Deco tea services, the style is often most vividly set by the shape employed for the teapot, which may be the most extreme and angular of all the items of tableware. In fact, ever since tea was first imported into Britain in the mid-seventeenth century, ceramic designers have experimented with the shape and decoration of teapots, producing in the eighteenth century hexagonal shapes and novelty shapes, like a house, squirrel or pineapple.

The Cube Teapot was the most forcefully advertised and successful of the geometric shapes of the 1920s, but it was not the only one on the market. The established teapot manufacturer James Sadler produced a 'Hexagon' teapot in 1924 (described by the company as 'The Premier Spoutless Teapot of the Day'); Wade Heath launched the six-sided *Compacto*; and octagonal shapes were also marketed. The teapots were intended to represent a practical and streamlined modernity, but were seen by some as extreme, and even silly, designs. A charming parody of exotic teapot shapes appeared in the *Pottery Gazette* in June 1925, submitted by an anonymous correspondent under the title 'A Tea Pot Fantasia':

> Sitting at ease in a tea lounge and contemplating dreamily the rectangular teapot from which had just been poured an appropriate libation, we were inspired to meditate upon the changes which might be induced by the adoption of this geometric form . . .
>
> . . . How many times, in these later years, have we seen that, once a thin trickle of innovation pierces the barrier of convention, the gap tends to grow broader and deeper, until every restraint is swept aside and riotous revolution works its will. So it may be conceived that this simple and logical invention might bring all sorts of startling possibilities in its train. If a teapot can be made rectangular, why not triangular or even rhomboidal?

The correspondent goes on to describe, and illustrate with comic line-drawings, a range of impossible teapot designs cleverly adopting some fashionable motifs, for instance in the shapes of a five-pointed star, a Chinese lantern, a disc, a coiled snake, a Diplodocus dinosaur. Although the article was clearly intended to amuse, its publication in 1925 coincided with the more serious criticisms of the 'new' voiced after the Paris *Exposition*, and it contains a sharp reminder of the desirability of utilitarian restraint in design. By the 1930s, manufacturers were actually to produce teapots in inappropriate animal and other novelty shapes.

James Sadler and Sons (Burslem) were established in the late nineteenth century, producing almost exclusively teapots, and their novelty products of the 1930s represent both the best and worst of such designs. By 1934, they had designed one of the most famous and enduring novelty teapots of the age, the *Motor (or Racing) Car*. The car stood five-and-a-half inches high, had a four-cup capacity, and came in white and other coloured glazes. It could be detailed in black and finished off with silver mudguards; its driver's head formed the lid and its registration plate bore 'OKT42'. The car was a streamlined piece of teapot sculpture, perfectly representing the mechanization and speed images of the age in a simply shaped and decorated item of tableware. It was even later

supplied with a hook-on sugar-bowl trailer! The teapot was so popular that production continued until the late 1950s.

Sadler's other well-known teapot fantasy, aimed at a more sentimental market, was the Bunny, launched in 1938. The Bunny was moulded, its ears and back of neck forming the lid, and came in a variety of plain and matt glazes. Pale blue, green and pink were favourites. The Bunny was endearing, unlike another matt-glaze Sadler production of 1938, Ye Daintee Ladyee, a grotesque crinolined triangular woman in the worst of nostalgic taste.

1938 was also the date of Sadler's launch of the Soccer teapot. The handle was a footballer bent backwards to form an arc, as if throwing in the ball from the touchline; the pot itself was, of course, a spherical football; the spout was moulded like a referee's whistle; and the knob of the lid moulded like the prized English Cup. A clever marketing ploy allowed for the footballer handle to be painted up in the colours of any club, depending on local markets. Sadler's other novelty productions included Pixie (the seated pixie forming the knob, the pot decorated as a thatched cottage); Doggie (a Scotch terrier on the same principle as Bunny); and a Santa Claus, specially designed for the 1939 Christmas trade. The company also produced more serious modern teapot shapes, including the ribbed Radnor, described in soft coloured glazes.

Other companies, particularly specialist firms, produced similar novelties. In 1930, **Gibson and Sons (Burslem)** devised a teapot in the shape of an alarm clock, with painted clock hands and numbers, and the greeting 'Good Morning' on the clock face. **Lingard Webster (Tunstall)** made cottage, wishing well and Mr Pickwick teapots. **R. Sudlow and Sons (Burslem)** produced 'The only Tea Plane on the Market' in 1938. The aeroplane teapot owed its streamlined design to Sadler's Motor Car, and was produced in yellow, green or ivory glazes, all over-painted in silver. The lid consisted of the projecting wings of the plane and the pilot's head, and when not in use could be upturned with wings lying parallel to the body of the plane for storage.

At the opposite design extreme, **Price Brothers, Beswick** and **Grimwades (Royal Winton, Hanley and Stoke)** specialized in nostalgic 'cottage ware' teapots. Most were shaped like square thatched and half-timbered cottages. Beswick produced a Bus teapot in 1938 and a Panda with one leg and paw as the spout and a piece of bamboo as the handle in 1939. Such styles were perfectly suited to the talents of Clarice Cliff, who designed a wigwam teapot with a red Indian as the spout, Gnome Ware teapots, and a Corn Cob as part of a range of tablewares reminiscent of similar Victorian majolica shapes and earlier, eighteenth-century pineapple and cauliflower embossed designs.

Even companies of the stature of Mintons turned again to novelty teapots, reviving some of their earlier designs. For the Christmas 1932 trade they produced a cheap earthenware copy of their 1873 majolica Monkey design. The oval body of the teapot was in the form of a yellow gourd, its stem forming the spout; the gourd is hugged by a monkey wearing a smart blue floral outfit; his tail curves up and round as the handle, and his head constitutes the detachable lid. The late nineteenth-century enthusiasm for the oriental was added to by Mintons in the 1932 range by a Chinaman teapot, and also by a Chanticleer cockerel.

□ Nursery Ware

No branch of 'twenties and 'thirties tableware was more fashion conscious than that made for the nursery. The principle of fashionable designs made to be replaced within a few years was obviously particularly apposite here – infant users would soon graduate to adult tableware or drop their little bowls from the high chair. In consequence, manufacturers were quick to respond to nursery vogues that were created by popular children's book illustrations, cartoon films newly imported from the USA and even famous animals at London Zoo.

Ashtead's (see pp. 36–7) use of simple patterns in strong colours lent itself well to nursery designs. They produced a number of wares with simple animal decorations, such as outlined rabbits and ducks, and then in about 1927 secured the services of E. H. Shepard to reproduce his famous illustrations to A. A. Milne's stories and poems. The series of nursery ware was called *Christopher Robin*, and when the Duke and Duchess of York visited Ashtead in 1928 they were presented with a 23-piece nursery set for the young Princess Elizabeth. A different A. A. Milne design was drawn for each piece by Shepard, depicting characters from *Winnie-the-Pooh*, *When We Were Very Young* and *Now We Are Six*. The under-glaze decorations were subsequently put into general production, and the second set was presented to the son of the author, Christopher Robin himself.

Shelley Potteries had secured the talents of another famous illustrator, Mabel Lucie Attwell, whose pudgy-cheeked children and friends adorned a very successful nursery range from 1926. Within months of the launch, a nursery teaset was specially modelled, with a toadstool-house teapot, toadstool sugar-basin and 'Boo Boo' character milk-jug. Plates and mugs were illustrated with children and events from the stories. *Homes and Gardens* described the wares in a suitably sugary editorial in January 1929:

> Her teapot is the toadstool house of a wee gnome. It has a little window in the roof and a chimney at the top. Nor is this all its enticement, for the door is open with the gnome just about to say 'Good Morning'. The sugar-basin is also in the shape of a toadstool, but one does not know if it is inhabited. This fact lies hidden in the world of conjectures called 'Perhaps'. The milk-jug is a great favourite. It is in the shape of a Brownie saluting the little ones and this never fails to bring delight.

Mabel Lucie Attwell subsequently designed for Shelley in the thirties an animal tea set and statuettes of fairies and characters like 'Diddums' and 'The Toddler'. Her wares were very successful, and were developed again after World War II.

In 1928, the children's illustrator Hilda Cowham also designed nursery ware for Shelley, with pictures of children having a jolly time. Her teapot was modelled as a tent, with an umbrella-shaped top, and the tent flap drawn back to reveal a girl and a boy looking at a picture book. A mug was shaped and painted to represent a seaside bucket and depicted children playing on the beach.

Midwinter's coup was in securing the considerable skills of Heath Robinson in 1928. Twelve traditional nursery rhymes – such as 'Jack Spratt' and 'Old King Cole' – were drawn with a verse from the rhymes for lithographic reproduction, which meant that the wares sold comparatively cheaply. The illustrations representing the rhymes were treated with characteristic Heath Robinson humour and charm, and each was bordered with round children's heads. A large plate had as many as 50 heads comprising its border, each one entirely different. The *Pottery Gazette* reported enthusiastically on the nursery ware launch:

> . . . the portrayal of his ideas [is] so ingenious and amusing, that even the parents are likely to find as much entertainment in these drawings as the wee bairns themselves. The designs bristle with the richest humour, and they have been rightly described everywhere as amazingly clever, highly original, and, above all, delightfully sympathetic; they have the lightness of touch and studied perfection of a masterpiece, and a live interest which will appeal to the children.

Paragon China were known for their nursery wares even before the 'twenties, when they commissioned designs by artist Beatrice Mallet. These hand-painted wares were particularly admired for their practical shapes – teapots and milk jugs with extended bases which made it virtually impossible for a young child to upset them. In 1929 Paragon produced 'The Dainty China' nursery ware decorated with a photograph of a bubble-haired, pearl-wearing young Princess Elizabeth. This soon proudly became *Princess Elizabeth Nursery China*. Alphabet Nursery Designs were advertised as 'attractive, interesting and educational', and *Animal's Alphabet* followed, in which every initial letter was made the key to the name of an animal. By 1930, a tea-service of traditional design, of rose and heather sprays supporting two love birds, was designed to commemorate the birth of Princess Margaret Rose.

The majority of Paragon's publicity in 1930 was reserved for their launch of *Mickey Mouse* nursery ware for the Christmas trade. A trade advertisement of July 1930, depicting the original Mickey, declared proudly: 'Paragon China Ltd. secures World's rights to reproduce the famous Mickey Mouse on Paragon Bone China'. (The first Mickey Mouse film was *Steamboat Willie*, copyrighted in September 1928, although his early incarnation was as Mortimer Mouse in 1927.) Each Walt Disney illustration on the china conveyed a story about Mickey or his friends, and a series of 12 subjects started off production. Faint printed outlines of the patterns were filled in with vivid enamel colours. The series was added to with fresh incidents from the famous Mouse's adventures. **Wade, Heath and Co. (Burslem)** launched their own *Mickie Mouse* (and *Minnie* and *Pluto*) nursery ware in 1934, Paragon's valuable world rights having presumably expired. Each Wade Heath character was claimed to be personally drawn by Walt Disney himself, and boxed sets of baby plate, cup and saucer were marketed with the free gift of a specially boxed Mickey Mouse mug for the Christmas trade.

Paragon did not stop at the nursery, but went on in 1935 to produce 'Children's China', with designs by Ellen Soper depicting early 'Janet and John' style children with cats, dogs and farmyard animals.

Meanwhile, at **A. J. Wilkinson**, Clarice Cliff's promoter Colley Shorter was publicizing the work of another young woman designer, his nine-year-old daughter Joan. The idea worked, reported by the *Pottery Gazette* in June 1930:

> These are genuinely original, child-like conceptions of nursery rhymes, which seem to ring as true to the mentality of a child as did the illustrations in 'Daddy Longlegs'. But in some respects these designs are even better, because Joan has been entrusted to suggest the colourings as well as the drawings. One cannot wonder that the Joan Shorter nursery ware has met with such a remarkable reception; it is simply that child is communicating with child in native language, instead of a grown-up person striving to reproduce the psychological atmosphere of a juvenile mind.

Joan, with her fringed juvenile bobbed hair, appeared in publicity photographs and in public like a miniature Clarice Cliff.

In 1938 the most famous of all Disney's children's films, *Snow White and the Seven Dwarfs*, was copyrighted, and appeared as a feature-length cartoon which became a box-office smash. **Wade, Heath and Co.** responded immediately with novelty moulded *Snow White* jugs, teapots and biscuit barrels. The dwarfs, predictably, were used for moulded cruet sets. Wade Heath were again quick off the mark in 1939. On Christmas Eve 1938, London Zoo acquired the first giant panda in Britain, the baby Ming. Ming was shown to the public first in early 1939, and Wade Heath's *Panda* nursery ware was launched soon after, with the bear as motif and moulded as an accompanying china figure.

Other companies were competing in the nursery market: **R. H. and S. L. Plant** had *Tuscan* nursery designs by Gladys Peto by 1929; **E. Brain (Foley)** had a *Toy Soldiers* design in the early 'thirties; **Carter, Stabler and Adams** had designs by Dora Batty; Charlotte Rhead designed tube-lined children's mugs for **A. G. Richardson** in about 1934; and in about 1928 Susie Cooper had designed nursery ware for **A. E. Gray**. The female nursery designer became quite a cult, with her name always incorporated in advertising material. **Bourne and Leigh**, for example, advertised *Leighton* nursery ware *Pixie* and *Elf* designs 'by Renée Pemberton, a young lady designer'.

One of the most famous nursery ware designs of all, still in production, was **Royal Doulton**'s *Bunnykins*, designed by Barbara Vernon and first launched in 1934. Doulton had an eminent history of nursery wares: a stunning series decorated with scenes from *Alice in Wonderland* was in production from 1906, *Alice Through the Looking Glass* from 1908, and nursery-rhyme designs were produced from the 1900s through the 1920s. Barbara Vernon's whimsical rabbit family, whose stories were told in pictures, not words, was an imaginative invention of a woman who had spent a secluded life. She was a daughter of Cuthbert Bailey, general manager of Doulton, and had spent most of her adult life enclosed in a convent. The successful illustrated *Bunnykins* wares were supplemented with a teapot in 1940 – a brown-rabbit moulded shape with green leaves whose head and ears formed the lid. Since its launch, over 150 designs have appeared from *Bunnykins* nursery ware in both earthenware and china, most with the familiar border made up of leaping rabbits.

Artists employed by **Josiah Wedgwood** also worked on nursery designs. Daisy Makeig-Jones, creator of the famous *Fairyland Lustre* (see page 194), designed *Brownies* and *Noah's Ark* nursery ware in about 1914, followed between 1916 and 1923 with a number of patterns, including *Chicken, Rabbits, Thumbelina, Golliwog* and *Yellowstone Zoo*. In 1937, Eric Ravilious (see p. 200) designed his beautiful, simple *Alphabet* nursery ware, which was printed in sepia on earthenware with hand-painted bands of pale colours over the letters. The letters correspond to appropriate motifs – a kettle on the hob, a sun, moon, Indian's head, umbrella, pair of twins.

The nursery was certainly better equipped for the young follower of fashion than it had ever been before. No market could be ignored during this competitive period.

CHAPTER SEVEN

Design Theory and Action in the 1930s

Although the pottery manufacturers who produced novelty tablewares were pleased by their commercial success in mixing function and ornamentation, it comes as no surprise to learn that their views were not shared by serious design commentators. Critics from outside the pottery industry were, by the early 1930s, tearing their hair over the interpretations of 'modern art' which had issued from the industry during the previous years. The simple forms and restrained decoration which they had championed after World War I had been largely ignored in favour of a riot of colour and, as they saw it, an improper use of materials. (The criterion of 'fitness for purpose' was hardly achieved with Y*e Daintee Ladyee* teapot.) The precepts of 'modern art' had been adhered to only in the superficial elements of the Jazz Modern style (as it then came to be disparagingly known), and these elements, which were in fact structural, were misused as decorative motifs, and often bore no relation to the pottery shapes onto which they were painted. Worse still, Jazz Modern had deflected attention away from what was really modern in contemporary art and design. Needless to say, the charm and humour of much that had been produced was considered unimportant.

We have seen in our discussion of the designs of individual potteries that as the 1930s progressed a new Modernism of design, quite different from that of Art Deco, was being tentatively introduced by a variety of manufacturers. Such patterns were greatly simplified, colours more subdued, and often featured small motifs and coloured bandings. These designs were English pottery's response to the International Modern style developing in Europe, and such mid to late 1930s English productions had many similarities with pottery designed some years earlier on the continent.

The International Modern style (also known as Modernism or the International style) was a term coined to describe avant-garde architecture of the 1920s and 1930s. The use of the term to describe elements of modern industrial design associates it with the activities of the Bauhaus in Germany, a school of art and design founded in 1919 by the influential architect, Walter Gropius, with

Items of tableware (coffee service in Kestrel shape of 1932) by Susie Cooper at the Crown Works. The freehand-painted geometric pattern dates from c. 1932. (Page 189)

the purpose of uniting the arts. The Bauhaus developed out of the Deutsche Werkbund which, as we have seen, owed much of its own inspiration to an extension of British Arts and Crafts ideologies. British designers and design theoreticians were increasingly exposed to Bauhaus ideas, and a number visited the school in Dessau and were impressed by its design mix of order and progressiveness. In 1934 Walter Gropius himself fled to England, although he was quickly disillusioned about what he could achieve in Britain, and moved to the US in 1937.

Although the influence of Germany was keen, there was still a resistance in Britain to anything issuing from the country of the late enemy, and as a result British pottery owes much of its interpretation of the International Modern style to the ceramics of Scandinavia. Danish pottery had been much admired by Gordon Forsyth at the 1925 Paris *Exposition*; and an exhibition of Swedish Art was mounted in London in 1931, largely as a result of behind-the-scenes work of members of the DIA. The simple shapes and decorations and the modest approach of Scandinavian ceramics represented for many the true Modernism towards which the British pottery industry should aspire (although always, of course, maintaining its own national character).

The need to consider Modernist ideas was also becoming pressing with regard to the industry's export markets. Britain was in competition with sophisticated modern designs, increasingly demanded by the buying public, from other countries exporting to its major foreign markets, and from the home products of the markets themselves. Influential architects and designers had settled in the USA, for example, where the industrial designer now had a recognized role, and market research entailed a better understanding of retail selling.

The gradual adaptation of Modernist principles in Stoke-on-Trent was reflected in the revived debates about art and industry in general and in a plethora of didactic publications on the subject which appeared during the 1930s. Pottery manufacturers had put discussion of art and industry on one side during the previous years while they concentrated on the survival of their businesses during the Depression. Such was the apathy towards any serious discussion of design issues that the Art Section of the Ceramics Society had dwindled until it disappeared completely in the late 1920s. By the early thirties, the manufacturers were if anything more hardened than ever by circumstances in their straightforwardly commercial approach to production.

The Society of Industrial Artists was formed in 1930, and one of its first regional branches was established in North Staffordshire in 1932. This was to provide a new forum for discussion in the Potteries. Once again outsiders, inspired by what they had seen in Europe, were fired with enthusiasm to spread the gospel of new design. In November 1932, the architect Serge Chermayeff addressed the North Staffordshire Branch on the subject of art in industry from 'A Modern Designer's Point of View'. Chermayeff had directed a modern art studio set up by the furniture manufacturers Waring and Gillow from 1928, and from 1931 had been in private practice as an architect. Although he had himself been influenced by Art Deco design, his work by this time was in sympathy with the International Modern style.

Chermayeff's message to the potters was clear: elaboration was useless; simplicity was essential; a fresh outlook was needed rather than adaptations of old ideas; and the intelligent use of machines for mass-production could produce fine design that was cheaper than 'the rubbish with which we had hitherto been content' (as the *Pottery Gazette* reported his speech.) He submitted four maxims by which he himself worked:

First of all there must be that familiar slogan of the DIA fitness for purpose . . . Secondly, form and colour were *of* a thing and not *on* it. For example, if they [the potters] wanted to introduce a cheerful note of yellow into a tea-set they should have a yellow tea-set, or yellow insides to cups and saucers; they should not put on each cup and saucer a bunch of daisies or a canary.
Thirdly, meaningless decoration, as such, was desecration . . . If a job required, when finished, the addition of ornament, this could only mean that it had failed in the first place.
Fourthly, simplicity was essential in a scientific age if we were to retain our sanity. We required of art a direct contrast to the bustle, noise, and complexities of life in order to give our nerves a well-earned rest.

These words were obviously a clear criticism of recent tablewares, which had willingly adopted daisies or canaries as their whole design. His call for simplicity as a necessary antidote to everyday life was also the very antithesis of the potters' own assumption that colour and pattern were needed to brighten up dull lives and living conditions. Furthermore, Chermayeff was chipping away at the fashion for non-mechanistic hand-painting, and suggesting that considerable economies in the work force would be necessary if the industry were to survive in a properly industrial climate.

To a large extent Chermayeff was preaching only to the converted, as few pottery manufacturers had been moved to attend the meeting. Those that were there argued that if they were to produce such modern styles they would be labelled highbrow; that such austere wares would become monotonous; and that although such 'absolutely modern' styles would be a credit to the Potteries they would most likely put them all out of business when they were seen by ordinary shoppers. The discussion was bitter, with Chermayeff informing an outspoken producer of old-fashioned lithographic transfers that it would seem he had no reason for living. Susie Cooper raised the point that such a design revolution would mean considerable unemployment amongst craftsmen and technicians, and the speaker replied that the issue should rather be addressed to the Prime Minister in an economy where old industrial practice had become obsolete. The problem was a complex and deep-rooted one, and there was also a degree of snobbery about the idea of machine-produced wares being widely available to many people – a concept repugnant to some of the few in a position to purchase the most exclusive and best.

By the end of the meeting few could have been left in any doubt that the implications of the machine age had to be faced more positively than they had been previously, and that the revival of hand-painting, however refreshing, served also to postpone the day of reckoning. However, the contrasting camps of commentators and manufacturers remained opposed, the former considering the commercial successes of previous years as artistic failures, and the latter believing that their attempts at simple modern design would be commercial failures.

Later in the same month Cuthbert Bailey, General Manager of Doulton and Co., addressed the Branch on the subject of modern art 'From the Point of View of the Average Person' (which as an interested party he could hardly claim to be). He proposed that artists were always arguing with each other and that the public were completely uninterested in internal squabbles, and that the modern school were possessed of an irritating superiority complex which left them contemptuous of the pleasures required by the average person. Gordon Forsyth, with characteristic tact, tried to sum up the arguments by making a point that illustrated the continuing lack of understanding between the various parties. It was reported in the *Pottery Gazette* thus:

> He thought the whole trouble really lay in that modern artists were fighting a war for good art, whereas in the Potteries they were fighting first and foremost for pottery quality.

Little seemed to have changed: the artists were not trained to understand their materials and the manufacturers were not trained to understand their artists. As a result, the central issue about pottery forms, or shapes, being more important than applied decorations was still rarely in evidence in actual tableware production.

□ The Exhibition of Contemporary Art for the Table

In this context it is interesting to look at a brave but flawed experiment carried out jointly by the manufacturers E. Brain and A. J. Wilkinson. In 1932, Thomas Acland Fennemore, Managing Director of E. Brain and Co., producers of Foley China, approached twelve artists who all had some experience of design to submit pottery decorations for Foley China. The intention was to arrange a prominent exhibition of the resulting tableware in June 1933. Enthusiasm for the project was such that the list was extended to a final total of twenty-six artists, many of whom had had no previous involvement in industrial design.

The artists were given very little guidance in the execution of their designs. The *Pottery Gazette* reports the method adopted by Fennemore:

> We understand that no restrictions of any kind were placed in the way of these artists in the production of their designs, it being felt that absolute freedom in subject, treatment and colours should be left to them. At the same time, consultations and adjustments proved to be necessary in a number of cases whilst the designs were being evolved, mainly on technical grounds, though also on the all-important question of price . . .

The problems of producing the designs so that they could be purchased with the average purse led to the involvement of A. J. Wilkinson, where Clarice Cliff was responsible for translating some of the patterns for hand-painting on earthenware, to be produced as Royal Staffordshire Pottery.

Two patterns for china tea, coffee and breakfast sets designed in the early 1930s by Millicent Taplin for Josiah Wedgwood (and Sons): coffee pot, cup and saucer and milk jug in the Globe shape of c. 1935 with Falling Leaves pattern; pattern book showing instructions for the Green Lattice pattern on Globe shape. (Pages 194–6)

Both Clarice Cliff and Thomas Acland Fennemore also designed pieces themselves, thus finding a place on the eminent list of artists involved. These were Thomas Acland, John Armstrong, Freda Beardmore, Angelica Bell, Vanessa Bell, Frank Brangwyn, Clarice Cliff, Eva Crofts, John Everett, Gordon Forsyth, Moira Forsyth (Gordon's daughter), Duncan Grant, Milner Gray, Barbara Hepworth, Laura Knight, Paul Nash, Ben Nicholson, Dod Proctor, Ernest Proctor, Anne Riach, W. P. Robins, Albert Rutherston, Graham Sutherland, Allan Walton, Billie Walters and Michael Wellmer. The artists were paid £10 for each design, plus royalties.

The exhibition of the china and earthenwares was mounted at Harrods store in November 1934, under the title 'Exhibition of Contemporary Art for the Table', and the catalogue invited all those interested in the progress of art in industry to visit this unique exhibition. Harrods had some need to promote its image in this respect, having been repeatedly attacked in the design press. In July 1929, for example, the DIA Quarterly had commented:

> To be almost libellously frank, one can walk through whole departments at the said store and not see one object that bears the mark of contemporary design, or which is the creation of living artists.

The designs produced by the artists spanned a fascinating range of styles, from colourful rustic and old-English themes, bold areas of limited colours from the Bloomsbury artists, through to simple linear designs in two colours by the Modernists. Between one and three designs by each artist were produced, totalling about one hundred, and only a representative few are described here.

The most generally popular and widely reported design was Dame Laura Knight's *Circus*. A dinner service in the design had a different subject on each piece, brightly coloured predominantly in yellow, red and green. Performing seals, horses, bareback riders, acrobats, clowns, lion tamers, performing bears, tightrope walkers and other elements of English low-brow culture were depicted in nostalgic, highbrow artistic idiom. Although the designs were beautifully conceived, they seemed part of the 'rustic' pottery fashion which was by now hardly new in principle (and was being squeezed into a back seat). Other Laura Knight designs were titled *Cupids*, *Plumes* and *White Dove*.

Vanessa Bell had designed ceramics for the Omega Workshops around the time of World War I. Her designs, such as *Vanessa*, were adaptations of Bloomsbury florals, simplified and produced in a limited range of colours. Duncan Grant and Angelica Bell followed suit with patterns such as *Fleur* and *Daisy* respectively.

Paul Nash produced marvellous bold splashes of unusual colours for *Tiger*, painted in brown and blue; *Gay*, which consisted of jazzy circles, irregular stripes and dots in brown, blue, black and sepia; and *Forest*, where blocks of suggested foliage were coloured dark green with brown and light orange. Nash's characteristic painting palette was unmistakable in these designs.

Gordon Forsyth produced simple sprigs of flowers; Milner Gray (who had experience of designing packaging) simple modern outlines and squiggles for *Celia*, and some patterns involving lustre and sgraffito techniques; John Armstrong produced a modern *Fish* design, and stylized horses for *Chevaux*.

Ernest Proctor adopted traditional subjects with modern drawing techniques in *Courtship* and *The Hunt*, and Clarice Cliff had moved with the times in decoration (although she still used the angular *Biarritz* shape), producing very simple lined and banded pieces.

The most fiercely modern and exciting designs came from Ben Nicholson and his wife Barbara Hepworth. Nicholson designed a simple pattern in shades of grey groundlay with bands in reddish brown which inspired the caustic wit of Anthony Blunt in the closing words of a *Spectator* review: 'Dare we say, finally, that in his exquisite breakfast set in dove-grey and crimson Mr Ben Nicholson has at last found his cup of tea?' Barbara Hepworth produced the simplest design of all, a grey groundlay which allowed the white china to show through, with an enamelled abstract design in brown.

The exhibition was very widely reported, typically with praise: 'The results … are remarkably successful and constitute numerically, and perhaps specifically, the biggest influx of new ideas that the pottery industry has received for a very long time' enthused *Country Life*. Others were more properly critical. In an article entitled 'Saucers and Socialism' in the *New Statesman and Nation*, Raymond Mortimer commented:

> The earthenware is sound enough, but most of the china has a hard, rigid quality which contrasts unpleasantly with the free brushwork of the decoration. Moreover, some of the shapes (vegetable-dishes and soup-cups, for instance) are modernistic in the ugliest sense of an ugly word. The manufacturers have shown enterprise and goodwill in commissioning the artists, and it would be graceful if these would show their appreciation by a closer study of the material. There is still a long way to go before pottery of this sort can be marketed at prices possible to the great mass of the public. But how can it ever reach them unless the intelligentsia have the intelligence to give the lead?

Although the declared intention had been to market the wares at a reasonable price, they were in fact produced in limited signed first editions, ranging from £2. 10s. for a tea-set for six to £35 for a full dinner service for 12. They were, after all, exhibited at Harrods, not Woolworth's, and were inevitably snapped up by informed middle-class buyers with an eye for the work of contemporary artists and a view to the future exclusivity of their purchases. Even Clarice Cliff later admitted that the experiment had been a commercial flop.

The exhibition may be seen as successful in drawing wider attention to the need for new ceramic design and for artists and industry to co-operate, but it had little impact on the wider pottery industry. Some pertinent excuse could be made for the absence of new shapes, which would have entailed substantial outlay for new moulds, which may have been an unrealistic expense. But despite the publicity conscious Colley Shorter having talked in the *Daily Mirror* of 'a careful alliance of art and industrial production', there was no real integration of the designs and the industrial technicalities, or of the decorations and the pottery shapes. In retrospect, it can be seen as marking the end of an era by employing artists who had little or no experience of pottery manufacture to submit designs for ceramics. Although it did result in some

Pieces from a Susie Cooper
earthenware Kestrel shape
(1932) coffee service,
washbanded and enamelled with
spots, and dramatically striped
banded tea service, both probably
c. 1934; the freehand-painted
geometric pattern plate dates
from 1932–33. (Pages 189–90)

very attractive new decorations and brought the question of new design down to a manufacturing level, both the central issues of the current debate were entirely glossed over by an experiment that purported to be taking new design seriously. In spite of being greeted with considerable interest and some enthusiasm, it must be judged as something of a red herring in terms of contemporary design debates, and particularly to the issue of economic mass-production.

□ Other exhibitions, 1933–5

The mid-thirties spawned a number of exhibitions of contemporary design which included sections of pottery. A Board of Trade Committee on Art and Education, under the chairmanship of Lord Gorell, had produced a Report in 1932 that concluded that if the public were to become conscious of what constituted good design they should be shown examples. The obvious way in which to do this was through exhibitions. An exhibition of 'British Industrial Art in Relation to the Home' was mounted at Dorland Hall in Lower Regent Street in June–July 1933, and Lord Gorell wrote the foreword to the exhibition catalogue. The idea for such an exhibition was already under discussion by members of the DIA after the success of the Swedish Exhibition in 1931. The pottery section was supervised by a committee which included Gordon Forsyth and Harry Trethowan.

The china and earthen tablewares displayed at Dorland Hall demonstrated a pleasing simplicity of design – modern floral sprays, lines and banding were much in evidence, and Art Deco patterns, when they occurred, were less extreme that they had seemed in the very early 1930s. The purists in particular recommended the most simple and basic utilitarian wares that represented the best of Englishness. Harry Trethowan wrote in *The Studio*:

> . . . without question the kitchen things were the good wares. Form was based in the uses, and quality was an essential because the tests to be applied in daily use would be served. They were intended, and thus formed for a definite service. Simple forms of sound construction, a sound pot with true English character to be used daily in an English home. In our modern trend the English character must be preserved.

Although the exhibition was considered a success, many of the exhibits in the pottery section had been specially made, and were thus hardly representative of the industry as a whole.

The same charge was one of many that were levelled against another exhibition, 'British Art in Industry', which was mounted at the Royal Academy in 1935 in conjunction with the Royal Society of Arts. It was an adventurous move for the Royal Academy to admit industrial products through doors which were usually closed to all but the fine arts. The organizing secretary was John de la Valette, an ardent nationalist who was keen to show that British industry and British artists could work successfully together to produce everyday items of beauty by mechanical means. He was strongly antagonistic to the influence in

Britain of the International Modern style, which he identified as issuing from a despised Germany.

Although the avowed intention of the exhibition was again to show what could be produced by mass-production for the majority, criticisms again focused on the exhibits being untypical of the industry, extravagant examples aimed at gracious upper middle-class living. W. A. Thorpe, reporting on the exhibition for the *Pottery Gazette*, resented the didactic tone of the organizers:

> The authorities of the Royal Academy and the Royal Society of Arts have stated officially that the first purpose of the Exhibition is 'to impress upon the public the importance of good design in articles of everyday use.' I do not like that word 'impress.' It smacks of an Academic schoolmaster whacking his opinions into the public flanks.

He went on to say that he felt 'as if I were spending forty pleasant evenings with the Smiths in their rather respectable, rather refined, English, middle-class home'. He was excited only by the excellent banding on many of the wares, which, he said, 'one is tempted to regard . . . as the most important tendency in pottery during the last hundred years.' The general feeling amongst the critics was that the Royal Academy was too far out of touch with business reality to exercise the necessary controls over the crassly commercial interests of the RSA. Herbert Read attacked the exhibition in a paper entitled 'Novelism at the Royal Academy' in the *Architectural Review*, and Paul Nash – among others – wrote a critical letter to *The Times*. Even the tactful Nikolaus Pevsner, assessing reactions to the exhibition in his *An Inquiry into Industrial Art in England*, published in 1937, concluded that the exhibition had failed to make its mark on the establishment of the Modern Movement in Britain.

In 1934, the Board of Trade had set up a Council for Art and Industry under the chairmanship of Frank Pick, a DIA member and ex-solicitor who, when chief administrator of the London Underground, had commissioned distinguished designers for buildings, tiles, fabrics and posters. Pick's council mounted an exhibition of 'English Pottery Old and New' at the Victoria and Albert Museum in 1935. By showing both past and present products of the potters, the slant this time was to illustrate a 'living tradition' of manufacture. More effort was made to show tablewares which could be purchased by those of modest means, although the products of Wedgwood and Worcester predominated.

The point about simplicity of form and decoration was treated seriously in the exhibition, to the extent of showing porcelain made for laboratory use by Doulton as examples of beautiful, unadorned shapes. A somewhat confused step towards the recognition of the new modern style was alluded to in the picture book which was produced after the exhibition:

> On mass-produced wares, bold and simple designs are more appropriate than the mechanical reproduction of elaborate painting . . . Unlike some other manufactures, pottery can seldom be completely mechanized and hand-work is commonly required at some stage or other. But the austere impersonal forms of the specifically modern style may fittingly symbolise the process of mass-production.

□ Influential opinions

However successful or otherwise, these various exhibitions did stimulate discussion and argument. Industrial design of everyday articles had become the 'buzz' subject of the mid-1930s. Yet more exhibitions of 'modern living' and 'everyday things' were mounted, by such widely differing organizations as the Royal Institute of British Architects (RIBA) and Whiteley's London store. A quotation from Herbert Read, the figure of whom all commentators spoke with reverence, sets the tone of the arguments put forward by the many publications of the time on the subject:

> The whole purpose of art in industry is to reconcile the necessary qualities of an object (material, working and function) with incidental qualities of beauty.

Read's position was that beauty in industrially-produced goods was to be achieved by addressing questions of surface, materials and colour rather than designing archaic ornamentation. This was a more sophisticated point of view than the simple fitness-for-purpose argument which had been put forward so consistently and forcefully by the DIA. As the decade progressed arguments such as Read's were developed by other commentators. Thus in the same year as Read's *Art and Industry* (1934), Geoffrey Holme, in his book *Industrial Design and the Future* added his qualifying principles to the DIA slogan:

> However much we may emphasise the doctrine of 'fitness of purpose', we cannot exclude or be blind to the value of decoration of the right kind and in the right place . . . Many of the most highly mechanized industries combine the accuracy of machine methods with the personality of hand-work, and from this combination there is much to be hoped.

Holme and other commentators were excited by new developments in aircraft, ship, railway and motor-car designs. These were all machines designed along increasingly utilitarian lines, and yet their aesthetic appeal was not lost on critics or many members of the public. John Gloag, in *Industrial Art Explained*, also published in 1934, was similarly stimulated by such new developments. He saw in the new Pullman railway cars evidence of a final abandonment of the influence of carriage design on railway vehicles, and the recent motor coach – which placed the driver in front of the engine – was a design where 'the ghost of the horse is laid for ever . . .' Gloag proposed the establishment of an Academy of Design through a merger of the DIA and the Royal Society of Arts. He also argued for the recognition of the architect as the 'proper consultant on all matters pertaining to design'. This was the same year as the great modern architects Mies van der Rohe and Walter Gropius left Germany for the English-speaking world, and Gropius read a paper to the DIA.

In the following year John de la Valette edited the provocative *The Conquest of Ugliness* and Noel Carrington published *Design and a Changing Civilization*. In fact, everybody who was anybody in the design world seemed to publish a book expounding his opinions, and by 1937 a wide audience was being addressed. The BBC broadcast a series of talks entitled 'Design in Modern Life'; there were travelling exhibitions organized by the DIA and mounted in retail stores; and a small, cheap and eminently readable book, *Design in Everyday Life* by Anthony Bertram, was published. This book was written for a lay audience and succeeds in being both clear and unpatronizing. Bertram too gained hope and inspiration from developments in car, ship and aircraft design, and made special commendatory mention of the public works of the London Passenger Transport Board, and of the Miners' Welfare Committee for their design of pit-head baths. He summed up the argument of modern design critics in the simple formulation 'We don't want to beat the machine . . . We want to use it'. Thus decoration was criticized, for 'all good ornament has been handwork'. He then takes as a case study the design of a teapot, and argues that 'The contemporary product should rely for beauty on its shape rather than its adornment'.

Every avenue for getting both the message and the resulting products through to the public had to be explored in this heated climate of opinion. The shops had come in for considerable criticism for offering so few examples of well-designed goods for the home to its buying public (with the notable exception of Heal's which, under Trethowan's influence, had made notable attempts to market new design). More specifically, the main targets for the pens and tongues of those who sought to educate were the shops' stock buyers, who were empowered to choose what should be offered for sale, and the salesmen, who could influence a customer's choice. It fell to these two key people in the chain to interpret the ever-burning question: 'What does the public want?' Maurice Rena, writing in *The Studio* in 1936, presents the issue of the 'middleman':

> It would be difficult to over emphasize the immense importance of this gentleman, unfortunately placed and saddled with disquieting responsibility. A plenipotentiary of public taste, it is not surprising that he is the object of constant criticism . . . it is up to him to foster good design, firstly by understanding what it stands for and then by presenting the best types to suit his public.

The conclusion was that closer relationships and exchange of opinions should be forged between manufacturers and retailers and that the designer should play a significant role in achieving these associations. Steps were taken to enlighten the retail trade: in 1933 a trade magazine entitled *Shelf Appeal* was started, and the Pottery and Glass Trades Benevolent Institution revised its 'Textbook for salespeople engaged in the retail section of the Pottery and Glass Trades'. The textbook endeavoured to teach the salesman technicalities of manufacture, because 'no one can sell an article effectively if the seller is ignorant of its manufacture and its special properties'. Ignorance was generally identified as the problem, leading to a timid approach to design by the shops.

Some degree of understanding was reached through all this rhetoric. We have seen how a handful of design commentators – and the retailer Harry Trethowan – had began to admit that the near-sacred phrase 'fitness for purpose' had outlived its purpose. 'Functionalism is not enough', declared Gordon Forsyth to the Newcastle-under-Lyme Rotary Club in 1936. 'Men are not merely material and physical, but endowed with a natural appreciation of beauty and a desire to create it.' Some even admitted that humour could be a worthwhile attribute of design. William Gaunt was reported in *Commercial Art and Industry*, the publication of which he was editor, as telling the North Staffordshire Branch of the Society of Industrial Artists in 1934 that 'He did not believe in making too solemn a gospel of industrial art, or attempting to abolish all whimsicality or fantasy in design'. The designer himself had to acquire a better sense of proportion, see the world, become closer to the views of the public. For their part, the manufacturers who were involved in the discussions recognized in principle that designers should be given a better status in their firms, with proper renumeration (the wages paid to decoration managers were fairly low), possibly on a freelance basis.

□ From theory to reality

At the very least, the terms of these discussions had moved significantly from that of *art* in industry to that of *design* in industry, and the role of the industrial designer as such was becoming recognized. However, once again, the moves that manufacturers did make towards simplicity of design in their wares were largely forced by economic necessity. Much of the most interesting discussion in Stoke-on-Trent revolved around the means of production itself.

One of the most important reported evenings at the North Staffordshire Branch of the Society of Industrial Artists was in May 1933, when discussion was on the topic of lithographs, whether they could successfully yield all the qualities demanded by good and reliable pottery. This question was absolutely central to the development of the industry, but had been largely ignored at a time when hand-painted wares could be cheaply produced. Gordon Forsyth was viciously attacked for the part he had played in encouraging hand-decoration, and accused of turning out stereotyped artists from the schools – very unfairly after all his work in art education. Although he responded mildly, Forsyth must have been hurt to hear his influence abused and himself resented as a 'dominating personality' on the industry. Hand-painting had, after all, offered a relatively successful way forward for modern designs for a number of years.

Opinions of the true role of the pretty paintresses who had provided such a publicity stunt during the previous years and facilitated the cheap production of the hand-painted wares began to emerge. It was this cheap and exploitative girl labour that had killed the trade in lithographs: some claimed that while 14-year-old girls worked, their skilled lithographer elder sisters were on the dole. Arguments were inconclusive as to whether the girls were paid a decent standard rate or whether in fact many were working for starvation wages of half-a-crown a week, but the fact was that the 'little girls' had to all intents and purposes beaten the machine.

Lithographic transfers came under attack from the opposite direction: Gordon Forsyth had complained of 'those anaemic, vapid, insensate transfers' that had been on the market, and called for improvement. The problems in achieving this were aired: if lithos were to be centrally marketed from stock how could they then be specifically designed for a particular shape? Could lithographs be produced successfully in more than two colours, and if not, how were these limitations to cope with public demand for colourful tablewares? How was the lithograph manufacturer to assimilate the high costs involved in producing enough designs to give the potter sufficient choice of the right one for his wares? Did the manufacturers even properly understand the principles and subtleties of good lithographic reproduction?

With the future of exclusively handcraft production in doubt and these questions about lithographic decoration in mind, the climate of opinion amongst the potters finally began to lean towards simple designs which would be relatively easy and economic to achieve. If only two colours could be well executed, then why not have two-colour designs? The decisions about future design were thus largely made by the practical men of the Potteries, not by the idealists and intellectuals up from London.

One manufacturer in particular had already begun to set an example. Susie Cooper was present at the May 1933 meeting, and called for collective endeavour and co-operation between all involved in the production of pots. Her powers of analysis pin-pointed the underlying fears of the potters, who had lived through not only a world war, competition from abroad, a Depression, General Strike and extended coal strike, but also attacks from those who felt themselves superior in artistic judgement, all of which had crippled their ability to find a way forward. The *Pottery Gazette* reports her argument:

> . . . one of the things that was contributing to wreck the lithograph trade at the present time was the bee that the manufacturer had in his bonnet of producing something for less and less. To rectify this, one of the first obstacles to be overcome was fear – fear of their competitors, fear for their supply, fear of unemployment, and the ability to do, to have, and to be.
>
> They did not want onlookers in this society; they needed workers; acting and thinking members, if they were to bring about that most desirable state, stability and prosperity.

□ The Susie Cooper Pottery (*Chelsea Works and Crown Works, Burslem*)

Susie Cooper practised what she preached. Although she had successfully adhered to the production of hand-crafted pottery in earlier years, she was to move with the times and develop sophisticated techniques of lithographic decoration in the mid and late 1930s.

Susie Cooper had anticipated that her time spent in the early 1920s as a designer for A. E. Gray would lead to a scholarship to the Royal College of Art in London, but as she developed her skills she decided that the best possible training was a practical one within the industry. Her intention was not to become a studio potter but to effect changes in the design of industrially produced goods for an inexpensive market. However, the outlets at A. E. Gray for her own ideas were limited, and in October 1929, at the age of exactly 27, she

Part of an earthenware dinner service designed by Susie Cooper at her Crown Works Pottery; the shape is Kestrel of 1932, and the lithographic printed pattern Dresden Spray, *used in conjunction with shaded washbanding, dates from* c. 1935. (Pages 190–91)

decided to establish her own pottery-decorating business to give her scope to experiment. In April 1930 the *Pottery Gazette* described her motivation:

> ... Miss Cooper decided that it was essential if she was to carry forward the ideas upon which she has obviously set her mind, that she should have freedom of opportunity to evolve such new styles of design as she feels to be based on right lines.

Although in subsequent interviews she has played down the business implications of this decision, it was a very brave step to take at the end of the Depression years, characterized by a poor market which resulted in pottery closures rather than start-ups. The subsequent success of her venture put her in a strong position to comment later upon the fear shown by less determined manufacturers. Even Gordon Forsyth had advised her against her risky endeavour.

Her first premises were in rented rooms of a pottery in Tunstall, where she set up in partnership with her brother-in-law Jack Beeson, who was to become her very enterprising London agent. Her first landlord was made bankrupt soon after, so it was not until the spring of 1930 that the Susie Cooper Pottery started production in earnest from the Chelsea Works in Burslem. The experienced potter A. G. Richardson advised her on the technical side of the operation.

As a decorating firm, Susie Cooper was obliged to buy in undecorated white-ware from other manufacturers. The 'blanks' were purchased from a number of firms, including Wood and Sons. The early decorated wares were similar in style, although more varied and original, to the pieces she had executed for A. E. Gray – brightly hand-painted geometric, stylized floral and wash-banded wares. The standard of painting was high, and her paintresses, unlike Clarice Cliff's, reproduced exactly her own designs and were not at liberty to make their own freehand interpretations. Instructions for the paintresses in the firm's pattern books are very detailed, at times precisely indicating the shading, angle and intensity of the brushstrokes necessary to achieve a design. From the outset, Susie Cooper's was a very professional operation.

Even during this period of bright fashionable wares a distinctive Susie Cooper style is evident; her products could not be confused with those of any other pottery. There was a restraint and sparingness about the designs which was commented on by the *Pottery Gazette* in June 1931:

> ... she is a gifted, creative artist of the modern school of thought, one who reveals in her work a lively imagination combined with a unique capacity to achieve the maximum degree of effectiveness in pottery decoration by recourse to the simplest modes of expression.

In the summer of 1931, Susie Cooper Pottery moved to the Crown Works, Burslem, leasing space from her now major white-ware suppliers, Wood and Sons. One of the great attractions of this alliance was that the company had offered to produce new shapes to Susie Cooper's own designs. This was essential to the development of integrated shapes and decorations which she fully recognized to be a prerequisite of good modern ceramic design.

In consequence, in 1932 the first of the bird-named shapes, *Kestrel*, appeared and was exhibited to considerable acclaim at the British Industries Fair of the same year. The *Kestrel* shape bore few similarities to the geometric shapes which were being produced by comparable firms at the time. Its streamlined outline was curvaceous and Modernist, a delicate shape that was nevertheless produced in earthenware, not china. The name was suggested in particular by the hollow-ware – coffee- and teapots, for example, which had sleek curves, beak-like spouts, and lids topped with crest-like slanting knobs. The shape was designed with more than aesthetic considerations in mind – practicality, indeed 'fitness for purpose', was always a prime consideration of Susie Cooper's work. The vegetable dish of the dinner service, for example, had a bowl-shaped lid which could be upturned to rest on the table (its handle was at the side) while vegetables were being served, or could be used in its own right as an additional serving dish or soup bowl. And spouts, however stylish, were first and foremost designed to pour well. Coffee-, tea- and dinner-ware were all produced in the *Kestrel* shape, which was so adaptable and popular that it remained in production until the late 1950s.

Other bird shapes followed: *Curlew* in about 1932 and *Falcon* in about 1937; a further shape, *Wren* (modified as *Jay*) was designed especially for Wood and Sons in about 1934 (see page 192). The *Curlew* shape was slightly more angular and rotund, the bird inspiration most evident in the vegetable dish, whose downward-pointing handles resembled the wings of the bird when not in flight. In character with its name, it was a pert shape, less streamlined than *Kestrel*. *Falcon* was less recognizably bird shaped, although like its namesake it was a simple, perfectly balanced design, having an almost semi-circular open handle, streamlined spout and open ring knobs to the lid for tea- and coffee-pots.

In the early years of their production, these shapes were treated with a variety of carefully hand-painted decorations, both over and under the glaze. As their designer, Susie Cooper benefited from her training as a paintress, which had taught her the extent and the limits of what could be achieved. It had also made her a perfectionist, demanding very high standards of craftsmanship from her paintresses. She provided pounces (tissue paper was pricked out with holes around the pattern outline, laid onto the white-ware and dusted over with charcoal to provide an impression), or sketches for the paintresses to work from, and broke each pattern down into simple operations which could be learnt systematically. This approach also meant that the expertise or limitations of each paintress could be taken into account and the work which they were to do planned accordingly. Some of the simplest patterns, for example, the polka dots and dashes for which she was to become famous, were designed in part in order to train the women in simple painting skills. Consequently, a high standard of quality was maintained in the finished wares and time was well spent, in keeping with her declared business 'bible': 'The maximum out of materials from the minimum capital outlay.'

Kestrel, *Curlew* and *Falcon* (for later decorations) were painted with beautiful banding and lines in such colour combinations as grey, brown and purple-brown or pink, yellow, brown and grey. Very bright shades of colour were largely abandoned in the very early 'thirties for these subtler colours of a Modernist palette. Amongst the simple hand-painted patterns were *Polka Dot*, done in blue, tangerine or apple green with lined edges on the white body; *Exclamation Mark*, the simplest downward brushstroke and dot; and leaf, flower, and fern patterns which were also easily executed.

Susie Cooper, unlike the vast majority of Stoke-on-Trent potters, was not content to follow a supposed taste demanded by the public. She took the responsibility, so much talked about by design commentators, of being innovative, and actually moved demand forward by marketing her new designs. She was constantly experimenting with decorating techniques for her wares, setting a lead for other manufacturers. She used a technique of crayoning, where colours made up into sticks were used to draw with onto the wares, as in the *Crayon Loop* pattern, which created an effect of cobblestones. She perfected techniques of aerographing, where areas of the wares were coloured using a spray gun, a tool previously only exploited to the full by the advertising world. The water-based aerographed colours were not as hard as ordinary groundlay, and enabled her to develop new techniques of *sgraffito*, where patterns of outlined flowers and small abstract motifs were incised through the colour to reveal the white underneath, as in the *Scroll* and *Astral* (stars) patterns. She experimented with 'in-glaze' decorations in which the colours appeared to have added depth, sunk in the glaze. She used tube-lining for entire patterns, and decorative wares were incised and treated with matt glazes. Her careful integration of materials, forms and techniques was noted by the trade press, who also frequently commented on the advantages of a woman designing for a predominantly female buying public (although Susie Cooper herself considered her gender an irrelevance). In August 1935 the *Pottery Gazette* talked of her designs in terms more characteristic of DIA journals:

> Form, decoration and even texture in the Susie Cooper ware are part of a considered scheme; it is not merely a case of sticking a decoration on to a pot regardless of context; and in addition to all this there is, in the background the whole time, the woman's point of view, which counts for a good deal – in domestic pottery at all events.

By the mid-1930s the market was responding well to her tableware designs – she had successfully created a demand for her products. She had gradually won the vital confidence of the retailers: '... ledger accounts talk, and it is no secret that some of those dealers who, at first, were inclined to toy with some of the Susie Cooper fantasies have summoned up more courage as they have continued' reported the *Pottery Gazette* in 1935.

By this time, however, she was well aware of the serious need to develop good lithographic transfers for pottery decoration. Characteristically she was not content simply to argue about the difficulties which lithography presented to the industry. She produced her own sophisticated modern designs involving a number of colours, and persuaded lithography manufacturers to produce them specially for her to the required high standard. This lead was subsequently followed by other potteries, but in his *Survey* of 1937, Nikolaus Pevsner cites her as the first to introduce such a working practice.

Lithographic designs such as the now-popular pastel-shaded stylized floral

Dresden Spray, used in conjunction with wash-banding, continued in production for many years. Other successful designs of the 'thirties include a version of the leaping deer, a stylized rustic floral, *Nosegay*, a modern English *Patricia Rose* and various other subtly coloured floral, fern and leaf patterns. The quality of these lithographic decorations was such that at first glance they could be mistaken for hand-painting.

Although the mainstay of Susie Cooper's productions were the basic tablewares, supplementary items and decorative wares were considered important additional productions. Vases, jugs, animal and figure models, wall masks, lamp bases, table-centres, water and lemonade sets, cruet sets, cheese stands, candlesticks, ashtrays, hors d'oeuvres sets and nursery wares were all produced during the 1930s. She was also aware of domestic changes, in particular smaller houses with less storage space, built for smaller families, which created a market for smaller tableware services. Her economical 15-piece dinner-services were all that were needed by many families.

In 1940, her innovative skills were formally recognized when she was appointed a Royal Designer for Industry, an honour bestowed by the Royal Society of Arts – she remains the only woman in the Potteries to receive such a decoration. She had demonstrated that it was commercially viable to lead the market with good, modern design, and had proved that there was a buying public possessed of good taste but limited resources who would select such wares from modest retail outlets and department stores when presented with the choice. She had put paid to the deeply conservative design attitudes of the majority of the manufacturers, not with rhetoric but with a flourishing business founded on modern industrial design principles.

Perhaps her greatest achievement was in a brilliant fusion of International Modern principles and English style. However streamlined her shapes, they could never be mistaken for more austere Continental models. Her patterns relied for effect on their quality of drawing, not on the crude geometric lines which appeared so 'foreign'. The unusual pastel shades of her gentle wash-bands, drooping flower sprays and understated dots and dashes created a style which was fresh and new yet unmistakably English. Susie Cooper had created the English modern ceramics with good lithographic decorations that everyone had been begging for – and she had sold them cheaply to a willing public.

□ Wood and Sons   (*Trent and New Wharf Potteries, Burslem*)

Wood and Sons, manufacturers of earthenwares and ironstones, were founded in 1865. Although they are comparatively sketchily recorded in the twentieth century, they had working connections with many of the most important designers of the period, in particular Susie Cooper, for whose work they provide a footnote.

In his studies of the Rhead family, Bernard Bumpus has recorded that Frederick Rhead worked as art director of Wood and Sons between the years 1913 and 1929, during which time he designed quantities of tableware and hotel-wares, and introduced tube-lining techniques to the firm. During this period, his daughter Charlotte trained under him at Woods, leaving for Burgess and Leigh in 1926.

The quality of potting and earthenware shapes produced by Wood and Sons was such that both A. E. Gray, and subsequently Susie Cooper at her own potteries, chose to buy in the firm's white-ware. The company controlled a number of individual potteries, each specializing in a type of ware, for example, tablewares, teapots or ornamental wares, which provided a wide range of blanks from which others could select. Consequently, many of the most elegant decorated pieces of the day are pottery actually made by Wood and Sons.

In the early 1930s, some of the tablewares produced by Wood and Sons themselves were of the brightly coloured rustic floral variety, many constituting quite crude interpretations of the style. Hand-painted naturalistic sunbursts were mixed rather indiscriminately with bold stylized florals, and some of the angular earthenware shapes had a very heavy appearance. However, as early as 1931 Wood and Sons were experimenting with streamlined new shapes and colourful lithographic patterns for their *Ivory Ware*, treated with a mellow glaze. The colours of these lithographs were powerful enough to prompt the *Pottery Gazette* to make a general point in relation to Wood and Sons, in September 1931:

> . . . To view such a striking collection of samples is to be struck with the tremendous changes which have come about in the decoration of semi-porcelain tablewares during the past few years. Strong colour, at one time used only with temerity by the manufacturers of ordinary priced earthen-wares, seems to be now the very backbone of many of the most popular treatments.

From 1932 there is little doubt that Wood's productions as a whole were influenced by their close association with Susie Cooper, who made occasional designs for them and whose company became an associated member of Wood and Sons in 1933. In 1932 Wood and Sons launched a new angular floral pattern called *Capri* and a 'diaper' effect banded tartan design. Susie Cooper's *Wren* shape was designed for them in about 1934, advertised early in 1935, and exhibited at the Royal Academy exhibition in the same year. The compact and rotund shape, particularly suited to small services, was enhanced with tooled incisions in the body of the clay on handles, spouts and lids. Freehand decorations for *Wren* were very simple and restrained, in two or three colours. The shape was subsequently modified as *Jay*. In addition, Susie Cooper improved some existing traditional Wood and Sons shapes, *Classic* and *Rex*, for the firm, and also decorated examples at her own pottery. Other contemporaneous tableware designs, such as the *Charnwood* design, resembling embroidery stitches, still showed the influence of the Rhead family.

CHAPTER EIGHT

Towards an English Modernism

□ Josiah Wedgwood (and Sons) *(Etruria and Barlaston from 1940)*

The tablewares produced by Wedgwood, the best-known pottery company of all, in the 1920s and 1930s are also very significant in the history of British Modernism. It is interesting to contrast the achievements of this large, well-established firm with those of a small, new pottery: Wedgwood was a giant at the opposite extreme to Susie Cooper's small business. Nevertheless, from these different positions within the industry, the two firms can be said to have produced between them the best Modernist ceramic designs seen in Britain before World War II. Whereas Susie Cooper's pottery demonstrated what could be accomplished by a fresh, new enterprise headed by a far-sighted young designer, Wedgwood illustrates how good Modernism could be a valuable part of the output of a pottery that had more reason than most to be aware of the powerful dictates of traditional English manufacture.

Wedgwood had long had a reputation for treating artists and designers seriously and for innovative pottery techniques. Josiah Wedgwood had opened his factory at Etruria in the Potteries in 1769, and from the start had employed talented artists, notably the Neo-classical sculptor John Flaxman and animal-painter George Stubbs, to design for ceramics. From the beginning, then, Wedgwood had been concerned with uniting art and industry and aligning itself with contemporary design.

Although this reputation waned along with the company's overall prosperity at the end of the nineteenth century, in the early twentieth century efforts were made to recapture the artistic verve of Wedgwood's products, and under Art Director John E. Goodwin, talented artists were once again brought into the company. Alfred Powell, born in 1865, had trained as an architect and was heavily influenced by Arts and Crafts ideologies. Designs by Alfred Powell were first accepted by Wedgwood in 1903, and a design studio for Powell and his new wife Louise (born into a distinguished artistic family in 1882) was established in London in 1907. The Powells' involvement with craft manufacture led them to suggest as early as 1909 that some of their designs should be hand-painted. This decision led the way to the important establishment of a handcraft department at Wedgwood in the 1920s, and neatly illustrates the progression from Arts and Crafts thinking to the hand-painting of the period.

Many of the most interesting patterns produced by Wedgwood in the 1910s and early 1920s were decorative wares rather than tablewares. The Powells were interested in re-establishing lustre decorations, but it was a member of Wedgwood's ordinary design department, Daisy Makeig-Jones, who produced the most spectacular lustre designs of the period for her *Fairyland* series, produced from 1915 and popular throughout the 1920s. The designs depicted elves and fairies in exotic natural and fantasy-castle landscapes, decorated in vibrant lustre colours. Wedgwood's decorative *Rhodian* ware, influenced by earlier work of the Powells, was launched in 1920, and consisted of a range of ornamental wares hand-painted in lavish Islamic style. It was followed by a similar series of *Persian* ware.

As these wares became popular the need for hand-paintresses at the Stoke-on-Trent factory at Etruria grew. In 1926, a small handcraft studio was opened, employing young women, some of whom had been trained under Gordon Forsyth at the local schools of art, to decorate patterns designed largely by Louise Powell. The most talented and important of these paintresses was Millicent Taplin, who from 1928 started to implement her own designs in addition to those she was executing to the Powells' instructions. The handcraft patterns were designed for and executed on both earthenwares and china, and during the 1920s and 1930s some very striking new tableware designs were produced in some quantity.

Wedgwood's earthenware pattern books of the late 1920s and early 1930s show a sophisticated use of stylized and rustic floral elements of the Art Deco style – in particular, zigzagged and interlocking line patterns. One tea-ware pattern called *Futurist* of 1929 took its inspiration from the decorative works of primitive civilizations, with crossing lines and semi-circular 'eyes' painted in black, brown and orange; others were painted with large poppies and other florals in such bright colour combinations as orange, red, yellow, green and black. Zigzags and polka dots, stylized fruit and flowers, and wiggly lines were used as decorative devices. Millicent Taplin's *Sun-lit* pattern, a combination of stylized florals and border-line pattern with an overall Islamic feel, appears in 1930 on a cane-coloured earthenware body. Lustre tableware designs were mostly floral, the curvaceous forms simpler than they had been earlier in the century.

Most of these tableware patterns were applied to the *Concave* shape, a gently curving but streamlined shape which derived from traditional Wedgwood designs – nothing remotely angular was produced by the factory during this time, except for the ubiquitous Cube Teapot, designed as part of services for shipping lines and hotels. The patterns were also applied to different-coloured bodies used for the shape – celadon green, cane and lavender.

Millicent Taplin designed a large number of striking Modernist patterns for china tea-, coffee- and breakfast-sets during the 1930s. *Falling Leaves* was a simple design of stylized single leaves in grey and green with silver finish;

Moonlight was a striking design combining areas of silver-grey groundlay with broken straight and wiggly lines in silver, finished with fine black lines. The latter was exhibited at the Royal Academy in 1935, along with an unusual pattern with 'diaper' border in green finished in bright platinum, called *Green Lattice*.

A number of other artists and designers was employed on a freelance basis to produce patterns for tableware. In 1931 the *Pottery Gazette* illustrates and comments upon the design *Sunbirds* by Sir Charles J. Holmes, Director of the National Gallery, London: this was a marvellous pattern with arching rainbow-like semi-circular bands and stylized birds. In 1933 a pattern of disconnected, half-circle bands of silver by Harry Trethowan was exhibited at Dorland Hall. Star Wedgwood – one of the Wedgwood dynasty – designed the *Stars* pattern, with large white stars touched with gold on a blue background (and other combinations); she also designed some fine small floral-motif designs and a *Coronation* pattern in 1937. Rex Whistler's classical views of *Clovelly* were used on Wedgwood ceramics from 1933. The use of freelance artists to produce good contemporary designs for ceramics was once again very much in evidence.

Veronese wares were introduced in about 1930. Simple forms, decorated with a range of glaze colours, they were introduced in part to provide work for the hand-throwers when demand for traditional expensive wares was low. In her book *Wedgwood Ceramics 1846-1959*, Maureen Batkin categorizes the wares thus: '*Veronese* wares represent the transition between the handcraft styles produced by Millicent Taplin and her paintresses and the architectural Modernism of Keith Murray'. The glaze colours used for decorative wares – bowls, vases, ashtrays, etc – included plum, celadon green, pink, crimson, black and Barnstaple blue. Decorations included bronze and silver lustres and hand-crafted simple floral and leaf motifs. The glaze techniques used on the *Veronese* wares were developed by Norman Wilson, who had been appointed works manager in 1927. His technical skills were to be exploited to the full in years to come in the development of new glazes.

The first move towards dramatically Modernist shapes in tableware was made by Art Director John Goodwin and (Clement) Tom Wedgwood, who together designed the *Annular* tableware shape in about 1932. *Annular* was plain and sculptural, with wide ribbed bands down the body of the durable earthenwares. Norman Wilson had developed a *Moonstone* glaze for the shape, which advertising material described as '. . . a semi-matt glaze like driven snow', while '. . . the modern shapes are designed for strength and cleanliness as well as beauty'. Decorations were clean and Modernist, often incorporating silver lustre designs or graduated coloured lustres following the ribs of the body. Others had simple lines between the ridges in green, light and dark brown, blue, or dark red. Some later examples, of about 1935, were decorated with other plain matt glazes – green and straw – developed by Norman Wilson. The *Pottery Gazette* responded almost archly to the scantily decorated *Annular* shape, describing it in October 1934 as '. . . a form which reveals rippled bands of clay, and which is being decorated in a number of elegant, if restrained, styles for the requirements of people whose artistic sensibilities are such as to befit them to appreciate such efforts.'

Tom Wedgwood and John Goodwin had secured the advice of a very important designer when developing the *Annular* shape. Keith Murray, a New Zealander by birth, was a distinguished but often unemployed architect who undertook freelance design commissions, predominantly in ceramics, silver and glass. As we have seen, design commentators had already identified the architect as the single most important individual in the design firmament, and the designs which Murray was to execute for Wedgwood during the following years were met with the highest praise, the like of which had not been heard during the whole century. Murray's association with Wedgwood started at the invitation of Josiah Wedgwood V, who, like his ancestors, actively encouraged associations between artists and designers in the ceramics industry. From 1933, an arrangement was confirmed whereby Keith Murray would work as a designer for Wedgwood for three months of each year.

Murray immediately came to grips with the important issue of modern shapes as opposed to new decorations. The vast majority of his ceramic designs were for simple, Modernist, architectural shapes, which were decorated in a variety of plain-coloured glazes developed by Norman Wilson. Here at last was an industrial ceramic designer who concentrated on form rather than decoration, and who designed shapes which were simple, modern, yet thoroughly English, containing echoes of traditional Wedgwood classical shapes. Advertising material at the time boasted:

> He has seen how to build on the Wedgwood tradition an entirely new style of design, making full use of Wedgwood craftsmanship and fineness of material. His designs are characterized by virile shapes and clear cut outline, and are, in the large majority of cases, executed by the traditional methods of Throwing and Turning, in which Wedgwood craftsmen excel.

This latter point should be borne in mind: because many of Keith Murray's wares were produced by hand-throwing, and were then hand-turned to achieve their architectural outlines, they were not suitable designs for large-scale mass-production.

The majority of Murray's new shapes were for ornamental wares – jugs, bowls, vases, trays – in a variety of ribbed and fluted modern forms. Tableware shapes included an elegant, tall coffee-set with straight-sided cups, stepped lids to pot and sugar box, and turned-effect decorations at the centre of each piece of hollow-ware. The coffee-set was decorated with the *Moonstone* glaze, and had optional platinum handles. Murray also designed ceramic cocktail cups, one design featuring a fluted triangular-shaped base, and cider or beer mugs, designed in ivory-glazed traditional Wedgwood *Queens Ware*. Perhaps most influential of all was his set of beer mugs and three-pint jug designed in 1934, in a form gently tapering towards the rim, with turned decoration at the base. The set was produced in *Moonstone*, *Matt Grey*, *Straw* or *Green* glazes, and a non-matt glaze in shades of Champagne, white or green. 'Apart from their good looks, they have other advantages,' ran Wedgwood's promotional blurb. 'They are particularly pleasant to drink from, because of their smooth surface, and they have a positive gift for making good beer taste even better.' The ultimate in fitness for purpose! The beer mugs were illustrated as examples of good

modern design in many important books of the period.

Keith Murray designed a large variety of other shapes for mugs, and other supplementary useful wares included powder-, cigarette- and multi-purpose covered boxes, ashtrays, ceramic inkstands and tobacco jars. The glaze effects used on these and on the ornamental wares were many and sophisticated, including both matt and satin finishes, and opaque semi-matt black glaze, while others were produced with bronze basalt and red stoneware bodies.

The earliest Keith Murray wares were exhibited at Dorland Hall in 1933, but their real impact was only felt at the Royal Academy exhibition two years later. They were very well received, although the *Pottery Gazette* remained sceptical. It commented, for example, on the turned coffee-pot: 'We would prefer to reserve our judgment as to whether it has power to *sell* . . . it seemed a trifle lacking in plasticity and flow, as is natural enough in an architect.'

Keith Murray also designed a number of patterns for Wedgwood's more conventional tablewares, consisting of small motifs, including *Lotus*, *Iris* and *Silver Willow*. These were applied to modern shapes designed in the mid-1930s, and often incorporated platinum in the decorations. His most important commission of all from Wedgwood was an architectural one – the design of the new factory at Barlaston, outside Stoke-on-Trent. This work was done in conjunction with his partner C. S. White and with Tom Wedgwood and Norman Wilson, who were responsible for planning the factory itself, and designs were complete by 1938. Much of the building work had been carried out by 1940, and as a necessary industry, Wedgwood was allowed to carry on building to a certain extent during World War II.

John Goodwin retired in 1934, and was replaced as Art Director by 25-year-old Victor Skellern, another protégé of Gordon Forsyth's Burslem Art School, who had joined Wedgwood as an apprentice in the decorating shop in 1923. The modern trends which had begun under Goodwin were to be carried forward forcefully by Skellern during the latter half of the 'thirties. Many of Keith Murray's and Millicent Taplin's designs, described above, were devised under his directorship. Most importantly, from a commercial design point of view, Skellern concentrated much of his energy on the production of tableware lines, both in earthenware and china, rather than on ornamental items.

New tableware shapes designed by Norman Wilson were simple, clean-lined and modern, but almost always referred back to classical and traditional shapes produced earlier in Wedgwood's history. The *Globe* china shape, delicate, tall, with elongated curves, appeared in about 1935 and was used for a large number of Skellern's patterns throughout the 1930s. Many of his patterns incorporated simple floral motifs, others simple lines and bandings, while yet others showed Persian influences. Some were very unusual, for example the varied star patterns of *Snow Crystals*, designed about 1935, or *Astral*, of about 1938, which incorporated an extraordinary planet and shooting arrows motif on a polka-dotted background.

The careful combination of new shapes and patterns was not the only concern, and the glazes and bodies of the wares were not neglected. In 1936 an *Alpine Pink* coloured body was introduced and used for moulded shell-shaped wares. Also in about 1936 a *Green Glaze* was introduced and used for embossed

Vases and bowls designed by Keith Murray for Josiah Wedgwood (and Sons), 1932–39. The bowl and vase (centre) are treated with a celadon satin glaze; the vases (top and bottom left) are in matt green glaze; the vase (centre) in matt straw glaze; and the vase (right) in semi-matt white Moonstone glaze. (Pages 196–99)

leaf-shaped dishes; and others, for example in the shape of a sunflower, incorporated both yellow and green glazes. At about the same time Norman Wilson devised simple tablewares, undecorated but with bodies in two contrasting colours: *Summer Sky* (lavender and white), *Winter Green* (celadon and cream) and *Harvest Moon* (champagne and ivory).

Although considerable progress in modern design had been made with the new shapes, coloured bodies and glazes, and hand-painted decorations, Victor Skellern was keenly aware that the future of industrial ceramic decoration would be invested in lithographs. During the second half of the 1930s, he was investigating the development and application of lithographs for Wedgwood's general tableware production, although full-scale production of lithographed wares did not get under way until after 1945.

Tentative steps towards modern lithographic techniques were helped by Wedgwood's employment on a freelance basis of the artist Eric Ravilious. Born in 1903, by the 1930s Ravilious was developing a keen interest in lithography as an art medium which could combine drawing and printing. He was introduced to Wedgwood in 1935, and until 1940 designed a number of printed patterns for both earthen and china tablewares. Many of the patterns were not actually put into substantial production until after 1950, although Ravilious himself died in 1942, lost on an air patrol over Iceland in the course of his work as an Official War Artist.

Ravilious's works in general demonstrate a unique fusion between cool Modernist lines and colours, machine technology, and a sensitive feeling for the English landscape and life. His designs for Wedgwood, although applied to traditional (but plain) ceramic shapes, were amongst the finest patterns to be devised for industrial tableware during the inter-war years. Certainly, they were superior to any produced by the artists involved in the 1934 Harrods exhibition: his patterns looked as though they were really intended to be industrially reproduced, and he did not make the mistake of earlier artists of trying to make mass-produced designs appear hand-crafted.

The majority of the tableware patterns were intended to be printed in one colour and then tinted by hand with one or more additional colour. In this respect they provided a half-way stage, and an acceptable compromise, between true modern lithographic printing and the old detailed skills of hand-painting. Perhaps the most famous design of all was *Persephone* of 1938, printed in grey to be tinted with either yellow, green or blue. A border of swirling continuous lines is centred with motifs of fish, fruit and other produce. First produced in earthenware, the pattern was later made on bone china. English domestic life was exploited for *Afternoon Tea*, c.1937, and *Garden Implements*, c.1938 and *Garden* of c.1939. *Afternoon Tea* was printed in sepia on fine bona china, again tinted in yellow, green or blue. The vignette patterns show a bench and tea-table, laid out with pots of jam, loaves of bread and so on – many backed by exterior landscapes, emphasizing Ravilious's love of the outdoors. The motifs indicate an afternoon tea taken in the garden on a summer's day.

Garden Implements, perhaps the most charming of all Ravilious's ceramic designs, was a thoroughly outdoor scene for outdoor tableware: an earthenware lemonade set complete with large jugs. A large motif of the implements themselves covered one side of the jug and the beakers: an old barrel cascading flowers displays fork, rake, hoe, scythe, broom, pruning shears and lawn-edging tool like a bunch of flowers; a watering can stands alongside. On the reverse side, nine vignettes arranged circularly depict greenhouse, wheelbarrow, vegetable patch, beehive and other garden scenes, including a curled-up sleeping cat. The printed pattern was highlighted with pink lustre and enamel. *Garden*, devised for earthen tablewares, depicted vignettes of larger garden landscape scenes, most incorporating trees and sketchy figures sitting or working in the gardens. Post-war productions of the pattern were printed in two-colour lithography.

In all these patterns, Ravilious has used outdoor domestic scenes graphically, so that although detailed and descriptive, they form the simple lines of an overall pattern. They also all contain a marvellous, gentle humour, a comedy of English middle-class manners, which is an element missing from other more self-important modern designs.

Ravilious's fascination with technology in the landscape was indulged in his *Travel* pattern of about 1937, in which trains, boats, planes and even balloons are depicted in action. The pattern was printed in black on grey *Queens Ware* and tinted with colour. In addition, he designed *Alphabet* nursery ware in 1937, with the letters illustrated with pictures and the pattern printed and washed with bands of colour; a Coronation Mug for Edward VIII, quickly adapted for George VI; and a magnificent *Boat Race Day* cup and large bowl, where the vignettes concentrate on the celebrating crowds gathered in Piccadilly Circus. In 1939 he designed a mug to commemorate Wedgwood's move to Barlaston, which was the first of his designs to be produced entirely by colour lithography.

Ravilious's designs, particularly tablewares, did not meet with enormous commercial success – although it is interesting to note that their recent popularity encouraged Wedgwood to reissue one or two in limited editions in 1987. Ravilious himself was not entirely at ease: he felt that Wedgwood thought his designs too highbrow, and he himself regretted that they had not been manufactured on lighter ceramic bodies. Wedgwood evidently felt that, yet again, the artist did not have sufficient understanding of his materials. In the book published to accompany the 1986 exhibition of Ravilious's works at the Towner Art Gallery, Eastbourne, Norman Wilson is quoted as recalling, in 1982, that:

> . . . Ravilious patterns did not sell well and only progressive buyers like Heal's and Liberty's showed much interest. The individual items were more saleable than the tableware. *Persephone* sold fairly well but *Travel* was a flop. Buyers and customers alike thought the pattern a joke . . . It is worth mentioning that very few outside artists made a success of graphic design at Wedgwood's. In my time from 1927 to 1962 there were many famous artists who were quite unsuccessful on pottery, largely because they failed to learn the problems.

Whether or not the Ravilious wares were a commercial success, his patterns did make more impact on the world of industrial ceramic decoration than perhaps any others produced by contemporary artists. Writing in a mid-century survey

A selection of tablewares designed by Keith Murray from 1932 for Josiah Wedgwood (and Sons). The part tea set is in the *Annular* shape designed by Murray, John Goodwin and Tom Wedgwood c. 1932 and, together with the dinner plates, is decorated with matt straw glaze; the beer mugs and three-pint jugs are shown in a variety of glaze finishes – matt straw, matt green, semi-matt white Moonstone *and* celadon *and* grey-blue satin. (Pages 196–99)

of British industrial design in 1955, Michael Farr firmly states:

> The first designer to demonstrate the creative possibilities of modern decoration applied to traditional shapes was the late Eric Ravilious. The shape is late eighteenth century and the *Garden Implements* design has made the set the most famous in modern pottery.

Wedgwood were to continue to commission artists to design tableware patterns after World War II, but during the 1930s much of their most successful use of outside artists was for ceramic sculptures and decorative wares. Perhaps the most important of these was the Norwegian-born sculptor Eric (Erling) Olsen, who began working for Wedgwood in 1931. He produced earthenware vases, bookends, ashtrays, inkwells and lamp bases in embossed relief designs, which were decorated with one-colour matt or Veronese glazes or modelled in *Queens Ware*. These pieces had a Continental Art Deco flavour, often employing stylized animals – for example, a vase with monkeys and a jungle scene in relief; *Stag and Tree* bookends, and stepped fan-shaped *Pan* bookends. Another favourite for Olsen's embossed motifs was the conch shell, sometimes stylized into a pattern. In 1935 Olsen left Wedgwood for W. T. Copeland where he produced similar wares (see p. 141).

The sculptor John Skeaping was employed from 1926, and modelled a series of 14 animal sculptures, 10 of which were in production throughout the 1930s and well into the 1950s. They were simple and Modernist, their clean lines and indentations well adapted to the medium of ceramics, with reflective, semi-matt and matt glazes. The ten produced were *Polar Bear*, *Bison*, *Sea Lion*, *Fallow Deer*, *Monkey*, *Buffalo*, *Kangaroo*, *Tiger and Buck*, *Duiker* – both standing and lying. The models were available with a range of glazes: plain cream, moonstone, celadon or black basalt. Skeaping's sculptures were advertised in Wedgwood's publicity leaflets alongside the new wares designed by Keith Murray. They stood between 5 and 9 inches high, and could be bought with or without black wooden stands. Alan Best, an American-born sculptor, designed six athlete models for Wedgwood in about 1934–5, together with a superb Art Deco *Panther* and a *Mandarin Duck*.

Wedgwood's management and art directors of the 1920s and 1930s took a very serious and well-informed view of the artist working in industry. The company was willing to employ good designers both on a full-time and freelance basis, and to accord them a proper role and proper remuneration. Nevertheless, as Norman Wilson himself indicated when talking about Eric Ravilious's designs, even the power and experience of a Wedgwood could not really crack the problem of artists working in industry, particularly in the area of tablewares. The general public still did not immediately associate the name of Wedgwood with the modern wares described here, but rather with the traditional bone china, *Jasper* and *Black Basalt* wares that were produced concurrently and had been associated with Wedgwood for generations. Although progress was made in the early decades of the twentieth century, it is significant that Wedgwood's major advances in contemporary design for tablewares, and the company's extensive use of colour lithographs, only really developed after the restrictions imposed by World War II were lifted.

□ Trends in the late 1930s

By the late 1930s, everyday British tablewares were, in general, considerably better designed than they had been ten or fifteen years earlier. There were at last indications of progress: some design developments had already been achieved, and others were likely to follow. Nevertheless, as we have seen, the developments were both slow and limited, and problems still remained. Surface decoration of tablewares was still seen as more important than changes in shape: hand decorations, however liberating in their own right, had diverted attention from fully industrialized techniques. Artists and designers were by no means fully integrated into the industry; and none of the parties concerned in the chain of manufacture – designers, industrialists, marketers and public – were sufficiently educated in one another's needs and capabilities. The potters, still steeped in the traditional atmosphere of Stoke-on-Trent, showed only limited enthusiasm for modern designs, and the mainstay of their industry remained the old, traditional tableware manufacture.

By the middle of the decade it was possible to feel either encouraged or disappointed by the developments that *had* been made during the preceding years. In conclusion, we will look at two such contrasting opinions: those of an optimist operating within the atmosphere of Stoke-on-Trent, Gordon Forsyth, and the more cautious words of a stringent observer from outside the industry, Nikolaus Pevsner.

Gordon Forsyth's 20th Century Ceramics was published by The Studio magazine in 1936. Its text is short, and it is illustrated extensively with Forsyth's selection of British, European, American and Far Eastern contemporary ceramics of good modern design. In addition to the international mix, he includes both industrially produced and hand-made 'art' pottery. The result (and Forsyth's clear intention) is that the selection of British industrially produced tablewares, although they do not exactly lead the design field, certainly hold their own by comparison with the foreign wares depicted. The British showing alongside its foreign competitors now appears much more creditable than it did a decade earlier at the Paris 1925 *Exposition*.

In his text, Forsyth does not ignore the difficulties which faced the pottery industry in Britain – the need to bring artists and studio potters into collaboration with industry, for example – but he sets out to place the best possible interpretation on recent productions. The desire for novelty, he points out, may have prompted 'inartistic' designs, but it is also a prerequisite of the evolution of 'artistic' ones; the old 'fitness for purpose' argument of the 'extreme functionalist' may lead him to ignore the visual and aesthetic need for good decoration, which should also be recognized. He concedes that modern British ceramic design is less than perfect, but 'in the main, pottery is striving towards harmony and modern ideas'. His use of the word 'striving' is significant: it implies activity and good intentions, but is unspecific about the degree or speed of success. Forsyth is able to be encouraging while at the same time gently pointing to limitations and problems which still have to be tackled: his book reflects the tactful and unhurried way in which he had tried to effect change in the pottery industry since 1920.

Most important of all, Forsyth has recognized that the pressures of the

Overleaf Two patterns for Josiah Wedgwood (and Sons) china by Victor Skellern: pieces from a Globe shaped coffee service in Snow Crystals pattern of 1936, printed in gold; and pattern book showing Winter Morn of 1934, hand-painted on blue groundlay. (Page 199)

market-place have finally begun to prompt simplification of design. He thus feels able to report:

> The need for low prices on the world markets, forcing simpler and more rational shapes and decoration, has been the finest thing that has ever happened to the English pottery industry. Dinnerware made in the Potteries to-day, from the many first-grade firms, is unbelievably cheap and good.

His optimism is thus realistic: the potters are 'striving' to produce good design, and in addition they have been 'forced' into this position by the need for economic production. Although he refers to the good tablewares of many firms, for his selection of illustrations of British industrial tableware Forsyth picks examples from a comparatively small number of companies which by no means represent the hundreds of potteries operating at the time. The best of British Modernism, as he depicts it, comes mainly from the large, well-established companies, many of whom feature more than once in his choice.

Nevertheless, the pieces which do appear are encouraging. More Wedgwood pieces are illustrated than those of any other company. The tall, elegant and curved *Globe* shape appears in a variety of guises: with simple champagne glaze and gold finish; with a floral motif in bronze and red designed by Keith Murray; with the white and gold on blue *Stars* design by Star Wedgwood; and as part of Wedgwood's range of two-colour *Sylphides* ware, here in cream with pink handles and knobs, finished with silver lines. Other Wedgwood ware illustrated includes another simple floral in red and black by Star Wedgwood; Victor Skellern's traditional *Seasons* series; Millicent Taplin's hand-painted silver and *Green Lattice*; and examples of *Alpine Pink* and *April Green* coloured wares. W. T. Copeland are represented by Agnes Pinder Davis's *Country Souvenir*, with its fawn and grey reeds and grasses on a cream ground, and by two simple dinner services designed by Tom Hassall – one with pale yellow bands, silver lines and central floral motif, and the other a restrained floral, *Rosemary*. There are dinner services by John Wadsworth for Mintons and Jack Noke for Doulton.

The smaller companies that do appear are those that had made the most considerable design changes or those that had been consistently praised by the design pundits throughout the previous decade. Susie Cooper is represented by a *Kestrel* shape dinner service hand-painted with a modern fish design. A. E. Gray's example is a dramatic tea- or coffee-service decorated with radiating gold and silver stripes, designed by Sam C. Talbot. The Royal Staffordshire Pottery (A. J. Wilkinson) is illustrated by Clarice Cliff's *Corncob* embossed jug and teapot with a shiny honey-coloured glaze and by a plain-coloured glaze breakfast set, *Meadow Green*. E. Brain (Foley) is represented by a silver lustre on white breakfast or tea service designed by Milner Gray, and John Adams's *Everest* ware appears for Carter, Stabler and Adams.

Almost without exception, all the shapes chosen in the selection are extremely simple, rounded, twentieth-century models with traditional, eighteenth-century overtones. Decorations are both hand-painted and modern lithographs, banding, lining or all-over coloured glazes. From the evidence which he presents, Forsyth is able to show that by the mid-thirties there did exist a clean, simple, but recognizably British Modernism, informed by the best of traditional wares rather than the worst. He is also obviously at pains to point to the successes of designers working in industry: nearly all the pieces he chooses to illustrate are accompanied by captions naming their designers, who are either freelance artists or the best of the art directors of the period. Forsyth's book shows the manufacturers that they have much to be proud of, although it by no means reflects the products of the industry overall.

As we saw in Chapter 5, Pevsner, writing in 1937 in *An Inquiry Into Industrial Art in England*, was less than impressed with overall standards of design throughout the industry. His book was concerned with investigating the industry as a whole, and his conclusions were backed by convincing statistical evidence. Despite such observations that the 'use of freelance artists is very rare in the pottery trade' and that 'manufacturers are far readier to turn out new patterns than new shapes', he still succeeds in finding innovations worthy of commendation, such as Susie Cooper's modern lithographs and T. G. Green's *Cornish Kitchen Ware*. His rather austere admiration is reserved for 'stoneware pans' and Royal Doulton's functional Acid Jars, which had received a cult following of like-minded critics for their natural and unpretentious simplicity. Nevertheless, he does imply some hope for the future of ceramic design, linked to the technology that was forcing the industry to take a new direction:

> Moreover the new processes of pottery mass production should raise new problems of design. For whereas to-day many of the factories still keep the same blackened sheds and the same kilns which they have had for more than a hundred years – another fact, incidentally, that shows how alive tradition is in the English pottery trade – there cannot be any doubt that the methods and requirements of a changed era are bound to react on the artistic appearance of pottery in the near future.

The enormous and colourful array of British Art Deco tablewares which are discussed in Chapters 3, 4 and 5 make no appearance at all in Gordon Forsyth's summary, except obliquely in his suggestion that novelty is responsible for both good and bad design. Pevsner is straightforwardly dismissive: he refers to 'any amount of jagged handles, square or polygonal plates, wrongly balanced pots, etc' as 'thoughtless in design, and hardly meant to be of lasting value'.

Design was still no laughing matter. The enthusiasm, the humour and the possible value of the fanciful and the kitsch demonstrated by pottery of the Art Deco period were not qualities which were recognized by the highest authorities of their age. The designs were, as we have seen, bought in their thousands, faithfully recorded by the trade journal the *Pottery Gazette* and no doubt innocently enjoyed by many who were unconcerned with the niceties of good design and good taste. From a vantage point of fifty years or so, it is possible both to enjoy the excesses of Art Deco and to recognize the important problems facing the development of more serious modern industrial design. It is also possible to feel both charmed and frustrated by the stubbornness and lack of understanding of those on both sides of the ceramic design debate, and to recognize that even today not all the answers to these problems have been provided.

Tablewares designed by Eric Ravilious for Josiah Wedgwood (and Sons): *jug and two handled beakers from lemonade set in the* Garden Implements *pattern of* c. 1938 (left); *plate and saucer in the* Garden *pattern of* c. 1939 (top); *covered vegetable dish in* Persephone *of 1938* (centre bottom); *preserve jar in* Afternoon Tea *of* c. 1937 (top right); *and* Edward VIII *coronation mug, 1937. (Pages 200–4)*

The 'First Effects of War News' upon the industry were recorded in the *Pottery Gazette* in October 1939:

> The first definite information of war having been declared upon Germany, although it had not been unexpected (since everyone knew that it simply *had* to come), seemed to strike the Potteries, and everyone connected with the pottery industry, with an almost paralysing force . . . As we write now, within a month after the outbreak of the war, the general feeling is that if it cannot be a case of 'Business as Usual,' as was the motto in the last war, it must, at least, be 'Business as Near as Possible to Usual' . . .

The editorial gives itself away, sounding quite like those that were written in the same journal more than twenty years earlier during the outbreak of World War I. But this was a different war, and the Potteries were to find themselves in an ever less 'usual' climate. After 1945, a new country had to be developed, not a pre-war one reinstated, and their traditionalism and patriotism were not going to be sufficient to see them through.

Ironically, it was the war that delivered the final design blow to the pottery industry, which was once more forced – this time by law – to move its ideas in the direction of the simply shaped, unadorned, industrially produced tablewares that had been the subject of anguished debate for a quarter of a century. During the first few years of the war restrictions were placed upon the quantities of tableware produced for the home market, although there were no regulations restricting design or decoration. From 1942, however, Utility restrictions were imposed on the potters by Government legislation, and persuasion and argument were no longer needed to effect simplification of design and means of production. Only plain undecorated wares could be produced for the home market, and only a limited number of shapes and pieces, each of which had to be registered by the manufacturers. Moreover, these had to be churned out by wholly industrial methods by companies sufficiently rationalized to make economic sense in a time of organized modern war effort. Thus the potters were now obliged, albeit reluctantly, to give away to the 'New Look' of their own wartime and post-war industry.

Select Bibliography

General: industrial design and ceramic history between the Wars

Battersby, Martin, *The Decorative Twenties*, London, 1969

Bennett, Arnold, *Anna of the Five Towns*, London, 1902 |Penguin, 1986|

Bertram, Anthony, *Design in Everyday Life*, London, 1937

Cameron, Elisabeth, *Encyclopedia of Pottery and Porcelain: the Nineteenth and Twentieth Centuries*, London, 1986

Carrington, Noel, *Design and a Changing Civilization*, London, 1935

Carrington, Noel, *The Shape of Things*, London, 1939

de la Valette, John, (ed.), *The Conquest of Ugliness*, London, 1935

Dorfles, Gillo, *Kitsch*, London, 1973

Dowling, H. G., *A Survey of British Industrial Arts*, London, 1935

Farr, Michael, *Design in British Industry: A mid-century survey*, Cambridge, 1955

Forsyth, Gordon M., *20th Century Ceramics*, London, 1936

Forsyth, Gordon M., Chapter on 'Pottery' in 'Reports on the Present Position and Tendencies of the Industrial Arts as indicated at the International Exhibition of Modern Decorative and Industrial Arts, Paris, 1925', Department of Overseas Trade, 1927

Gloag, John E., *Artifex, or the Future of Craftsmanship*, London, 1926

Gloag, John E., *Industrial Art Explained*, London, 1934

Gloag, John E., (ed.), *Design in Modern Life*, London, 1934

Godden, Geoffrey A., *Encyclopaedia of British Pottery and Porcelain Marks*, London, 1964 |1987|

Godden, Geoffrey A., *British Pottery*, London, 1974

Haggar, R. G., *100 Years of Art Education in the Potteries*, 1953

Haggar, R. G., et al., *The Staffordshire Pottery Industry*, Staffordshire County Library, 1981 (reprinted from the Victoria History of the County of Stafford)

Hannah, Frances, *Ceramics* (Twentieth Century Design series), London, 1986

Hillier, Bevis, *Art Deco of the 20s and 30s*, London, 1968 |1985|

Holme, Geoffrey, *Industrial Design and the Future*, London, 1934

Lancaster, Osbert, *Homes Sweet Homes*, London, 1939 |1953|

Lesieutre, Alain, *The Spirit and Splendour of Art Deco*, London, 1974

MacCarthy, Fiona, *All Things Bright and Beautiful: Design in Britain 1830 to Today*, London, 1972

MacCarthy, Fiona, *British Design since 1880*, London, 1982

Pevsner, Nikolaus, *An Inquiry Into Industrial Art in England*, Cambridge, 1937

Préaud, T. and Gauthier, S., *Ceramics in the 20th Century*, Oxford, 1982

Read, Herbert, *Art and Industry*, London, 1934

Rosenberg, Harold, *The Tradition of the New*, London, 1962

Sparke, Penny, *Consultant Design: the History and Practice of the Designer in Industry*, London, 1983

Street Porter, J. and T., *The British Teapot*, London, 1981

Stuart, Denis (ed.), *People of the Potteries: A Dictionary of Local Biography* (Vol. 1), Keele, 1985

The Thirties: British Art and Design Before the War, London (Hayward Gallery Exhibition Catalogue), 1980

The following works relate to (and are given in alphabetical order of) individual potteries or designers:

May, Harvey, et al *The Beswick Collector's Handbook*, London, 1986

Wentworth-Sheilds, Peter and Johnson, Kay, *Clarice Cliff*, London, 1976

Clarice Cliff, Brighton (Museum and Art Gallery Exhibition Catalogue), 1972

Eatwell, Ann, *Susie Cooper Productions*, London (Victoria and Albert Museum Exhibition Catalogue), 1987

Woodhouse, Adrian, *Susie Cooper: Elegance and Utility*, Barlaston, 1978

Atterbury, Paul and Irvine, Louise, *The Doulton Story*, Stoke-on-Trent, 1979

Eyles, Desmond, *The Doulton Burslem Wares*, London, 1980

Niblett, Paul, et al., *Hand-Painted Gray's Pottery*, Stoke-on-Trent, 1982

Atterbury, Paul, *The story of Minton*, Stoke-on-Trent, 1978

Atterbury, Paul and Dennis, Richard, *William Moorcroft and Walter Moorcroft 1897-1973*, London (Fine Art Society Exhibition Catalogue), 1973

Hawkins, Jennifer, *The Poole Potteries*, London, 1980

'A Century of Poole', *Tableware International*, April 1973

Eric Ravilious 1903–1942: A re-assessment of his life and work, Eastbourne (Towner Art Gallery Exhibition Catalogue), 1986

Bumpus, Bernard, *Rhead: Artists and Potters 1870-1950*, London (Geffrye Museum Exhibition Catalogue), 1986

Bumpus, Bernard, 'Pottery Designed by Charlotte Rhead', *Antique Collector*, January 1983

Watkins, C., Harvey, W. and Senft, R., *Shelley Potteries*, London, 1980 |1986|

Shelley Potteries, London (Geffrye Museum Exhibition Catalogue), 1980

Copeland, Robert, et al., *Spode/Copeland 1733-1983*, Stoke-on-Trent, 1983

Batkin, Maureen, *Wedgwood Ceramics 1846-1959*, London, 1982

Niblett, Kathy (ed.), *Wedgwood of Etruria and Barlaston*, Stoke-on-Trent, 1980

Sandon, Henry, *Royal Worcester Porcelain from 1862 to the Present Day*, London, 1973 |1975|

Periodicals and yearbooks: relevant issues range in date from 1914—1940

Architectural Review
Commercial Art and Industry
Design for To-day
DIA Journal
DIA Quarterly
(Our) Homes and Gardens
Journal of the Royal Society of Arts
The Pottery Gazette and Glass Trade Review
The Pottery Gazette and Glass Trade Review Diary and Trade Directory
The Pottery and Glass Record
The Studio
The Studio Year-Book
Transactions of the English Ceramic Society

Pattern books for the following potteries, dating from the 1920s and 1930s, can be examined, with appropriate permissions, at the given locations. The number and condition of extant pattern books varies.

Sir Henry Doulton Gallery, Royal Doulton UK Ltd, Nile Street,
    Burslem, Stoke-on-Trent ST6 2AJ:
Adderleys (Daisy Bank Pottery, Longton)
Booths (Church Bank Pottery, Tunstall)
Colclough (Royal Vale China, Longton)
Doulton and Co. (Royal Doulton Potteries, Nile Street, Burslem)
E. Hughes (Paladin China, Opal Works, Fenton)
Shelley Potteries (The Foley, Longton)
Shore and Coggins (Bell China, Edensor Works, Longton)

The Wedgwood Museum, Barlaston, Stoke-on-Trent ST12 9ES:
William Adams and Sons (Titian Ware, Tunstall and Stoke)
Susie Cooper Pottery (Chelsea Works and Crown Works, Burslem)
Josiah Wedgwood and Sons (Etruria and Barlaston)

Coalport, Minerva Works, Park Street, Fenton, Stoke-on-Trent ST4 3JB:
Allertons (Park Works, Longton)
Bishop and Stonier (Hanley)
E. Brain and Co. (Foley China Works, Fenton)
Crown Staffordshire Porcelain (Minerva Works, Fenton)
George Jones (Crescent Pottery, Stoke)

Stoke-on-Trent City Museum and Art Gallery, Bethesda Street, Hanley, Stoke-on-Trent
    ST1 3DW:
S. Fielding and Co. (Crown Devon, Devon Pottery, Stoke)
Shorter and Sons (Stoke)

The Minton Museum, Minton House, London Road, Stoke-on-Trent ST4 7QD:
Mintons (Stoke)

Royal Worcester Spode, Spode Works, Church Street, Stoke-on-Trent ST4 1BX:
W. T. Copeland (Spode Works, Stoke)

The Dyson Perrins Museum Trust, Severn Street, Worcester WR1 2NE:
Worcester Royal Porcelain Co.

Horace Barks Reference Library, Stoke-on-Trent City Library, Bethesda Street, Hanley, Stoke-on-Trent ST1 3RS:
The Newport Pottery Co. (Newport Lane, Burslem)
A. J. Wilkinson (Royal Staffordshire Pottery, Burslem)

Factory Index

General Index

Photography Acknowledgements

The items that appear in the book were photographed courtesy of:

Beverley, Alfie's Antiques Market, London, pages 2, 78–9;
John Miles, Bizzare, Deco Warehouse, Birmingham, England, front jacket and pages 30–1, 35, 38–9, 46, 50–1, 54–5, 94, 151, 163, 198, 202–3;
Rita Smythe, Britannia Antiques, Gray's Antiques Market, London, pages 154–5;
Pat and Howard Watson, Castle Antiques, Warwick's Art Deco Shop, Warwick, England, pages 26–7, 59, 62, 70, 74–5, 86–7, 90–1, 159, 186–7;
Alastair Hendy, Alfie's Antiques Market, London, back jacket and pages 18–19, 66–7, 171, 178–9;
Brian Parkes, page 15;
Connie Speight, Gray's Antiques Market, London, pages 98–9 (Myott and Rhead);
Judy and John Kassman, pages 22–3, 98–9 (Booths and Hancock);
The Dyson Perrins Museum Trust, Worcester, England, pages 146–7;
Royal Worcester Spode Ltd, Worcester, England, page 143;
The Minton Museum, Royal Doulton Tableware Ltd, Stoke-on-Trent, England, pages 10–11, 106, 114, 118;
The Spode Museum Trust Collection, Stoke-on-Trent, England, pages 134–5 (Queen's Bird) and 138; pages 130–31, 134–5 (Christmas Tree), 139, are from a private collection;
The Trustees of the Wedgwood Museum, Barlaston, Stoke-on-Trent, England, pages 174–5, 195, 206, 207, 210–11.
The photographs that appear on pages 6, 102, 110, 122, 126–7 were loaned by Royal Doulton Tableware Ltd, Stoke-on-Trent, England.